MW01492222

**Evolution, Welfare, and
Time in Economics**

Evolution, Welfare, and Time in Economics

Essays in Honor of Nicholas Georgescu-Roegen

Edited by

Anthony M. Tang
Fred M. Westfield
James S. Worley
Vanderbilt University

Lexington Books
D.C. Heath and Company
Lexington, Massachusetts
Toronto

Library of Congress Cataloging in Publication Data

Main entry under title:

Evolution, welfare, and time in economics.

  Includes index.
  CONTENTS: Heard, A. Foreword.—Tang, A. M., Westfield,
F. M., and Worley, J. S. Preface.—Evolution as opposed to circular
flows: Boulding, K. E. The great laws of change. Spengler, J. J. The
population problem. Kuznets, S. Aspects of post World War II
growth in less developed countries.—Some welfare question: Chipman, J. S. and Moore, J. C. The scope of consumer's surplus arguments. Tinbergen, J. Equitable income distribution: another experiment. [Etc.]
  1. Time and economic reactions—Addresses, essays, lectures. 2.
Economics—Addresses, essays, lectures. 3. Georgescu-Roegen,
Nicholas. I. Georgescu-Roegen, Nicholas. II. Tang, Anthony M.,
1924– III. Westfield, Fred M. IV. Worley, James S.
HB199.E84   330   76-14664
ISBN 0-669-00736-6

Second printing, January 1979

Published simultaneously in Canada

Printed in the United States of America

International Standard Book Number: 0-669-00736-6

Library of Congress Catalog Card Number: 76-14664

CONTENTS

Foreword

Vanderbilt's centennial theme is phrased "The Uses of Knowledge and the Consequences of Knowing." In adopting this theme, we acknowledge that a university should go beyond its conventional missions of generating and transmitting knowledge and seek to understand the uses to which knowledge is put and the consequences of knowledge for personal values, ethics, and public policy.

The life work of Nicholas Georgescu-Roegen, Distinguished Professor of Economics, anteceded us in this centennial theme. No one on any faculty anywhere has addressed himself or herself more directly and pertinently to the uses of knowledge and its consequences. Especially in recent years, his work on the relation between the law of entropy and the economic process has exemplified the prophetic vision of the scholar who looks to the future of mankind and our planet.

It is thus with a special sense of significance, on behalf of the University, that I applauded the conference of distinguished economists held on the Vanderbilt campus, as one of our centennial undertakings, to pay tribute to Professor Georgescu. I welcome this book as its aftermath. The title itself is a summing up: *Evolution, Welfare, and Time in Economics: Essays in Honor of Nicholas Georgescu-Roegen.*

We are grateful for Professor Georgescu's contributions to Vanderbilt during the last twenty-seven years and recognize as well the contributions of his wife, Otilia, in the support of his career and as a member of our community. Escaping the adverse political conditions of their native Rumania in 1948, Professor and Mrs. Georgescu first went to Harvard, where he had been Visiting Rockefeller Fellow from 1934 to 1936. It was our good fortune that he came to Vanderbilt in 1949 to join the faculty of the Department of Economics and Business Administration. Through the years he has been accorded many honors, both at Vanderbilt and elsewhere. One honor received here is the Harvie Branscomb Distinguished Professor Award, which recognizes talents and achievements we identify as desirable in a university faculty member: creative scholarship, teaching that results in learning of a high order, and service to the university and society at large.

Professor Georgescu is a thorough man of the academy. He has consistently demonstrated rigorous intellect and by all reputation has

---

This foreword is based upon remarks made by Chancellor Heard at a banquet honoring Professor and Mrs. Georgescu during the conference, "Economics: A New Look," at Vanderbilt University, October 22–25, 1975.

viii

been a demanding and meticulous teacher. He has been sufficiently universal to make the ultimate fate of the universe the unavoidable and practical concern of the university.

I think it proper to say that Nicholas Georgescu-Roegen represents the "Centennial Intellect," not only an intellect fitting our centennial theme, but one worthy of this and any other century. And if the century to come pays heed to his concerns, it will prove worthy of his legacy.

ALEXANDER HEARD

Preface

This volume honors Nicholas Georgescu-Roegen on his seventieth birthday. The papers collected herein were prepared for this occasion by his peers, some of the world's most distinguished economists, on themes suggested by his own intellectual contributions. With the exception of Jan Tinbergen, all traveled to Vanderbilt University during the university's centennial celebration in 1975 to present their papers and honor Professor Georgescu-Roegen in person.

Nicholas Georgescu-Roegen was born on February 4, 1906, in Constanza, Romania. He lost his father when he was eight and was brought up by his mother, a schoolteacher, in the modest surroundings that her earnings could provide during World War I and its aftermath. At age ten, he won a full scholarship to the Mânăstirea Dealu, the Romanian "Eton," an extraordinarily demanding high school, and every year stood at the head of his class. Then he went on to the University of Bucharest to study mathematics, obtaining his "license," equivalent to the master's degree, in 1926.

His outstanding achievements at the university led to the award by the government in the following year of a scholarship for study at the Sorbonne in Paris; and three years later at age twenty-four, he was awarded his doctoral degree in statistics with the distinctive citation, "avec les félicitations du jury," inscribed on his diploma. This honor earned him an extension of his government scholarship for two more years of postdoctoral study under the great statistician Karl Pearson in London. On his return to Romania in 1932, he was appointed Professor of Statistics at the School of Statistics of the University of Bucharest, at the same time occupying a position with the Central Statistical Institute.

He came to the United States first in 1934, as a Visiting Rockefeller Fellow, and spent most of his time at Harvard. Here, under the decisive intellectual influence of Joseph A. Schumpeter, he became an economist. During the two years of "apprenticeship"—as he has called this period at Harvard—he published three pathbreaking papers of singular import to economic theory that were to launch his brilliant career. Georgescu's work in choice theory, which as Samuelson has aptly said, "will interest minds when today's skyscrapers have crumbled back to sand," had its foundation laid during these formative years in Cambridge.

Schumpeter and Harvard tried very hard to keep him, mindful of the important role which he could play in the development of mathematical economics there. Georgescu returned instead to Romania, feeling that the need of his native land for his services was greater than Harvard's. He taught and held various government positions until "purged" by the Iron

Guard—the Romanian Nazis. Later, he was reinstated by the Antonescu regime. In 1944–45, he served as Secretary General of the Romanian Armistice Commission. In that capacity, he risked personal safety to defend his country's interests and soon aroused the hostility of Soviet military and civilian occupation officials. He was "purged" again in 1946. In February 1948, stowed away, he fled the country to Istanbul together with his wife, Otilia Busuioc. In the United States, Harvard at once found room for him.

The distinguished economist George W. Stocking (later a president of the American Economic Association) was, as head of Vanderbilt's Department of Economics and Business Administration, able to entice Georgescu to accept an appointment as professor of economics, beginning with the fall quarter of 1949. It is at Vanderbilt during his twenty-seven-year stay that his career as economist and teacher came to full flower.

On campus and off, he has received almost every imaginable honor. On campus, he was appointed Distinguished Professor of Economics in 1969, having previously received the annual Harvie Branscomb Distinguished Professor award. He has been a visiting professor or lecturer at the great universities of North America, South America, Asia, Africa, and Europe. He is a Richard T. Ely Lecturer and a Distinguished Fellow of the American Economic Association, a Fellow of various scientific organizations, including the American Academy of Arts and Sciences and the Econometric Society, and a member of numerous others. For seventeen years he was an associate editor of *Econometrica*. He has held the Guggenheim Fellowship and the Fulbright Scholarship and in this, the year of his retirement from Vanderbilt, was elected to an honory membership of Phi Beta Kappa.

A prefatory note is not the place to make a serious appraisal of the life work of a scholar of Georgescu's stature. In any event, it is much too soon in his case. His scholarly output is still growing, at an increasing rate, and the growth is not merely quantitative. He continues his study of the most fundamental problems in economics: choice, production, and human welfare. This he does from an ever broader and deeper perspective. A bibliographical postscript is appended to this volume to serve as a convenient guide to his work. For a one-paragraph summary of his rich and varied career, we can do no better than to borrow (with permission) the citation drafted by William H. Nicholls and presented to the American Economic Association upon naming Nicholas Georgescu-Roegen Distinguished Fellow of the Association:

We honor Nicholas Georgescu-Roegen, whom Paul Samuelson has called "a scholar's scholar and an economist's economist." Ever since the publication of his path-breaking paper on the Pure Theory of Consumer's Behavior 35 years ago, Georgescu-Roegen has been a seminal writer on utility theory, in which almost every important theoretical problem or relevant issue bears the mark of his pen. In production theory, where he has been one of the pioneers of the theory of linear systems, his contributions extend from the two most important theorems in the input-output analysis to a radical reformulation of the concept of production function. No American economist has more successfully combined in his training and publications the fields of economics, mathematics, and statistics. Yet Georgescu-Roegen has remained a signal defender of the view that many important problems are beyond the reach of numbers. Unique also is his keen knowledge of past and present human institutions. To this knowledge, which ranks very high in his intellectual hierarchy, we owe his penetrating adaptation of analytical tools to a complex structure. A recent product of his broad range of knowledge is his new book, *The Entropy Law and the Economic Process*, in which he develops the revolutionary view that economic activity is an extension of man's biological evolution—an entropic process rather than the mechanical analogue traditional in mathematical economics. At the same time, Georgescu-Roegen has been and still is a great teacher. Every one of his class lectures is a work of a long-mastered art, the pride of all those who were fortunate to be his students and to know his continuous and friendly devotion to their academic progress and career. To Nicholas Georgescu-Roegen—the scholar, the teacher, the humanist—we pay homage as a true Renaissance man. [*American Economic Review* LXII, no. 3 (June 1972): frontispiece.]

As former students and long-time associates of Nicholas Georgescu-Roegen, it has been our pleasure to serve as the Festschrift Committee and as editors of these essays in his honor. In this undertaking, which is best thought of as a labor of love, we have acted on behalf of all of his colleagues at Vanderbilt as well as his students, past and present. We wish to thank all those who made it possible for us to complete the organizational and editorial tasks. We are very grateful to the contributors of the papers in this volume for accepting our invitation. We owe a special debt to Chancellor Alexander Heard for his encouragement and support and to a Vanderbilt Centennial Fellowship for providing generous financial assistance. Our deepest gratitude is to Nicholas Georgescu-Roegen himself for giving us the opportunity to celebrate. And to Otilia, without whose unfailing understanding and encouragement Nicholas would have been a far lesser man, we express our affection and esteem.

Vanderbilt University
Nashville, Tennessee
May 1976

ANTHONY M. TANG
FRED M. WESTFIELD
JAMES S. WORLEY

**Part I
Evolution as Opposed to Circular Flows**

1 The Great Laws of Change

Kenneth E. Boulding

Laws of Change—Generalization and Foundation

In thinking about the laws of physics, and especially the three famous laws of thermodynamics, I have sometimes been surprised at the extent to which they can be generalized to more complex systems. Yet, I suppose one should not be surprised; for after all, these are on the whole laws of change, and change is a universal phenomenon in all systems. Nature is a Heracleitan flux, and we never step into the same river twice. All equilibria are temporary. Indeed, equilibrium is a fiction of the human imagination and is really unknown in the real world. "Time," in the great hymn of Isaac Watts, "like an ever-rolling stream, Bears all its sons away." Fortunately, not all of them "Fly forgotten as a dream dies at the opening day," for they do leave traces, and we do keep records, and out of these we are able to piece together the laws of change. Most of the great laws, however, have a strong element of the *a priori* about them. They are the way we know things must be rather than the way we have observed them. There is a certain myth among scientists that the great laws of science are derived by induction from observation and tested by the confirmation of predictions. This may be true of the small laws, but it is not really true of the great ones, which are derived on the whole from identities that we discover in our imaginations.

The First Law: Conservation

The first great law, of course, is the *law of conservation*. This states that if we have a fixed quantity of anything, then all that can happen to it is to be shifted around among various parts of the system. This might almost be called the "law of shifting cargo." In itself, this is an identity, not an empirical law. The empirical part of it consists of the study of *what* things, in fact, are conserved—that is, what things exist in a fixed stock, and what things may be added to and subtracted from. For whatever exists in a fixed stock, however, the principle holds. For a *conservand* (whatever it is which is conserved), if there are any exports of it from one part of the universe, these must equal the imports into the rest of the universe. If there is a fixed stock of money, then the sum of all balances of payments must be zero, for the diminution in the money stock of one person or one

3

group must be equal to the increase in the money stock of everybody else. If matter is a conservand, then any matter that leaves one part of the universe must end up in some other part. If energy is the conservand, the same principle applies. In thermodynamics, we often think of the conservation of energy in terms of energy moving into and out of several different forms (electrical, mechanical, chemical, and so on); but these different forms are simply different parts of the total energy stock, and what leaves one part must end up in another part.

The tricky empirical question, of course, is what is it that is conserved? The answer to this is not altogether clear. From Einstein, we know that neither matter nor energy is conserved in itself, because either can be transformed into the other, and we have to expand the old first law into a law of conservation of "mattergy," or whatever we are going to call it, which is the total of energy and its equivalent in matter. We are not even really sure that mattergy is a conservand. If Fred Hoyle is right, it is being created continuously throughout the universe, and unless we suppose that the total amount of mattergy in the universe has existed for an infinite time, there must have been some time at which it was created or during which it increased or diminished. The awful truth is that we have only explored an almost infinitesimally small sample of the universe, and we really do not know very much about it. We certainly know that the law of conservation of money breaks down in inflation and in deflation, and that this law is only a very, very rough first approximation. We are pretty sure that information is not conserved at all insofar as it relates to replicable structures. Every living creature is a printing works, turning out its genetic instruction book in vast editions all through its life. It is this nonconservation of information, indeed, which makes evolution possible.

The Second Law: Entropy

The second great law is the *law of increasing entropy,* the generalization of the famous second law of thermodynamics. This can be stated in a good many different ways even in thermodynamics, and Professor Georgescu-Roegen has argued, without, as far as I know, getting much attention from the physicists, that some of these ways even in thermodynamics may be better than others. I have always thought it was a rather unfortunate historical accident that entropy was defined in negative terms—that is, as negative potential, entropy being what goes up when potential runs down. This is a characteristic which the entropy concept shares with the much more disreputable concept of phlogiston, which turned out to have a negative weight and to be, indeed, negative oxygen. Another negative concept which caused much trouble was that of saving in economics. Until Keynes recognized that saving was not an act but a residual, just the difference between production and consumption or income and expenditure, the concept caused endless trouble. It is like asking somebody, "What didn't you do yesterday?"—a question which is much harder to answer than "What *did* you do yesterday?"

It is a little surprising that the negative definition of entropy has not caused more trouble in thermodynamics. It represented a kind of residual in the system anyway, so that perhaps the algebraic sign really did not matter. When it comes to generalizing and interpreting the entropy principle, however, it is very much better to reverse the algebraic sign and to think of it as potential. Then, the second law can be restated in its most general form as: If any event happens, it is because there was previously a potential for its happening, and after it has happened, that potential has been used up; so, it cannot happen again unless there is recreation of potential. In a closed system, of course, we suppose that there cannot be recreation of potential, and that hence the system simply goes on using up its initial potential until it is all gone. In a closed system, the first law says that all that can happen is rearrangement; the second law says that if rearrangement happens, it is because there is some kind of potential for rearrangement, and as rearrangement goes on, potential is gradually reduced to zero and we get to the point where nothing further can happen.

In thermodynamics, the "something happening" is the transfer of energy from one form into another because of some potential difference in the form (for instance, of temperature differentials), but as this transfer proceeds, the potential difference declines. In temperature, for instance, hot things get colder, and cold things get hotter; everything ends up at the same temperature, and then nothing further can happen. If the universe is a closed system—and this is something we do not really know—the transfer will lead ultimately to the "heat death" of the universe, in which everything is at the same temperature in a kind of thin, brown soup and nothing else can happen.

In Regard to Matter

In open systems like the earth, of course, the second law is considerably modified, and even the first law no longer applies with absolute strictness. In respect to materials, the earth receives a small amount of matter from meteorites and presumably loses a little matter into space in the outer atmosphere and a little from radioactivity. These gains and losses are so small, however, that for all practical purposes, we can assume that the earth has constant stocks of all its various elements, and that all that has been happening to these in geological history with plate tectonics and in human history with the production, distribution, and consumption of commodities is that these materials have been rearranged in space, compounds, and instructives.

The second law in regard to materials is best seen as the law of diffusion—that concentrated things tend to become diffuse in the course of activity. A great deal of activity like solution, erosion, and mining is entropic in this sense, but in the history of the earth, these material entropic processes have been frequently, and indeed perhaps constantly, offset by antientropic processes which have continually restored the potential for diffusion which the diffusion processes proceed to exhaust. We see this, for instance, in plate tectonics and orogeny—that is, mountain building. If the earth had started with a fixed complement of mountains and continents, the processes of erosion would soon have reduced this to featureless plains and swamps, or would even have produced an ocean over the whole of the earth's surface. The enduring variety of earth landscape and the continued existence of mountains are results of the fact that erosion is offset by mountain-building processes. Ultimately, perhaps, these will come to an end as the potential for them in tectonic energy (whatever it is that pushes up the mountains) is exhausted and the earth moves toward topographical equilibrium. For the last 3 or 4 billion years, however, the earth has not been in topographical equilibrium, and while there have been periods perhaps in which the earth's landscape has been a good deal flatter than it is now, the forces of erosion have been continually offset by the forces of mountain building. If this had not been so, evolution would have taken a very different course. If there had been no land, there certainly would not have been any human beings, although we might have had a great race of intelligent dolphins. One suspects that even the constant seesawing between mountain building and erosion contributed a great deal to the actual course of biological evolution.

In Regard to Energy

In regard to energy, the earth has always been an open system, receiving energy constantly from the sun and losing it into space. The record of biological evolution suggests that the temperature of the earth has been astonishingly constant over 3 million years; otherwise, evolution would never have taken place. Life can only develop within very narrow temperature limits. This must mean that for a very long time now the amount of energy received from the sun or from radioactive elements has been almost exactly equal to what has been radiated off into space. There have been minor variations responsible for alternating genial climates and ice ages, but the overall record has been astonishingly stable.

It is, however, precisely this throughput of energy from the sun which has permitted biological and now social evolution to take place. If the earth had simply been a pleasant, warm planet without a sun, it is very doubtful whether evolution would have gotten underway. And if it ever had, it certainly would not have lasted very long, as the earth would simply have cooled off. The evolutionary potential would soon have been exhausted. This is not to say, of course, that the second law has been repealed; it is simply that the sun has a very large potential for exporting energy, and it has continued to do so for several billion years without this potential having been exhausted. Indeed, I understand that there is a very good chance of its going on for several more billion years. Even though entropy is increasing in the system as a whole, therefore, as the sun does get used up, the earth benefits from this arrangement in the sense that it does not have to rely on its own energy potential.

In these open systems, it is important to emphasize that the second great law always operates but is not aggregative. Potential, as it is realized, is always used up, but then potential can be recreated. Whether or not the original potential of the universe can be recreated, we do not know. This concerns an obscure matter of cosmology, and with the extraordinarily imperfect and biased character of the record of the past, I think it is extremely improbable that we shall ever know. In regard to the earth, however, and particularly in regard to biological and social systems, this constant using up of potential through its realization and the equally constant recreation of potential is a key to the whole process.

The Third Law: Limiting Ultimate

The third law of thermodynamics, that we can never get to absolute zero, is relatively minor compared to the first and second laws. Even so, it is a proposition which is capable of generalization and perhaps might be generalized as a moderately great law. It can be generalized in the form that the closer any system gets to its ultimate condition, the harder it is to get any further. We see this principle apply, for instance, in Einsteinian physics in trying to attain the speed of light on the part of matter. The faster matter travels, the more its mass increases and the greater the force necessary to accelerate it, and so it can never achieve the speed of light, at which any existing mass would presumably be infinite. Similar principles apply in biology. No ecosystem ever really reaches the climactic ecosystem. No animal grows to exhaust its full biological potential and simply stays there; it always grows and then declines.

In social systems, the principle is even more striking. The elimination of any form of evil seems to be as difficult as getting down to absolute zero; the closer we come to eliminating it, the harder it is to go any further. There are some possible exceptions to this principle. We seem to be very close, for instance, to eliminating smallpox; even this, however, gets harder and harder as we get closer to the goal, and one has an uneasy suspicion that we are not really going to make it. We can push high school enrollment up to 90 percent of the age group; getting it up to 91 percent seems to run into insuperable difficulties. This is not, I think, an *a priori* principle like the others, though perhaps it is in thermodynamics. In its generalized form, one has to admit that there are possible empirical exceptions. After all, there have been a very large number of biological extinctions, the dinosaurs having reached their absolute zero quite a while ago.

The Fourth Law: Potential and Resistance

Going now a little beyond thermodynamics, we find another law of physics that is highly generalizable. This, our fourth law, is Ohm's law in electricity, which states that current is directly proportional to the potential difference between two points and inversely proportional to the resistance. In its general form, this law could be stated: If anything happens, it is because there is a potential for its happening, but the more resistance there is, the less will happen for any given amount of potential. This, again, in a pure form is an *a priori* law, but of course, what constitutes either potential and happening or resistance is an empirical matter. Even in thermodynamics there is a certain equivalent to Ohm's law in the principle of specific heat. The amount of heat, for instance, which it takes to vaporize or to freeze a given liquid varies a great deal with the nature of the liquid, and this variation is measured by the resistance, or the specific heat of freezing or of gasifying. Water seems to have a great deal more resistance to being turned into either ice or steam than some more pliable material such as alcohol or freon. We have similar resistance in the specific heat of solution or of crystallization.

As far as I know, the concept of resistance has never been worked out very well in biology, although I have a strong suspicion it could turn out to be important. We know very little, for instance, about resistance to mutation, simply because we know so very little about the mechanism of genetic mutation. It seems highly probable that some genetic structures are more resistant to change than others. This may be reflected in the existence of "empty niches" in ecological systems. An empty niche is an opportunity for a favorable mutation; if the system is resistant to genetic change, however, this favorable mutation may simply not take place, and the niche may remain empty, at least for a long period of time. Empty niches, of course, are extremely hard to detect, which is why we know so little about them and perhaps why these concepts of resistance have not been worked out very well in evolutionary theory.

Science has an extraordinary prejudice for studying what *is* rather than what *is not,* although very often what is not is the real clue to what is. The empty niche, again, is one of these negative concepts that are very hard to handle and yet may be important. The concept of the niche itself implies that there are resistances to the expansion of the population of a species beyond a certain point. A species which has a potential for filling a niche but has population which is below the equilibrium size needed for making the niche full will tend to expand its population. As it expands, however, the species runs into increasing resistance. Its death rate rises under increasing predation or conditions favorable for disease, while its birth rate diminishes under overcrowding; thus, the population increase slows down until the equilibrium population is approached. It may be, indeed, that because of the third law, the population is always approaching equilibrium at a diminishing rate, so that it is never actually realized.

In social systems, the generalized Ohm's law can be very important, although it is often hard to perceive examples of it. This is due to the fact that the current (that is, the change) is all that we perceive, and it is often hard to distinguish low potential from high resistance simply because systems cannot be experimentally manipulated. Is the success of a new religion, for instance, the result of its high potential for satisfying religious needs, or is it the result of low resistance to change on the part of people disillusioned with the old things and ready to accept almost anything that is presented to them? If any change takes place at all, this is clear evidence that some potential was able to overcome the resistance to it, but when the rate of change changes, it is often hard to tell whether this is the result of a decline in resistance or an increase in potential.

These kinds of considerations are important, for instance, in trying to answer the question that I have called the "Needham problem."[1] That is, why did science originate in Europe and not in China, which seemed to be much more ready for it in the year 1500? One is tempted to put forth the hypothesis that the potential for science may have been about equal in the two cultures in the sense that the Chinese, like the Europeans, were ingenious in material technology and in making inventions. Indeed, for at least 1,000 years before 1500, the Chinese seem to have been ahead of Europe in technical ingenuity in folk technology. In China, however, the resistance to new basic ideas was very well organized because of the internal unity and homogeneity of the society and the existence of a self-perpetuating Mandarin class. In Europe, the resistances were more scattered and fragmented. In China and Europe, both church and state resisted; however, in China the church and state were virtually a single organization, at least in the Confucian elements in society, whereas in

Europe there had always been separation between the emperor and the pope, not to mention the separation within the church, in the Protestant Reformation, and the division of Europe into many different states. Thus, official Europe did not present a united front against change, and science was able to grow in cracks of this somewhat fragmented structure. This is a little bit like electrons slipping easily through the cracks of copper wire in its more crystalline structure, whereas they get stopped cold by the solid front of insulating glass. Fragmented Europe was a conductor for new ideas; homogeneous China was an insulator. However, in 1949, after a hundred years of fracture, civil war, invasion, and disorganization, China was so fragmented that almost any new idea seemed better than the old ones. It is not surprising, therefore, that Mao was able to make such an enormous change in a comparatively short space of time.

The Fifth Law: Evolution

The fifth great law is, of course, the *law of evolution*. This is not really a law at all but a poetic vision of great power and complexity. It arises, in a sense, out of what appear to be exceptions to the other laws. This is possible, for instance, as we saw earlier, because information or know-how does not obey the law of conservation. It is this which permitted evolution even of the elements and compounds. In a certain sense, helium "knows" more than hydrogen, knowing how to have two electrons instead of one, and the development of the elements and the compounds is the record of increasing rearrangement or more primal stuff into increasing complexity, following a kind of phase rule. With the development of DNA, the first three-dimensional duplicating machine, replication became easy, and there was an enormous proliferation of complex structures involving information, at least in the sense of improbable arrangements of more primitive elements.

With the development of the human race and its extraordinary capacity for language, evolution passed into a new phase of accelerated rise in complexity, simply because each development permitted further developments. If we think of the cognitive structure of the human nervous system as essentially the genetic material of social production and social evolution in terms of human artifacts, even spoken language permitted enormous transfers of images from one mind to another. A human being can have images of things which are completely remote from personal experience. This is the fundamental change which put evolution into a new gear. Another fundamental development was the assembly or the classroom, in which one human being could transmit images to large numbers of others. With the development of writing, the number of people to whom one individual could transmit messages increased by another order of magnitude, with the additional advantage that messages could be transmitted from the past to the future and from the living to the unborn. We are still listening to messages from Plato and Aristotle. With the development of radio and television, of course, the capacity for replication of messages of the social genetic structure increased by still another order of magnitude.

These human knowledge structures which constitute the field within which social evolution takes place have to be coded in human artifacts. These may be material artifacts, from arrowheads to a space lab and the latest computer; they may also be organizational artifacts, from the family to NASA, or personal artifacts in the form of individual human beings with elaborate knowledge and behavior patterns, from the first caveman to Einstein. All of these are produced by an essentially similar process, as indeed genetic artifacts (phenotypes) are produced from genomes. The process starts with potential in the form of some kind of informational know-how. This is able to direct energy toward the selection, transportation, and transformation of materials into the improbable shapes which constitute the phenotype—the encoding of the knowledge structures. The production of a chicken from an egg and the production of an automobile from a blueprint are not essentially different processes.

Biological and Social Evolution Compared

There are, of course, profound differences between the overall processes of biological and social evolution. One major difference is that while biological evolution never developed more than two sexes, social evolution—that is, the evolution of human artifacts—is essentially multisexual. A horse can be produced by the fertilization of a mare's egg by a horse's sperm; an automobile is produced by the interaction of hundreds of different social species—engineers, designers, architects, chemists, metallurgists, factory workers, foremen, janitors, lawyers, executives, truck drivers, and so on in a very long list—all coming together in a single process which results in the automobile being born from the womb of the factory. This means that while in biological systems each species having sexual reproduction can draw on its own gene pool for rearrangements and recombination for the genetic structure of the individual, in social systems virtually the whole social gene pool of the human race—that is, the "noosphere," in Pierre Teilhard de Chardin's language—is available for recombination into the "genomes" of different artifacts. It is not surprising that social evolution has been in orders of magnitude more rapid than biological evolution. It has produced a variety and complexity of social artifacts which rivals that of biological species, even though it is still a long way from achieving the economy and complexity of biological production. No human artifact is as complex as a human being, or even as complex as an amoeba.

The other great difference between biological and social evolution is that social evolution involves human minds possessing self-conscious images of the future on a scale far beyond those even of the most complex prehuman animal. Social evolution, therefore, has teleological, purposive elements in it which biological evolution does not possess. A much greater importance is attached to decision—that is, choice among alternative images of the future—for humans have the capacity for directing the course of selection, even of mutation, toward "plans"—that is, highly valued images of the future. Where plans are widely shared, they will affect the whole future course of the system.

In biological systems, plans rarely go beyond epigenesis, the growth of a single organism. Every fertilized egg contains a plan for the organism that can grow from it. Each human being is indeed a planned economy, starting from the genetic plan of the fertilized egg in which each originates. This plan includes growth, development, aging, and death. It is only with the advent of the human race, however, that plans for whole ecosystems, such as we have in agriculture, or plans for whole social ecosystems which would expand some species and diminish others become possible. It is true, of course, that "The best laid schemes o' mice and men gang aft agley," as Robert Burns wrote. It is rare to find plans fully fulfilled. But it is rare also to find plans that do not have some impact on the future.

The movements of a human being have to be explained not in terms of a set of differential equations of any degree whatsoever but in terms of images of the future—that is, plans which are in the human's head. I read this paper at Vanderbilt University last October not because I was following a deterministic trend but because somebody had an idea which was translated into a plan, the plan was communicated to me, and I became part of it. I read the paper because the plan was fulfilled. The social egg produced a social chicken.

Equilibrium, Sustainability, and Evolution

The implications of this line of thought for the future are very important. We cannot simply think of the future in terms of entropy—that is, in terms of the fulfillment or exhaustion of existing potential. We have to think of it also in terms of recreation of potential, that is, evolution. This is particularly important when it comes to thinking about sustainability, of which there are several kinds. There is the essentially temporary sustainability of static equilibrium—the rock, for instance, which seems so stable but which is merely waiting to fulfill its potential for erosion and eventually will end up in the ocean. There is the temporary sustainability of homeostasis of the biological organism with its throughput and its capacity for behavior to correct divergences from the homeostatic equilibrium. All biological homeostasis, however, like the static equilibrium of the rock, is only temporary. We keep warm and we satisfy our hunger every day; every day we also age irreversibly along the road that leads to death. Social systems, likewise, exhibit homeostasis, at a low level like the Indian village; even at an advanced level like, for instance, the city of Warsaw, which was rebuilt after it had been destroyed in the Second World War, almost exactly as it was before, because of the homeostasis implied in the Polish imagination. There is a sustainability implied in climactic ecosystems, which in a sense exhibit homeostasis on a larger scale. All these, however, are essentially as temporary as the homeostasis of the human body. Time bears all its sons away, no matter who they are.

The most amazing and perhaps the only ultimate sustainability is that of the evolutionary process itself. This rests on the extraordinary capacity of knowledge structures once they have gotten underway to discover fresh sources of energy and materials to continue the processes of production. A good example of this in early evolution was the production of our present atmosphere by anaerobic forms of life, which produced oxygen as a pollutant. The pollution undoubtedly led to the extinction of most of the organisms that produced it, but the new potentials created by mutation enabled life to overcome this hurdle and start off on the development of oxygen-using organisms. I have sometimes said that evolution and pollution are almost the same concept, for evolution is the segregation of entropy into more complex forms, which requires, of course, more chaos elsewhere. It is even more remarkable than that, however, because it involves the creation of new evolutionary potential which can actually utilize the pollution of the older systems. One system's pollution is another system's nutrition.

These reflections, I confess, make me something of a long-run optimist about the future of the human race, mainly because of its enormous, and still largely unused, cognitive capacity. Because of this, the entropic processes of using up potential can be used to create further potential. That there will be disasters and catastrophes along the way I have no doubt—there always have been. Indeed, these catastrophes have not infrequently been favorable to the evolutionary process itself by destroying a premature equilibrium. That there might be an irretrievable catastrophe in this part of the universe is something to which one cannot quite give a zero probability. Failing that, however, the process is highly likely to go on to Tennyson's "far off divine event to which the whole creation moves" or Chardin's Omega point, though what this will be like is beyond our powers of imagination and prediction.

Note

1. Joseph Needham, *Science and Civilization in China,* Vol. I. *Introductory Orientations* (New York: Cambridge University Press, 1954).

2

The Population Problem: Its Changing Character and Dimensions

Joseph J. Spengler

"Our descendants, if ['precipitous decline'] should be their fate, will see poor compensation for *their* ills in the fact that *we* did live in abundance and luxury."

A. J. Lotka,
Elements of Physical Biology

"Every new source from which man has increased his power on earth has been used to diminish the prospects of his successors."

C. D. Darlington,
The Evolution of Man and Society

"There is no such thing as the cost of irreplaceable resources or irreducible pollution."

N. Georgescu-Roegen,
Southern Economic Journal

In this chapter I shall pass over the development and application, mainly since the 1880s, of demographic models and techniques, together with the comparative neglect of fertility-affecting institutions and motivations and wide variation in the long-run impact of catastrophe upon fertility behavior (e.g., cf. Ireland with India). I shall devote some attention to Georgescu-Roegen's contributions to his economicodemographic theory, his analytical tools, insights, and approaches, his discussion of interaction between man's institutions and environment, and his emphasis upon very long-run implications of population growth-rate differences. Important also is his emphasis upon the evolutionary nature of the process of change characteristic of societies and their economies, a process that makes anticipation of how the world economy and world population growth will continue to interact difficult (*AE,* pp. 414–15, also 66–71, 83–91).

Genesis of the Population Problem

The population problem has its origin in the presence of limitative factors, barriers not surmountable through substitution at the consumer level or

I shall use the initials *AE* and *EL*, respectively, to designate Georgescu-Roegen's *Analytical Economics* (1966) and *The Entropy Law and the Economic Process* (1971), both published by the Harvard University Press. Portions of this paper are by-products of research done on the economics of stationary populations financed by a joint Ford-Rockefeller grant.

through sufficient economy in the use of a limitative factor or its complete replacement at the producer level by as yet nonlimitative factors. For, as Georgescu-Roegen indicated in 1955, "a factor of production is limitative if an increase in its input is a both necessary and sufficient condition for an increase in output" (*AE*, Part 3, chap. 10, also chap. 7). The pace of growth of the food supply, or of some final bill of goods and services, will thus be set, as Dorfman, Samuelson, and Solow point out, by the "needed component of *slowest* growth." In Malthus's model, with the growth of subsistence dependent on that of available land, "the zero own-rate of growth of land would set the pace for organic food and for man, so that a stationary population would be reached in a technologically stationary society."[1] What proves limitative, of course, depends upon the composition of the final bill of goods sought by a population. Today, for example, with specialized materials essential to energy technologies, lithium could become a limitative factor.

Population theory, essentially a collection of concerns and techniques, originated in empirics, as did other sciences and mathematics, and like them suffers if it maps too closely or too remotely on the reality with which it is concerned. Population theory is not a theory *sui generis* but rather resembles engineering in that it consists of the use of quantitative methods, together with elements of economic, sociological, sociopsychological, geographical, genetic, and other relevant sciences, to analyze causes and consequences of population movements. The orientation of population theory at any time is dominated, therefore, by concerns of the moment—concerns associated with anticipated consequences of changes in population size, rate of growth, composition, and distribution in space.

The growth of population theory, together with ancillary sciences drawn upon to help resolve demographic concerns, illustrates both Georgescu-Roegen's thesis that theoretical science is "a living organism" (*AE*, pp. 14–16) and the implication that population economics cannot be based upon "mechanics" that "knows only locomotion" which is "both reversible and qualityless" (*EL*, p. 1; *AE*, pp. 83–91). Demographic concerns have been associated mainly with implications of changes in the ratio of organized communities of men to their environments (or portions of the world environment accessible to them) and secondarily with concomitants (e.g., horizontal and vertical mobility) of changes in population structure (e.g., age and space). These changes, in turn, are conditioned by the dissipatability of man's physical environment and biosphere, by the forces underlying want saturation (*AE*, Part II, chap. 1), and by the institutions that intervene between man and his physical environment or biosphere (*AE*, pp. 124–29; *EL*, pp. 320–25).[2]

What may be called the "population problem" is essentially a corol-

lary to the problem Hobbes posed in *Leviathan*, a problem whose antici-
pations are to be found in many ancient writings dealing with the maintenance of order through the establishment either of suitable mechanisms
(cf. John Locke) or of an authoritarian state. Malthus's approach to the
population question may therefore be described as being in the Hobbesian
tradition[3] in view of Malthus's recognition that the presence of physical
environmental constraints not surmountable by man make essential his
confinement of his numbers within the boundaries imposed by man's
environment and his capacity to exploit his environment—that is, within
the exosomatic and endosomatic boundaries confronting man at any
time.[4]

Man's rules governing factor use and rewards both condition his
response to population pressure and are shaped by it, a form of interaction to whose understanding Georgescu-Roegen has contributed notably
by developing a theory of agrarian economy that helps to explain man's
behavior within this economy (*AE*, chaps. 10–11) and points to how
agrarian overpopulation may be eased. In his discussion of the "marginal
productivity theory," a theory "at its best a translation of the economic
aspects of *some* social patterns compatible with a 'land of plenty,' "
Georgescu-Roegen shows how "in overpopulated countries the social
patterns differ from those of the more advanced communities." These
patterns "provide other rules than the principle of maximizing profit,"
conformity with which may prevent "the net product from reaching its
maximum" (*AE*, pp. 344–45, 351–54, 391), and they may prove
unfavorable to encourage the living standards of the landless (*AE*,
pp. 347–48). In his formulation of a sophisticated and applicable theory of
agrarian economics, Georgescu-Roegen contrasts problems and objec-
tives associated with overpopulation (which is tantamount to poverty in
nonlabor resources) with those emerging as a modern "land of plenty"
comes into being. He thus supplies insights both for the economicodemographic analysis of pre-nineteenth-century European
economies (*AE*, chap. 11) and behavior bearing upon barriers in the way
of fertility control (*AE*, pp. 383–86) and for the development of
effective international institutions to avert Meade's demographically
based "threat of Doom."[5]

Underlying man's demographic concerns, therefore, is the fact that
life is an intraspecific and interspecific struggle for natural resources and
income (e.g., *AE*, pp. 98–101), a struggle for existence as Malthus helped
Darwin to perceive.[6] More fundamentally, as Georgescu-Roegen implies,
it is a struggle against increasing entropy, or the second law of thermodynamics (*AE*, pp. 98–99); or, as Thomas Huxley put it, an intraspecific and interspecific struggle for space; or, as L. Boltzman held, one for
available energy; or, as still others hold, one for other components of the

biosphere. For, as Lotka pointed out, "man's industrial activities are merely a highly and greatly developed form of the general biological struggle for existence."[7] It will be conditioned in the near future by the degree to which technological progress can increase the fraction of man's limited environment subservient to his wants and thus partly counterbalance increasing entropy, and it will be conditioned in the remote future by how long man's environment remains a source of critical support. While the outcome will probably long favor the species that makes energy most subservient to its purposes,[8] that is, man, it will not favor all communities of men in the same degree and hence may be accompanied by intracommunity and intercommunity conflict. Family planning, resource conservation, migration, exchange, and the international diffusion of technology may depress conflict potential below the threshold level, but with difficulty as progress of exhaustion intensifies scarcity in a world of nations competing through trade and otherwise for critical and strategic resources.

It is not likely at present that institutional patterns can be developed to contain conflict in the manner of that pattern which came into being and produced stability within overpopulated peasant and feudal societies (*AE*, pp. 384–86). On the one hand, as Georgescu-Roegen points out, following Lotka, exosomatic instruments give or confer on some individuals (e.g., the privileged elite) and countries a differential advantage in the struggle for low entropy and hence for income, status, and luxury in a world capable only of limited output (*EL*, p. 306). On the other hand, even the common man usually lives in a world dominated by a set of commercial values designed to make an insatiable Sybarite of each and all. This relates well to Easterlin's finding that "economic growth does not raise a society to some ultimate state of plenty. Rather, the growth process itself engenders ever-growing wants that lead it ever onward,"[9] if only, as Keynes suggested, because of efforts to keep up with or outdo "the Joneses." In commercial economies characterized by overchoice (cf. *AE*, pp. 211–13), aggregate demand, if not forever insatiable given low entropy, is likely to remain unsatisfied until the time cost and the physical cost of consuming constrain this demand. Sir John Hicks's comment bears recalling:

One cannot repress the thought that perhaps the whole Industrial Revolution of the last 200 years has been nothing else but a vast secular boom, largely induced by the unparalleled rise in population. If this is so, it would help to explain why, as the wisest hold, it has been such a disappointing episode in human history.[10]

Numbers in a Two-Factor World

Prior to the nineteenth century, despite the fact that gross reproduction rates were relatively high, population grew very slowly over the long run in Europe and elsewhere, though rapidly enough at times in the shorter run to press heavily upon the land and cause concern lest population pressure persist. For example, Europe's population growth was interrupted several times with the result that it did not grow between A.D. 14 and A.D. 1000, or between 1340 and 1600, while Asia's did not grow between A.D. 14 and A.D. 1340 (see Table 2-1). Kuznets estimates that the world's population increased only about 0.3 percent per decade in the first Christian millennium, and about four times as fast, or about 1.3 percent per decade between 1000 and 1750. The latter global rate was less than the 1.6 percent rate experienced in the area of European settlement, and less than one-fifth of the world rate of growth between 1750 and 1960.[11] Responsible for the periodic declines in numbers were epidemics, famine, and food shortages caused by pests and crop failures, especially when food reserves were low despite public policies since ancient times to ensure the storage of enough grain to offset shortages. Adverse conditions, as noted by Polybius, Plato, and others, persisted into the late nineteenth century when famine alone eliminated perhaps 20 to 25 millions. As late as the early eighteenth century, suggests Fourastié, death was at the center of life and the churchyard was at the center of the village.[12]

Long before Malthus, note was taken of the seeming incapacity of the soil to meet the subsistence needs of Roman and other populations. For example, a contemporary of Julius Caesar, Lucretius (*De Rerum Natura*, Book VI, lines 1173–74) expressed the spirit of increasing entropy:

> That all things, little by little, waste away
> as time's erosion crumbles them to doom.

In A.D. 60, Columella observed that "nearly all writers on agriculture" believed (incorrectly, according to Columella, who believed that soil fertility could be maintained) that the soil was "worn out by long cultivation and exhausted," and is "suffering from old age." St. Cyprian, Bishop of Carthage, writing two centuries later, expressed the widely held end-of-the-world view of Christianity, when he said that the climate had changed, rainfall was insufficient, and mines and quarries were worn out. "The world has now grown old, and stands no longer in its pristine strength, nor has it the vigor and force which it formerly possessed."[13] Population growth, formerly a source of progress, was no longer desirable, asserted Tertullian (c. 150–200 A.D.). "We have grown burdensome to the world; the elements scarcely suffice for our support."[14] This opinion, compatible with early Christian asceticism and institutions unfavorable to propagation, was later modified somewhat in favor of marriage and fertility.

Illustrative of reactions to population pressure and associated unemployment long after their cooccurrence at the time of the Black Death[15]

Table 2-1
World Population to 1900
(millions)

	A.D. 14	600	1000	1340	1500	1600	1750	1800	1900
Africa	23	37	50	70	85	95	100	100	122
America	3	7	13	29	41	15	15	25	144
Asia	189	173	177	192	231	303	484	590	1007[a]
Europe	40	19	39	85	68	83	130	173	389[a]
Oceania	1	1	1	2	2	2	2	2	6
World	256	237	280	378	427	498	731	890	1668

[a]My estimate.
Source: Colin Clark, *Population Growth and Land Use* (London: Macmillan and Basingstoke 1967), Tables III–1 and III–15, pp. 64 and 108.

are three seventeenth-century statements cited by C. M. Cipolla.[16] Father Antero Maria di San Bonventura, survivor of the epidemic of 1657 which killed about three-fourths of Genoa's population, stated that were it not for the plague, Genoa would have become an even denser anthill, and there would not be enough food. He considered "the greater mortality among the poor to be the effect of Divine Providence for the good ordering of the Universe, since the poor are wont to breed beyond measure." G. B. Baliana (1582–1666) observed that "pestilence and war . . . cannot be escaped without our ultimately running into famine." In 1661, G. B. Riccioli stated that the populations of Bologna and Florence varied little in number since war, plague, and famine kept them within the confines of the available food supply. G. Botero (1540–1617) was of a somewhat similar opinion but more sophisticated and anticipative of Malthus.

Little explicit theory underlay statements of the sort cited. Seventeenth and eighteenth century "economists" proceeded upon the assumption that the economy was essentially a two-factor economy, with output being primarily the product of land and labor, albeit with the aid of some skills and man-made instruments. While land was thus likely to prove the limitative factor, the resulting constraint could be alleviated, Cantillon and later Sir James Steuart asserted, through exchange of labor-oriented for land-oriented products, essentially the policy pursued by Solon's Athens which, unlike a massive China or India, lacked unoccupied land into which to expand as numbers continued to grow. Adam Smith reinforced this approach with his concept of dynamic domestic and international division of labor as well as freed Malthus of the task of describing an economy in which men could pursue their self-interests within a generally accepted institutional setting and hence make effective use of their manpower.

Malthus, armed with the concept of diminishing returns and a distributive theory based thereon, conceived of the population problem in terms of an economy resting upon an essentially agricultural base, a base destined to begin gradually to give way to a mineral base within several decades. Living in the days of a fertility-conserving grass revolution, he found limits to the support of Britain's growing population, not in soil exhaustion, but in the principle of diminishing returns to which he and others had given expression. But in the *Essay on Population*, he opposed Britain's becoming very dependent upon external sources for food because these sources could eventually be lost through war or through population growth in export-supplying countries. He thus favored self-sufficiency, an objective sought in the German Empire in the latter part of the nineteenth century. It was essential, therefore, that Britain bring its numbers under control by preventing the introduction or continuation of institutions (e.g., "poor laws") conducive to fertility, by introducing institutional practices (e.g., deferment of marriage to the late twenties) less favorable to fertility, and by making manufactured products at prices attractive to workers while avoiding uneconomic cheapening of foodstuffs and thereby discouraging work and possibly stimulating fertility.[17] While Malthus's argument rested upon his view of land as the limitative factor, together with the limitations to which he found applied science subject, he could presumably have extended this role to other factors should man's numbers, together with his consumption pattern, have changed appropriately.[18] Malthus did not, however, favor a stationary optimum population such as Mill would favor because he believed growth of population constituted an essential stimulus to human activity.[19,20] Nor, as Georgescu-Roegen points out, did Malthus avoid the error of implicitly assuming "that population may grow beyond any limit both in number and time *provided that it does not grow too rapidly.*"[21]

In his *Principles*, John Stuart Mill, final formulator of classical political economy and Malthus's demographic model, also formalized a concept that had been lurking in the works of Cantillon, Steuart, the Physiocrats, and Ricardo among others: namely, the concept of optimum population size. Mill, however, doubted that it would come into being in the absence of state intervention, even given institutional improvements. He inferred that only under "the Communist scheme" or an analogous institutional arrangement would "public opinion" and, if necessary, penalties be directed against contributors to the "danger of overpopulation" since only under this scheme would the cost of overpopulation be quite visible and widespread. Mill's concept of optimum amounted to a corollary to Ricardo's concept of the genus "stationary state" whose members ranged from one in which wages, conditioned by the desired standard of life, remained at a subsistence level to one in which they were at a quite high level. Already in 1848, Mill observed that although old countries could support additional numbers, he could see "very little reason for desiring it" even if it were "innocuous." "The density of population necessary to enable mankind to obtain, in the greatest degree, all the advantages both of co-operation and of social intercourse, has, in all the most populous countries, been attained. A population may be too crowded, though all be amply supplied with food and raiment." He pointed to the opportunity for solitude and access to natural beauty that would be lost, and to the mental, moral, and social progress, the improvement in "the art of living," and the "abridging of labour" that would be gained. He did not propose maximization of a given social welfare index but instead reasoned as if further population growth was more likely to reduce than to augment the available and realizable options. Joan Robinson put it well over a century later: "The most noticeable effect of a growth in numbers, however, when it occurs at a high standard of life, is the way human beings destroy amenities for each other through cluttering up the country with their bodies, their houses, and their motor cars. The external diseconomies of consumption are then so marked as to leave utility theory completely in ruins."[22]

We may note in passing that Mill's physical vision of an optimum population was very simple compared to one appropriate to today. It ran essentially in agricultural and simple industrial terms. It implicitly postulated a very low rate of mobility and hence difficulty of access to nature's beauty even though railroads, condemned by early Victorians, were spreading; it thus overlooked the increase in desecration of attractive environments that would accompany great reduction in the physical cost of access to nature's beauty through replacement of man's legs by cheap modern vehicles. Finally, it postulated a simple environment and simple tastes rather than a Sisyphean pursuit of ever higher and more complex patterns of consumption in a wider environment become ever more complex and hence vulnerable to dissipation of limitative resources. Presumably his confidence in that eighteenth-century soporific, "almost inevitable progress," led him virtually to neglect warnings about the "exhaustion of mineral resources"—a neglect that, if averted by France, wrote Messance in 1788, would assure France's final triumph over Britain.[23]

Numbers in a Multifactor Western World

While factors substitutable for, or complementary to, land and labor had always been present in economies in some degree, their role continued to increase in importance after Malthus's *Essay* appeared, with the result that the final bill of goods grew in variety and complexity and its input composition became more vulnerable to the emergence of limitative factors. Moreover, since most factors in a multifactor economy are likely to be exhaustible, awareness increased respecting the likelihood of increasing economic entropy despite increase in the probability of finding actual or functional substitutes at the producer level for factors subject to depletion. Concern began to be focused upon possible barriers to the augmentability of output, particularly as it was observed that the rate of natural increase was not declining markedly. Would the chain of substitutes supposedly present in nature prove subject to discontinuities beyond the corrective powers of modern alchemy in a society that, as A. N. Whitehead later remarked, was inventing the very art of invention? Search for continuity therefore became the order of the day.

Of critical importance was the food chain, especially in the production of cereals (truly the staff of life), should soil fertility be dissipated by inappropriate methods of cultivation. Chemists of the early and middle nineteenth century demonstrated the essentiality of plant nutrients, especially nitrogen, and their fixation in the soil. Justus von Liebig's static theory of soil fertility, expressed in his "law of the minimum," pointed to the need for maintaining the stock of essential nutrients present in the soil, since yields were critically dependent upon a bottleneck factor —namely, that nutrient present in the smallest amount relative to the amount required.[24,25] Maintenance of yields therefore depended on the availability of plant nutrients, a shortage of which had contributed to the exhaustion of soil fertility in Roman times according to Von Liebig, an inference which Simkhovitch later independently put forward as the cause of ancient Rome's decline, which the planting of appropriate fertility-maintaining grasses might have prevented.[26] This thesis was later criticized but not wholly rejected by Usher, [27] Boak,[28] and others.[29] It was raised indirectly in 1898 when Sir William Crookes described the food supply as "a life and death question for generations to come. . . . England and all civilized nations stand in deadly peril of not having enough to eat," given low yields (0.4 of recent U.S. yields) and limited wheat acreage, unless atmospheric nitrogen fixation could make nitrogen economical enough as a fertilizer and science could be applied to solving the food problem.[30] Even so, in 1903, a royal commission inquired into the precariousness of Britain's food supply.

"In the present age," wrote Alfred Marshall in 1910, "the opening out of new countries, aided by low transport charges on land and sea, has almost suspended the tendency to Diminishing Return, in the sense in which the term was used by Malthus." But he added that Britain and other land-short countries would not long continue to be able to import landed products and raw materials in short domestic supply under essentially constant-cost conditions, should population continue to grow at even a quarter of its prevailing rate. Indeed, "aggregate rental values of land for all its uses . . . may again exceed the aggregate value of incomes derived from all sources."[31]

Two years later, J. M. Keynes suggested that the turning of the terms of trade against Britain revealed increase in population pressure. Still eight years later, he pointed out that the terms on which Europe and Britain traded with the New World had been worsening since 1900 and would continue to worsen should Europe's politicoeconomic system remain disorganized as a result of the war and its population continue to grow,[32] an unlikely outcome as E. Cannan[33] had pointed out already in 1895 and as French and other scholars had anticipated. Moreover, Sir William Beveridge[34] denied Keynes's assertion that Europe was overpopulated, and Hugh Dalton[35] described changes in the terms of trade as an ambiguous index of changes in population pressure.

W. S. Jevons was the first prominent economist to introduce so-called exhaustible natural resources into the Malthusian model and thus take into account the fact that an industrial economy rested on a natural-resource base as well as on an agricultural base, particularly if it had become dependent on foreign sources for produce. Believing coal to be the critical element in Britain's mineral base, Jevons in 1865 forecast the collapse of Britain's "industrial supremacy." For since it rested upon coal, whose cost was destined steadily to rise as easily accessible supplies were exhausted, "Britain may contract to her former littleness."[36] His scenario did not, however, arouse concern as did Malthus's forecast, perhaps because the impact of rising coal costs was hard to envision and the rising cost of coal proved less burdensome than expected,[37] or because solution in terms of a balanced autarky was not contemplated as in Germany.[38]

Despite discoveries by Lotka and R. R. Kuczynski (armed with refined measures based upon the stable population model perfected by Lotka) that fertility was near or at the replacement level in the United States and Western Europe, the 1920s found Malthusian concern as pronounced as in Malthus's time.[39] In the United States, the first conservation movement dating from the so-called disappearance of the frontier was still making itself felt.[40,41] Moreover, the capacity of the United States to support population growth at rising standards was put in doubt. In the 1923 *Agricultural Yearbook*, L. C. Gray and others put the country's population capacity at suitable standards at 150 million. A. G. Taylor wrote a year later that "when the ultimate population of the United States reaches 200 million," "one does not see how the country can raise the desired primary foods, domesticated animals, lumber, paper, and fibers."[42] In the same year, D. D. Lescohier anticipated that rising food costs throughout the world were "likely to check population growth as sharply as may prove necessary to maintain a twentieth-century civilization."[43] The modern point of view respecting energy was anticipated at that time by F. G. Tryon and Lida Mann, who pointed out the "barring some revolutionary discovery of science" (e.g., "utilizing the energy locked up in the atom"), the "rising cost of energy" would depress the standard of living. "A permanent civilization," they concluded, "must learn to balance its energy budget, to collect each year from the inexhaustible sources of water, wind, and sun as much power as it expends."[44] Confidence in technological progress, the economist's easy answer today to evidence of resource scarcity and increasing entropy, had not yet become the opium of the elite. After all, Julius Wolf had warned in 1912 that technicoeconomic progress was slowing down,[45] and sixteen years later a distinguished scientist, R. A. Millikan, dismissed exploitation of atomic physics as a potential source of power, pointing instead to the sun as the important source of power in the future.[46]

Ironically, already in the 1920s and especially in the 1930s, concern lest population cease to grow became manifest in a number of countries, and populationist measures were introduced, motivated in part by desires to reduce economic inequality.[47] Concern was expressed in America lest agricultural overcapacity might develop,[48] a concern accentuated by improvements in agricultural yields in the 1930s.[49] Soon to find expression as well was concern lest economies prove too inflexible to give rise to "full employment" in countries with little or no growth in population and hence reduced need for population-sensitive investment.

Population Growth Becomes a Matter of International Concern

While the population question has always been somewhat regional in scope, it did not become international in both fact and general awareness until the present century, particularly with the destruction of Euro-American hegemony by the first and second modern Peloponnesian wars and the emergence of population growth as a source of international instability. For with minerals and energy sources in exploitable concentrations distributed randomly over the planet, international interdependence has increased as more and more resources have moved into the orbit of use, with the requirements of many growing exponentially even though their inflow is subject to political as well as economic interruption (e.g., oil).[50] Meanwhile, with the release of the Malthusian devil in the underdeveloped world as a result of the introduction of death control, the rate of natural increase in population formerly below that in the developed world, has risen to levels more than double those in developed regions where fertility is often in the neighborhood of replacement. The population of underdeveloped regions, about 65 percent of world population in 1900, seems destined to exceed 80 percent within seventy-five years as it rises from over 2.5 billion in 1970 to between 9 and 12 billion in the twenty-first century. Until now, the introduction of Western capital, techniques, skills, and aspirations has failed to bring natural increase down and per capita output up (see Table 2-2) in keeping with post-1950 expectations based upon the experience of Japan and of the Marshall-Plan countries in Europe. In the absence of salutary revolutions, cultures change slowly, particularly in rural societies (e.g., *AE*, chap. 11), in which in 1950 only 11 percent of the population lived in localities of twenty thousand or more (compared with 40 percent in developed regions). Moreover, the rural population, given its high fertility, will long continue to grow (though not as fast as the urban population) since urban centers capable of supplying continuously growing employment to immigrants are too few and there are no longer foreign outlets comparable to those in the

Table 2–2
World Indicators, 1972

	Population		Gross National Product		
Group of Countries	Total (millions)	Annual growth rate (%)	Total (billions)	Per capita	Annual growth rate (%)
Developed	672	1.0	$2,033	$3,025	4.5
Non-oil-producing developing	1,624	2.4	390	244	2.6
Oil-producing[a] developing	264 (314)	2.5 (3.0)	58 (112)	221 (358)	3.3 (7.8)
Centrally planned	1,178	1.5	632	536	3.3
Total	3,738	1.9	3,133	838	3.5

[a] Data in parentheses estimated for 1978.
Source: *Finance & Development* 12 (March, 1975): 2–3.

New World, which prior to 1930 absorbed enough immigrants to enable cityward migration in northern and western Europe to absorb most of its excess rural population.

The future of the Third World is bleak in the absence of a speedy reduction of natality, an outcome hardly to be brought about by resolutions. Already about one-third or more of the populations of developing countries do not satisfy their calorie and protein needs. In his study of world food problems, Johnson concludes "that there can be no significant improvements in per capita food supply without declines in birth rates and reductions in population growth rates."[51] For while only about half the world's land suitable for crops and forage is in use, much of the nonused arable land is in Latin America and Sub-Saharan Africa and hence not easy of access to Asia's expanding population or as problem-free as land in use. Yields are susceptible to considerable but not unlimited increase on lands in actual or potential use, given continuation of favorable climatic and economic conditions, together with continuing access to requisite inputs (e.g., water, fertilizer, pesticides, suitable high-yield crops, and appropriate mechanization and practices).

Capacity to earn foreign exchange with which to import foodstuffs is quite limited in non-mineral-rich countries. Moreover, growth of their capacity for industrial development will be handicapped by rising energy and natural-resource costs. Thus, after examining the processes underlying slowly emerging functional and economic limits to the availability of utilizable geologic resources, together with consumption by increasing entropy of the utilizability of what is left, Earl Cook concludes:

Sometime in the not-too-distant future, Americans will look back with astonishment at our ignorance of the world we live in. Because of diminishing resources and continued population growth, we are heading for a planned, managed society. Just how restraining or undemocratic that society will become may depend in large measure on how quickly and successfully we move to minimize entropy increase and resource depletion—which, after all, are the same thing.[52]

The Future

Man's demographic future may be seen from four points of view: (1) identification and solution of particular problems, (2) age structure, (3) population optima, and (4) intergenerational relations. In these connections, especially regarding the latter, Georgescu-Roegen has made notable contributions to our knowledge.

Problem Identification and Solution

Most important here are: (1) fertility control; and (2) reduction in the rate of increase in resource exhaustion, together with resulting international externalities (e.g., pollution and uncontrolled exploitation of the seas) and their intensification by delay in reducing fertility, especially in various high-fertility countries.

In general, given fairly effective and safe methods of fertility control, fertility will be dominated by the time and other costs, together with the advantages, perceived as associated with family formation.[53] Differences in cultural and institutional environments, however, condition how actual costs and advantages are perceived and thus contribute to differences in fertility which may affect genetic selection adversely[54,55] or result in the rearing of a disproportionate number of children in unfavorable environments with the result, as Pigou observed,[56] that future generations in turn are affected adversely. Should a population become stationary or decline in number, fertility differences may be intensified unless countervailing policies are introduced; for those less sensitive to costs or to genetic or environmental shortcomings tend to be less disposed to curb fertility.

Economy is indicated in the use of natural resources since, as Georgescu-Roegen points out, they "represent the limitative factor as concerns the life span" of the human species. For although "in terms of low entropy, the stock of mineral resources is only a very small fraction of the solar energy received by the globe within a single year," the relative smallness of this stock and the fact that "the low entropy received from the sun cannot be converted into matter in bulk" together lead to the inescapable conclusion that it is "the meager stock of the earth's resources that constitutes the crucial scarcity." It is the size of this stock, together with the rate at which it is decumulated by population growth, that determines the duration of the "human species" (*EL*, pp. 20–21, 301–304).

Georgescu-Roegen points out further that technological progress is not the long-run offset to population growth even though it may temporarily increase the stock of utilizable resources. Thus far, he argues, "the price of technological progress has meant a shift from the more abundant source of low entropy—the solar radiation—to the less abundant one—the earth's mineral resources. . . . Population pressure and technological progress bring *ceteris paribus* the career of the human species nearer to its end only because both factors cause a speedier decumulation of its dowry. The sun will continue to shine on the earth . . . even after the extinction of mankind and will feed with low entropy other species, those with no ambition whatever." (*EL*, p. 304, also pp. 19–21).

Economy in terms of entropy consists in drawing upon relatively nonpolluting sources of energy, especially abundant solar power,[57] in utilizing methods, structures, forms of recreation, etc., that minimize the use of energy and natural resources, especially of those liable to become bottlenecks. Given our lack of knowledge of the future, however, action along these lines may be optimum-oriented and option-conserving; though not productive of an optimum solution, in effect, it can produce a second-best.[58]

Age Structure

Problems may arise with the response of a society to the advent of a stationary age structure. This age structure is favorable to per capita productivity since the relative number of working age will be at a maximum and since the savings potential is high and savings are not absorbed by net population growth.

While imbalance between savings and investment at the full-employment level could arise should the economy not prove flexible and its equilibrating mechanisms fail to function optimally, continuing increase in the fraction of GNP absorbed by government makes the feared imbalance unlikely. Dearth of savings is more likely. Of greater importance could be the impact of increasingly early retirement upon the economic security of the aged, both under more or less pay-as-you-go retirement systems and under so-called funded systems. For example, if, say, everyone retired at age 55 instead of at age 65, the ratio of population defined as of working age to those in retirement would be reduced from about 3.8 to 1 to about 1.73 to 1, and the fraction of working age would be reduced by about one-fifth. At the individual level, should a white male enter the labor force at 18 and retire at, say, 50 instead of 65, he will have worked only 1⅓ years for each year in retirement instead of about 3½ years.

Vertical mobility within the labor force will be significantly reduced in that movement from a given point to a given point in the employment hierarchy may take several years longer than at present.[59] This condition may call for reduction in the age-profile gradient of earnings insofar as they are affected by seniority; for greater pressure upon a limited number of so-called preferred situations by older workers will lower their relative incomes, whereas reduced pressure upon beginner employments will conduce to relatively higher starting incomes. No longer will someone with a Ph.D. proceed rapidly to a professorship or a lieutenant rise to the top as in a long war.

Aging will tend to diminish horizontal and geographical mobility, especially if information relating to opportunities is poor and financial costs of movement are incident on the mover.

Maintenance of optimum interoccupational and interindustrial balance tends to become more difficult when a population becomes stationary, especially if tastes and technology are changing. When a stable population is growing, the number of persons newly entering the labor force consists of r (replacements of withdrawals from the labor force) and a (additions); then $r + a$ are available to fill v (jobs vacated by withdrawals from nonexpanding employments, but in need of their replacement) together with e (newly developing jobs in expanding industries). When a population is stationary and hence only replacements are available to fill $(v + e) = r$, there is no problem; but if $(v + e) > r$, wages may have to rise slightly to restore balance. If, however, trade-union and other barriers slow transfer to jobs in expanding industries, upward pressure on wages in these industries, and sympathetically in other industries, is likely to result and could eventuate in some unemployment and/or real-cost-reducing inflation.

As long as a population is stationary and labor-force entries just balance withdrawals, absorption of young persons into the labor force presents few or no problems. An upsurge of births can, however, give rise to upsurges in children-oriented investment, later to upsurges in job-seekers, to unemployment should derived demand for labor not increase commensurately with the increase in the annual increment to the labor force, and finally to abnormally large numbers of unproductive aged.

Birth upsurges also generate future echo effects. Avoidance of birth fluctuations has become virtually essential to the avoidance of youth unemployment in a trade-union-dominated economy.

A population that is stationary could prove less dynamic than a growing one, even though the relative number of persons of inventive and innovative age is not materially affected. For the average age of a population, its labor force, and (most likely) its capital structure is higher, with the result that each embodies relatively few of the most recent improvements in technology, in part because an older population and business and governmental leadership are less likely to be agreeable to introducing either new and experimental methods or novel products. This shortcoming can be overcome in part by continuing education, but not entirely inasmuch as the cost of holding down the average age of capital could prove too high to pay off even though savings per capita should prove relatively high. To this cost there may be an offset insofar as an unused capital reserve functions as a price- and cost-stabilizing agency.

Generally, the degree of flexibility characteristic of a stationary labor force is conditioned by the degree to which human and other factors of production are nonspecific in character, or easily transformable through education, etc., from one specific orientation to another. There will be a growing need, therefore, for technologies and training that make for reduced specificity and for increase in multiple use.

Population optimization theory assumes two forms: that relating to distribution of population in space, and that relating to populations of states under given conditions. What constitutes an optimum turns on the welfare index subject to maximization under given but usually changing conditions; it therefore is subject to change since both the content of welfare indexes and the sociophysical environment of population movement and concentration change.

The efficiency-optimum size of a given state's population coincides with that at which economies associated with scale of activities counterbalance direct and indirect disadvantages of working with smaller per capita and per worker amounts of productive agents complementary to human agents; the welfare optimum lies just beyond this point.[60] This size changes with changes in trade relations and other conditions originally impounded in *ceteris paribus*. There is little or no tendency for deviation of population size from optimum size to produce a deviation-correcting feedback.[61] While the optimum concept is not easily actualized, it focuses attention upon the impact of change in population size on the options available to a population before, and expected to be available after, change in population size. It thus provides an impression of whether such change is immediately in a welfare-increasing direction though eventually productive of increase in both entropy and divers other costs.

It may be advantageous to compare large and small states in terms of their comparative advantages and disadvantages in a free-trade and nonfree-trade world. For conceptions of optimum size, as usually defined, do not take into account political and other noneconomic costs and benefits associated with size even though these may be more important than purely economic costs and benefits, particularly in a world in which the resource bases of economies are subject to contraction in the longer run.

Decisions respecting what constitutes optimum distribution of population in space or among cities of varying size may be directed to reducing energy and resource use as well as pollution and to increasing what Georgescu-Roegen calls "life enjoyment," an "immaterial flux" shaped by "exosomatic evolution" working through "cultural tradition" (*EL*, pp. 18–19, 282–84)—a flux whose volume will be conditioned by how skillfully and economically population concentrations are structured and distributed, particularly in underdeveloped regions where massive urbanward movements will long continue, given populations still about four-fifths rural in underdeveloped Asia and Africa though less so in Latin America. Were engineering science to concentrate upon miniaturizing technical determinants of economies associated with scale of production and concentration of complementary activities, it would often be possible to reduce city size, achieve wider dispersal of activities and people when compatible with supplies of water, etc., and reduce pollution and waste.

Emphasis upon the short run and virtual neglect of the long run have dominated practice and (in considerable measure) social theory in the so-called developed world for more than a century. Witness the neglect of reports of resource prospects in the United States,[62,63,64] now repaired in part by Resources for the Future. Yet, the welfare of future generations is conditioned in great measure by what the current and immediately succeeding generations do, by how rapidly they decumulate man's resource dowry, and by the degree to which they allow the mathematics of delay to make future populations, say, 40 percent or more higher than they would be given a net reproduction rate of 1.0 in the near future.

The impact of the decisions of present generations upon the options of future generations depends upon how technologically dynamic present societies are, together with the rate of change in tastes as they pass from one generation to the next. This impact in turn will set limits to the amount of knowledge a present generation can have of the wants and want-satisfying power of generations lying quite far in the future; even if some members of current generations had such knowledge, they probably would lack the power to shape current decisions appropriately. As a result, the probable impact of present decisions upon the welfare of vote-lacking persons several generations removed is unlikely to produce changes in tentative present decisions more in keeping with the supposed welfare of future generations. Indeed, as Georgescu-Roegen points out, economics in its supposed capacity of administrator of scarce resources "cannot even dream of handling" the distribution of mankind's dowry of natural resources "among all generations."[65] Economists do not live in a Laplacian world, nor have they the skill to foresee the optima formulated by those living a few centuries hence and facilitate the realization of these optima.

Intergenerational allocation favors current generations. For, as Georgescu-Roegen demonstrates, "the market system by itself results in resources being consumed in higher amounts by the earlier generations, that is, faster than they should be," thus confirming "the dictatorship of the present over the future." "The market mechanism cannot protect mankind from ecological crises in the future, let alone allocate resources optimally among generations, even if we would try to set prices 'right.' " Moreover, since resource depletion mainly affects future generations, it receives much less attention than pollution which is incident on the present generation, the very generation that produces it.[66]

Georgescu-Roegen points to a number of changes which, while not indicators of the optima likely to be chosen several or more generations hence, will increase the options available to these generations, or at least prevent their reduction. Most important is freedom of future generations from dictatorship by the present generation. Whence "until either the direct use of solar energy becomes a general convenience" (thereby greatly reducing the dictatorship of the present over future generations) "or controlled fusion is achieved, all waste of energy . . . should be carefully avoided, and if necessary, strictly regulated." He points also to the need to curb the use of natural resource and energy inputs by making possible elimination of military expenditure, by reducing the production and consumption of nonserviceable goods, by eliminating purposeful obsolescence, and by augmenting the durability of goods. He suggests, moreover, that since organic agriculture is not very dependent upon scarce-resource inputs, it needs to be depended upon in the future in greater measure even if some downward adjustment of population proves to be required.[67] To these suggestions may be added increasing use of labor-oriented methods of production, together with noncommercial rec-reation making little demand upon exhaustible resources.

If we follow Georgescu-Roegen's presentation of the population-resource problem, there are two alternatives. Should solar power, fusion power, and other essentially nonexhaustible sources of power become available and make possible the alchemy required to transmute abundant elements into that which is required, man can long live with the population-resource problem. Otherwise, he will need both to halt growth of population or even reduce it in size and to orient production, consumption, and recreation from dependence upon natural-resource-embodying products to much greater dependence upon labor-embodying goods and services. As Lapp aptly puts it, "the growth curves must depart from their vertiginous ascent—the twentieth century must, so to speak, begin to bend over." [68] And so must growth of the food supply bend unless solar energy is harnessed. For, as Chancellor and Goss conclude, "A calamity-free balance between energy and food depends upon the advent of a solar-powered world." [69]

Notes

1. Robert Dorfman, Paul A. Samuelson, and Robert M. Solow, *Linear Programming and Economic Analysis* (New York: McGraw-Hill, 1958), pp. 280–81, also pp. 245–47, 322–29.

2. N. Georgescu-Roegen, "Dynamic Equilibrium and Economic Growth," *Economie Appliquée* 27, no. 4 (1974): 529–64.

3. Talcott Parsons, *Structure of Social Action* (New York: McGraw-Hill, 1937), chap. 3.

4. A. J. Lotka, "The Law of Evolution as a Maximal Principle," *Human Biology* 17 (September 1945): 167 ff., esp. 188.

5. James E. Meade, "The Population Explosion, the Standard of Living and Social Conflict," *Economic Journal* 77 (June 1967): 233–55.

6. Peter Vorzimmer, "Darwin, Malthus, and the Theory of Natural Selection," *Journal of the History of Ideas* 30 (October-December 1969): 522–42.

7. A. J. Lotka, *Elements of Physical Biology* (Baltimore: Williams and Wilkins, 1925), pp. 36–37, 208, 355, 357.

8. Ibid., p. 357.

9. R. A. Easterlin, "Does Economic Growth Improve the Human Lot? Some Empirical Evidence," in P. A. David and M. W. Reder, *Nations and Households in Economic Growth: Essays in Honor of Moses Abramovitz* (New York: Academic Press, 1974), pp. 90–125, esp. 121.

10. J. R. Hicks, *Value and Capital* (Oxford: Clarendon Press, 1946), p. 302.

11. Simon Kuznets, *Economic Growth of Nations* (Cambridge: Harvard University Press, 1971), pp. 22–25.

12. J. Fourastié, "De la vie traditionelle à la vie tertiaire," *Population* 14 (1959.3): 418.

13. W. G. Simkhovitch, "Rome's Fall Reconsidered," in *Toward the Understanding of Jesus* (New York: Macmillan, 1921), 1937 ed., pp. 93–99.

14. A. O. Lovejoy, *Essays in the History of Ideas* (New York: G. P. Putnam, 1948), pp. 320–22.

15. A. R. Bridbury, "The Black Death," *Economic History Review* 26 (November 1973): 577–92.

16. C. M. Cipolla, "The Plague and the Pre-Malthus Malthusians," *Journal of European Economic History* 3 (Fall 1974): 277–84.

17. Joseph J. Spengler, "Malthus the Malthusian vs. Malthus the Economist," *Southern Economic Journal* 24 (July 1967): 1–12.

18. Idem., "Was Malthus Right?" reprinted with other papers in *Population Economics* (Durham: Duke University Press, 1972).

19. E. F. Penrose, *Population Theories and Their Application* (Stanford: Food Research Institute, 1934), pp. 24–34.

20. S. M. Levin, "Malthus and the Idea of Progress," *Journal of the History of Ideas* 27 (January-March 1966): 92–108.

21. Nicholas Georgescu-Roegen, "Energy and Economic Myths," *Southern Economic Journal* 41 (January 1975): 347–81, esp. 366.

22. Joan Robinson, *Economic Philosophy* (Chicago: Aldine, 1960), p. 116.

23. M. Messance, *Nouvelles recherches sur la population* (Paris: 1788), pp. 127–28.

24. Emil Lang, "The Law of the Soil," in W. J. Spellman and Emil Lang, *The Law of Diminishing Returns* (New York: World Book Co., 1924), Part 2.

25. F. L. Patton, *Diminishing Returns in Agriculture* (New York: Columbia University Press, 1926).

26. Simkhovitch, *Toward the Understanding*, passim.

27. A. P. Usher, "Soil Fertility and Exhaustion," *Quarterly Journal of Economics* 3 (May 1923): 386–411.

28. A. E. R. Boak, *Manpower Shortage and the Fall of the Roman Empire in the West* (Ann Arbor: University of Michigan Press, 1955), p. 120.

29. J. H. Clapham and Eileen Power, eds., *The Cambridge Economic History of Europe* I (Cambridge: University Press, 1941), chaps. 2–3.

30. Joseph S. Davis, "The Specter of Dearth of Food: History's Answer to Sir William Crookes," in Arthur Cole et al., eds., *Facts and Factors in Economic History* (Cambridge: Harvard University Press, 1932), pp. 733–54.

31. Alfred Marshall, *Principles of Economics,* Variorum edition (London: Macmillan, 1961), pp. xv–xvii.

32. J. M. Keynes, *Economic Consequences of the Peace* (New York: Harcourt, Brace, and Howe, 1920), chap. 2.

33. Edwin Cannan, *Economic Scares* (London: P. S. King, 1933), pp. 83–135.

34. Sir William Beveridge, "Population and Unemployment," *Economic Journal* 33 (December 1923), pp. 447–75, and "Mr. Keynes' Evidence for Overpopulation," *Economica* 4 (February 1924), pp. 1–20.

35. Hugh Dalton, "The Theory of Population," *Economica* 8 (March 1928), pp. 28–50.

36. W. S. Jevons, *The Coal Question*, 3rd ed., A. W. Flux, ed. (London: Macmillan Co., 1906), chap. 1, pp. 11, 232, 459–60.

37. H. W. Singer, "The Coal Question Reconsidered: Effects of Economy and Substitution," *Review of Economic Studies* 8 (June 1941), pp. 166–77.

38. A. O. Hirschman, *National Power and the Structure of Foreign Trade* (Berkeley: University of California Press, 1945).

39. A. B. Wolfe, "The Population Problem Since the World War: A Survey of Literature and Research," Pt. I-III, *Journal of Political Economy* 36 (October-December 1928), pp. 529–59, 662–85; 37 (February 1929), pp. 87–120.

40. S. P. Hays, *Conservation and the Gospel of Efficiency: The Progressive Movement, 1890-1920* (Cambridge: Harvard University Press, 1959).

41. H. J. Barnett and Chandler Morse, *Scarcity and Growth* (Baltimore: Johns Hopkins University Press, 1963), Part I.

42. L. I. Dublin, ed., *Population Problems in the United States and Canada* (Boston: Houghton-Mifflin, 1926), p. 110.

43. Ibid., p. 93.

44. Ibid., pp. 136–38.

45. *Die Volkswirtschaft der Gegenwart u. Zukunft* (Leipzig: Fischer, 1912), pp. 236–37.

46. F. G. Tryon and M. H. Schoenfeld, "Utilization of Natural Wealth," in W. C. Mitchell et al., eds., *Recent Social Trends,* I (New York: McGraw-Hill, 1933), p. 73 and note.

47. David Glass, *Population Policies and Movements in Europe* (Oxford: Clarendon Press, 1940).

48. O. E. Baker, "The Trend of Agricultural Production in North America and Its Relation to Europe and Asia," in Quincy Wright, ed., *Population* (Chicago: University of Chicago Press, 1930), pp. 211–80.

49. Lester R. Brown, *Increasing World Food Output* (Washington, D.C.: U.S.D.A., 1965), chap. 3.

50. S. R. Graubard, ed., "The Oil Crisis in Perspective," *Daedalus* 104 (Fall 1975).

51. D. Gale Johnson, *World Food Problems and Prospects* (Washington, D.C.: American Enterprise Institute, 1975).

52. Earl Cook, "The Depletion of Geologic Resources," *Technology Review* 77 (June 1975): 15–27.

53. E.g., see T. W. Schultz, ed., *Economics of the Family: Marriage, Children and Human Capital* (Chicago: University of Chicago Press, 1975).

54. Philip Handler, ed., *Biology and the Future of Man* (New York: Oxford University Press, 1970), pp. 478ff., 909–11, 917–19, 928.

55. Colin Clark, "Profit Maximization and the Extinction of Animal Species," *Journal of Political Economy* 8 (August 1973): 950–61.

56. A. C. Pigou, *The Economics of Welfare* (London: Macmillan, 1932), pp. 112–16.

57. Farrington Daniels, *Direct Use of the Sun's Energy* (New Haven: Yale University Press, 1964).

58. Harold Hotelling, "The Economics of Exhaustible Resources," *Journal of Political Economy* 39 (March-April 1931): 137–75.

59. Nathan Keyfitz, "Individual Mobility in a Stationary Population," *Population Studies* 23 (July 1973): 335–52.

60. J. E. Meade, *Trade and Welfare,* II (London: Oxford University Press, 1955), pp. 80–102.

61. Cf. P. A. Samuelson, *Foundations of Economic Analysis* (Cambridge: Harvard University Press, 1947), pp. 297–98.

62. C. K. Leith, *Mineral Valuations for the Future* (New York: American Institute of Mining, 1938).

63. President's Materials Policy Commission, *Resources for Freedom* (Washington, D.C.: U.S.G.P.O., 1952).

64. National Academy of Sciences, *Resources and Man* (San Francisco: W. H. Freeman, 1969).

65. Georgescu-Roegen, "Energy and Economic Myths," op. cit., pp. 374–75.

66. Ibid., pp. 375–77.

67. Ibid., pp. 377–78.

68. Ralph E. Lapp, *The Logarithmic Century* (Englewood Cliffs, N.J.: Prentice-Hall, Inc., 1973), p. 254.

69. W. J. Chancellor, Jr. and J. R. Goss, "Balancing Energy and Food Production, 1975–2000," *Science* 192 (April 16, 1976): 213–18.

3

Aspects of Post–World War II Growth in Less Developed Countries

Simon Kuznets

Introduction

In this chapter, we deal with selected aspects of economic growth since World War II in developing (less developed, or LDC for short), as contrasted with developed (or DC), market economies, excluding the centrally planned or communist countries (which in 1972 accounted for some 1.2 of 3.7 billion world population).[1] This exclusion is due partly to difficulties of securing comparable and meaningful estimates for these countries, particularly for the giant among them, Mainland China, but largely to problems involved in the analysis of economic growth in countries in which the trade-off between economic gain (in output or power) and individual welfare and freedom is so different from that in the less centralized market economies.

The LDCs are the countries in Asia, Africa, and Latin America that are characterized by low income per capita and a production structure that suggests a marked shortfall in exploiting the opportunities provided by modern technology. According to the *World Bank Atlas,* of the 1.85 billion people in the "developing" countries in 1972, close to 1 billion were in low-income countries whose per capita GNP averaged $110; and another 0.27 billion were in countries with "middle income"—i.e., a range of per capita GNP between $200 and $375, and an average of $260. By way of contrast, the average per capita income for developed or industrial market economies, with a population of 0.66 billion, was over $3,500.[2] United Nations estimates, a major source of comparative data, differ in detail of classification from those of the World Bank; but for our purposes, which involve general orders of magnitude rather than detail, the two sets of estimates are fairly comparable.

Our interest is in the growth of the poor LDCs. Not all the countries classified as "developing" by either the World Bank or the United Nations are poor, the striking exception being the oil sheikdoms with small populations and enormous oil revenues. Nor are all the countries classified as "developed" rich, as illustrated by several countries in Southern Europe. There is a twilight zone where a more discriminating classification would place countries that are backward but rich, those that are in the process of movement from LDC to DC status but have not yet attained the latter, and still others that may have regressed from apparent

DC status (possibly illustrated by Argentina). But these intermediate or mixed groups do not loom large enough within the LDC or DC categories to modify substantially the broader parameters of size, structure, and growth. This is especially true when we emphasize, as we should, the population weights in any aggregation of countries for establishing the growth of total and per capita product for large groups.

The broad topic covers a wide field for which, over the last quarter of a century, an enormous body of data, both descriptive and analytical, has accumulated. Indeed, it is hard to exaggerate the explosive acceleration in the flow of data and range of studies in this field, which before World War II was not of primary interest even for the developed countries and practically neglected for the rest of the world. No single scholar can deal with it either comprehensively or with full balance, and particularly within the limitations of time and space warranted on this occasion. The discussion that follows represents an individual's reflections on some of the questions raised by the broader type of aggregative evidence and analysis.

Diversity and Aggregation

DCs and LDCs Compared

For the LDCs as a group, the United Nations has estimated annual growth rates of total and per capita GDP (at constant factor prices) from 1950 to 1972.[3] The growth rate of per capita product was 2.5 percent per year from 1950 to 1960, and 2.7 percent from 1960 to 1972; and the combined rate for the twenty-two years was 2.61 percent per year. If this rate were sustained, per capita product would double in about twenty-seven years, with the further implication that between 1950 and 1975 per capita product must have risen by about 90 percent. For the poorer and most populous LDC region distinguished in the UN estimates back to 1950, East and Southeast Asia (excluding Japan), with a population by 1972 of over 1 billion, the growth rates in per capita product for 1950–60 and 1960–72 were 1.9 and 2.2 percent respectively. The combined rate of 2.04 percent implies a rise of close to two-thirds over twenty-five years and a doubling in a period somewhat short of thirty-five years.

Such growth rates are quite high in the long-term historical perspective of both the LDCs and the current DCs. While the historical data for the LDCs rarely provide a firm base for judging their long-term growth, the low levels of per capita product that characterize these countries in the early 1950s and even in the early 1960s clearly imply that rates of growth that mean doubling in a period from twenty-seven to thirty-five years could not have prevailed in the long-term past. For such rates, if applied to the years before the 1950s, would have meant impossibly low levels of per capita product and consumption at the beginning of the preceding quarter of a century. And for the current DCs, for sixteen of which we have measures of long-term growth, the observed rates are generally well below those cited for the LDCs in the paragraph above. For periods extending from at least half a century to the long period of their modern economic growth, Sweden, over the last century, and Japan, back to the late 1870s, are the only two of the sixteen countries with growth rates in per capita product that approached or slightly exceeded 29 percent per decade. Indeed, they are the only countries with growth rates above 22 percent per decade (unless one counts Italy, back to 1895–99, with a rate of 23 percent).[4]

A Puzzle

If growth rates in the per capita product of LDCs over almost a quarter of a century were so impressively high, one may ask why the reactions to them, as shown in the general flow of news about these countries and in the persistent concern about critical conditions with respect to supplies of economic goods, seem to ignore these growth achievements. The news, reactions, and concerns are not sufficiently tangible to be susceptible of easy quantification. Moreover, one cannot take measurements of this sort, even if quantitatively accurate, to reflect economic movements. It may well be that a rise in expectations has produced a negative reaction to economic attainments which otherwise might have elicited litanies of praise for economic "miracles." And, indeed, references have been made to such miracles for some limited periods and countries, in contrast to the more prevalent references to acute problems in the LDCs, and to the recurring flurries of concern among international agencies and developed countries over economic deprivation and dangers of collapse in the Third World. Perhaps the emphasis in the flow of news on the troublesome rather than favorable events, combined with the easier accessibility and wider communications, introduced a bias in recent decades that tended to conceal economic advance of major proportions. Still, even if we find, as we may later, grounds for inferring that there has been a change in expectations, and hence in the bases for evaluating the adequacy of modern economic growth, we should still examine critically aggregative measures of the type noted above. They may conceal more than they reveal, and the various kinds of aggregation that yield such measures may contain biases that should be identified, and their magnitude should at least be suggested.

This examination cannot deal with the question of accuracy of the basic underlying data, country by country, or even for a selected sample. The question is particularly relevant to the statistics of the LDCs, where the brevity of the period over which basic data have been collected and the limited scholarly resources for their analysis, combined with the difficulties of proper quantification of processes that do not naturally yield measurable results, limit the accuracy and adequacy of the data. And part of the problem lies in a system of national accounting concepts and classifications which is poorly fitted to the economic life and experience of the LDCs. But, taking note of the limitations, we assume that the basic data, while crude, are of the right order of magnitude for broad findings and inferences—which minimally can be used to generate plausible hypotheses, subject to test and revision as better data and study lead to an improved foundation.

The measures just cited, and widely used, are results of aggregation of: (1) populations, either within or among countries and regions, the products of whose economic activities are pooled together; (2) the outputs of the several production sectors viewed as contributions to, and the different uses of product viewed as drafts upon, that common pool of product; and (3) the movements of total product, or its parts, in relation to population, over the shorter periods within the total time span for which we derive the average growth rates. Because the measures are comprehensive in their coverage of product, of the relevant populations within and among countries, and of the different segments of the time span, the resulting aggregates are effective summaries of the net result of a wide range of interrelated activities over a long span of historical time. But the synthesizing function of such aggregation may involve sacrifice of important differences and variability and be attained along differing lines and with differing costs. These two aspects of aggregation and of the resulting measures will now be briefly discussed, with particular reference to the economic growth of the LDCs since the early 1950s and to the apparent puzzle set forth at the start of this section.

Variability: Temporal, Sectoral, and among LDCs

Let us take the growth rate of 2.6 percent per year in per capita GNP for 1960–72 derived for some sixty-seven LDCs, each with over 1 million population in 1972, and omitting major oil exporters, countries still in colonial status, and those affected by current wars in Indochina. Since the 2.6 percent rate is an average, it may easily be the result of a combination of some countries with no growth or even declines, with others having high growth rates. And, indeed, the *World Bank Atlas,* from which the average rate was derived, lists LDCs (with a total population close to 100 million) with a per capita product growth of less than 0.5 percent per year, and some of them showing no rise or even declines (Bangladesh, Ghana, Afghanistan, Senegal, for example). At the other end, eleven LDCs with a population close to 120 million have per capita growth rates of 3.5 percent per year or more, or an average (weighted by population) of 5.1 percent. Diversity of behavior within a comprehensive average is only to be expected; but this diversity in the growth records of the LDCs has some distinctive aspects, which will be considered after a brief comment on the implications of aggregation among sectors and over time.

Changes in per capita gross product are combinations of changes in per capita product of each of the n production sectors, appropriately weighted by the share of each sector in aggregate output. The important point to note in this connection is that the growth rate of the A sector (agriculture and related industries) has been markedly lower than that of the I sector (industry, including mining, manufacturing, utilities, construction, and transport and communication) and of the S sector (services, including trade, government, professional, and personal services). Moreover, in relation to total population (i.e., on a per capita basis), the growth of a basic products sector like agriculture has been low. Thus, calculated from quinquennial averages based on United Nations data for developing countries, the growth rate of per capita GDP over the 1950–72 period averaged 2.3 percent per year; but for the output of the A sector, the average was only 0.56 percent per year. [5] This finding of a low growth rate of agricultural output per head in the LDCs is corroborated by a recent study by the U.S. Department of Agriculture, which shows, for 1954–73, an annual rate of increase in per capita production of foods of 0.4 percent per year for the developing countries (compared with a rate of 1.5 percent for the developed countries).[6]

Short-term changes in subperiods of the time span for which the average growth rate is calculated do not necessarily cluster closely around the average. This is particularly true when total product comprises major sectors in which vagaries of weather from year to year may affect output (as is the case in so many LDCs), or when it is subject to short-term strains of changing markets and demand (as is the case in the smaller LDCs that rely heavily on export). Thus, even for a very large region, such as East and Southeast Asia, the indexes of GDP per capita, which rise over 1960–72, show a drop or stability from 1964 through 1966, and from 1971 to 1972. In other words, three annual rates out of a total of twelve represented contrary movements, while in two others the change was a rise of only slightly over 1 percent. The record for Africa, excluding South Africa, shows two declines in per capita GDP, one no-change, and two rises of barely 1 percent (YNAS, 1973, III, Table 6b). For individual

LDCs, sharp declines in aggregate product per capita and longer stagnation periods can easily be found within the period.

Distinctiveness of LDC Diversity

Diversity in per capita growth rates among countries and population groups within countries, in the growth performance of different production sectors, and in the records for shorter subperiods within the total time span could have been expected. However, some aspects of this diversity among the LDCs in the past quarter of a century are distinctive.

First, there is a clear suggestion that among the LDCs the combination of widely disparate per capita growth rates is a common occurrence. This diversity in country growth performance is far more striking than among the DCs. Indeed, of the eighteen DCs listed in the *World Bank Atlas* (excluding Puerto Rico), with a 1972 per capita GNP ranging from about $2,000 (for Italy) to about $5,600 (for the United States), not one shows a per capita growth rate for 1960–72 of less than 2 percent per year (the lowest being that of New Zealand at 2.1 percent). Leaving aside Japan and Israel whose growth averaged well above 5 percent, the rates for the other sixteen DCs fall within the narrow range from 2.1 to 4.7. With all the DCs included, the average per capita growth rate comes to 3.8 percent (YNAS, 1973, III Table 4b). In general, the world of the LDC market economies seem much more diverse than that of the DCs. The greater heterogeneity is found in the range of per capita product from less than $100 to over $700, in the duration of their existence as independent, sovereign states, in size, and in what might be called the distinctive long-term conditions that determined their historical heritage. The DCs, with their per capita incomes ranging from about $2,000 to less than $6,000, with their common origin within the framework of European civilization (except for Japan), and with the common impress upon them of the social and economic effects of modernization and industrialization, exhibit far less diversity.

Indeed, one could argue that diversity among the LDCs widened in the post–World War II period, if one can reasonably compare the contemporary setting with the earlier decades when most of the independent sovereign states of today in Africa and Asia were colonial possessions of Western powers. The multiplication of new sovereignties, in large numbers and at different dates, with varying degrees of preparedness and with diverse historical heritage that conditioned unity within and viability without of the new states of such different size and endowment, would in itself add to diversity in growth performance over the last two to three decades—setting aside the differences in purely economic factors. The difficulty that many of the new states faced—and still face—in attaining lasting consensus and unity needs no proof. It is evident in the incidence of civil conflicts and wars and in the widespread imposition of military dictatorships as a last recourse in stabilizing internal conditions to permit peace and some growth to occur. One could thus argue that the impressive rise in the *average* growth rate of per capita product among the LDCs, perhaps partly associated with the spread of political independence, has been accompanied by an almost inescapable widening of diversity in the growth rates among these countries. Since the number of units that have become independent sovereignties has increased tremendously, but at different times, during the last twenty-five years, it is not surprising that diversity in growth performance among periods has also grown. Stagnation or decline during some difficult political or other phase was followed by accelerated growth, at historically phenomenal rates, during the next subperiod.

Second, the particularly low growth rate in per capita output of the agricultural sector, and the wide contrast between it and the growth rates of the I and S sectors, raise questions that are specially relevant to the LDCs. To begin with, such differences mean that the weighting of the sectors in arriving at the aggregate growth rate is important. If the price structure is such that the I and S prices relative to A prices are higher than in the world markets, the I-S weights are exaggerated, and the aggregate growth rate is biased upward. A more critical factor is the susceptibility of the A sector to short-term fluctuations and to diversity of its short-term growth experiences among regions of a large LDC. This is the sector that is the major provider of the consumption needs of the populous low-income strata within any LDC. Thus, the sector's low growth rate of per capita output is associated with recurring declines or stagnation of the per capita supply of foods under conditions where such recurrent crises pose major organizational and political problems. In this connection one need not go far to find examples in recent years. The possible concurrent growth of industrial output or the S sector at a high rate, total and per capita, is not an effective offset. It is only an indication of the continuity in building the nonagricultural framework to higher levels and would be fully warranted only if long-term recovery of the A sector or long-term prospects of adequate substitution for the domestic supply of the A-goods can be expected. Here again, the natural diversity in the conditions of the A sector widens the disparity in aggregate growth experience among the LDCs.

Third, as already suggested, initial per capita product of most populous LDCs was, and is, quite moderate. With the usual internal inequality in the distribution of income within the countries, per capita levels were low indeed for large population groups. Hence, inadequate growth or regression and discontinuities over time are particularly costly in terms of human welfare—as they need not be in countries with relatively high per capita product and ample economic and social reserves for coping with short-term recessions or growth retardation. If diversity has been wide among the LDCs (in growth rates over the full span and in variability of rates from subperiod to subperiod, particularly in the A sector), the combination of a high average growth rate for the all-embracing group of all LDCs with a flurry of crises and deprivations affecting now some, then other, members of the group can be taken as "normal." The broader implications of such partial and temporary crises, particularly for policy choices and understanding of the immediate past and the proximate future, must be inferred from weighing of crises and deprivations against possible gains in the longer run. Such a calculus, admittedly difficult, is required if longer-term policies and prospects are not to be distorted by misinterpretation of partial and temporary difficulties.

The Question of Weights

Given diversity in growth rates of per capita product among the LDCs and their populations, or among sectors within a country, or variability of both sets of growth rates over subperiods, the proper choice of weights used for aggregation and averaging is important. The weights implicit in these summarization processes must, therefore, be examined for their effect on the averages of the type used above to initiate the discussion.[7]

If the levels of per capita product of the several population groups (within countries, or among countries or regions) differ at the start of the growth period, and if the growth rates of the per capitas also differ, the average growth rate for the aggregate will be much affected by the weights used. In the conventional calculations of the type used by the United Nations, the sum of all products is related to the sum of all populations at the beginning and end of the growth period; and the average growth rate is calculated from the changes between the initial and terminal ratios (or along a straight line fitted to the annual ratios). In this procedure, the average growth rate is affected by: (1) differences in the increase of populations with different levels of per capita product, so that if the population or richer LDCs grows relatively more than that of the poorer, the average growth rate in per capita product will be raised; (2) weights for the separate population groups, which are the size of population multiplied by per capita product, or total product. Neither implication of the procedure is defensible. Pooling among the LDCs, which would make the greater population growth of the richer countries meaningful to the poorer, is nonexistent. And there is no reason to assign greater weight to the per capita growth rate of a richer country than to that of a poorer. A more defensible procedure would be to hold constant the shares in total population of groups or countries with different initial product levels and, particularly, to weight each country's or group's growth rate in per capita product by population, not by product. Indeed, for more plausible welfare connotations, one might argue that the growth rates in per capita product for the poorer countries should be weighted by their population raised by a multiple over 1.0, and for the richer countries, by their population lowered by a multiple less than 1.0.

The distinction between the conventional and the population-weighted averages of growth rates is of particular relevance to the experience of the LDCs in the last twenty to twenty-five years. During this period, the richer of the LDCs (largely in Latin America) had the higher rate of population growth; and even more important, the richer LDCs showed higher growth rates in per capita product than the poorer LDCs, the latter being largely in Asia and Sub-Saharan Africa. Consequently, the conventional procedure yields an average growth rate in per capita product for the LDCs as a group that is biased upward. With the structure of recent growth experience as noted above, the adjustment based on the use of constant population weights is sizeable. Thus, for the sixty-seven LDCs covered in the *World Bank Atlas* for which we used growth rates of per capita GNP for 1960–72 and for which per capita GNP ranged in 1960 (in 1972 prices) from about $60 to about $500, the conventional calculation yields an average growth rate of 2.62 percent per year. The use of the 1960 population weights yields an average growth rate in per capita products of 2.01—a reduction of close to a quarter.[8]

If growth rates in per capita output of the various sectors differ, with that in the contribution of the A sector particularly low, the weights of the rapidly and slowly growing sectors obviously affect the combined product growth rate even for a single country; and we have already alluded to the possible adjustment for overvaluation of the industry and service sectors relative to that of the agricultural sector. But even more far-reaching questions arise concerning the character of some of the rapidly growing sectors—questions that have been discussed for decades in the national income literature. If the share of government (among other services) has grown as it has in so many LDCs in recent decades, indicating a higher than average growth rate for that particular subsector, and if much of it was for development of administrative, defense, and similar maintenance functions, one could view these outputs as intermediate—as costs of operation, not as final product. With the resulting narrower and purer definition of national product, the growth rate of the aggregate—in which a rapidly growing subsector was now assigned a weight of zero—would presumably be reduced. And this is, in fact, the result if we limit national product to the outputs of the A and I sectors, and either omit the S sector completely or reduce its weight substantially as compared with its weight in conventional national economic accounting.[9]

There is a related argument in connection with the variability of growth rates in total per capita product or important components over short subperiods. The argument is that an average growth rate over two decades of, say, 2 percent per year means one thing when the annual changes within the period range from 1.7 to 2.3 percent per year, and another when declines in several of the annual intervals are offset by higher than average rates in other intervals. The difference, of course, lies in the special difficulties created by variability over time, particularly in the output of final goods required for ''basic'' needs, and by changes that are nonsystematic and hence not easily foreseen. One could argue that in averaging annual changes over the span of two decades, the annual declines should be given greater weight and the high offsetting rates given lower weight than their mere arithmetic value—all of this compared with standard weights that would be attached to annual changes that are identical with, or close to, the simple average value over the full period. Use of such a weighting system would clearly reduce the averages for those LDCs for which the record shows a combination of annual declines or small rises in some intervals with explosively high rates in others; and these would be LDCs in which agriculture, sensitive to vagaries of weather, is of great weight, or the large number of those which, during the period since World War II, had major difficulties in establishing a peaceful and viable national state.

Even this brief note on the effects of diversity and variability on aggregation and averaging for the LDCs suggests a Pandora's box of difficult and question-provoking adjustments. It is impossible here, and would be difficult elsewhere, to approximate and test the magnitudes of the warranted modifications. Illustrative calculations in an earlier paper by the author, which did not touch on effects of the variability of growth rates over time, reduced substantially the aggregate average growth rate for per capita product of the LDCs (limited to East and Southeast Asia and Latin America). For the period 1954–58 to 1964–68, the conventional rate of some 2.0 percent per year dropped to between 1.1 and 1.4 percent.[10] And the effect is all the greater, because for the DCs the application of some of these adjustments raised rather than lowered the average growth rate in per capita product.

With no way of advancing the subject further, one may conclude with three general observations. First, the diversity and variability in the growth patterns of the LDCs, or within the individual countries, are an important datum in judging the significance of the averages for the LDCs as a whole, both for translating the current changes into long-term trends and for any general hypotheses about factors affecting the economic growth of the LDCs. Second, the conventional aggregates and averages tend to exaggerate, to bias upward, the composite measures for the LDCs—which they do not do for the DCs—the main reason being that, at least over the last two decades, the poorer LDCs showed lower growth rates in per capita product and more vulnerability to variability over time than the richer LDCs, an association not found among the DCs. Third, the limitations of the conventional aggregative measures of growth cannot be easily removed by simple adjustments. The choices involved in weighting the several sets of growth rates—for societies at different levels of economic development, for the several production sectors and income classes within these countries, and for the shorter subperiods in any longer span over which growth must be observed—raise difficult questions. The latter can be effectively answered only if they are clearly recognized and the quantitative record explored much further than the conventional aggregates allow.

Population Growth and Institutional Innovations

Output and Population Growth: LDCs and DCs Compared

The growth of per capita product among the LDCs was attained in decades marked by a high rate of population increase. According to the annual indexes of total and per capita GDP, available from the United Nations for 1950–72, for the LDCs as a group (conventional procedure) the growth rate of per capita product for the twenty-two years was 2.53 per year; that of population, 2.43 per year; and that of total product, 5.03 per year.[11] For the DCs, the same series show a growth rate of per capita product of 3.29 percent per year, of population only 1.09 percent per year, of total gross domestic product 4.42 percent per year—or almost a third higher, or less than a half, or about a tenth lower, respectively, than those for the LDCs.

It thus appears that failure of the growth rate, conventional or adjusted, in per capita product of the LDCs to keep up with that of the DCs lies in the much higher rate of population growth in the former. And one can easily calculate that with the same growth rate of total product, but much more moderate rate of population increase of, say, 1 percent per year, the rate of increase in per capita product for the LDCs would climb to almost 4 percent per year. Or, as has often been said, population growth has been eating up the fruits of the growth of product, leaving a small residual for the rise in per capita income.

Whatever our judgment of the threatening implications of population increase in the LDCs for the longer-term future, the suggestion that the high rate of population growth is an explanatory determinant of the moderate growth in per capita income is both easy and misleading. In and of itself, the rate of population increase is an inadequate explanation of either the success or failure of growth measured on a per capita level. In this connection, the population growth variable is significant largely in that it reflects the institutional and social conditions of a country.

To begin with, the higher rate of population growth of the LDCs than of the DCs is a recent phenomenon. For decades before the 1930s, and back to the early nineteenth century, the rate of the former was markedly below that of the latter.[12] To be sure, this was due to a much higher death rate in the less developed regions, which kept the rate of natural increase down despite fairly high crude birthrates—an extremely inefficient method of population control, and one that could not contribute to social and economic productivity. But it is important to recognize that only in the 1930s, and especially after World War II, did the LDCs begin to show significantly higher population growth rates than the DCs. Further, while some birthrates did rise, the trend was due largely to a rapid reduction of death and morbidity rates—one of the first requirements of, and a most important and valuable ingredient in, modern economic growth.

Second, if population, viewed as a collective of consumers, grew more rapidly in the LDCs, and thus can be debited with a greater proportionate draft upon the fruits of economic growth, it also grew more rapidly as a collective of potential workers and should be credited with a greater contribution to total product. One source shows that for a less developed group of regions (Africa, Latin America, and South Asia), whose total population grew from 1.08 billion in 1950 to about 1.75 billion in 1970, or at an annual rate of 2.43 percent, population aged 15–64 and thus classifiable as the potential labor force grew from 602 to 940 million, or at a rate of 2.24 percent per year. In the developed regions, including North America, Australia-New Zealand, Japan and Europe, and excluding Eastern Europe, total population grew from 563 to 701 million, or at an annual rate of 1.1 percent, and so did the population aged 15–64, rising from 361 to 449 million.[13] Thus, the rate of growth of population of working age in the LDCs was more than twice that in the DCs; and one may ask why these additional workers could not have contributed at least to about the same proportional rise in total product in the two groups of countries.

Third, while in comparing LDCs and DCs as groups, we find that a higher rate of population increase in the former is associated with a lower growth rate of per capita product, at least for the past twenty or twenty-five years, this association does not hold for the individual countries within the LDC group. Using the sixty-seven LDCs, with the records for

1960–72 found in the *World Bank Atlas,* we classified them by their rates of population increase over these twelve years, which averaged 2.5 percent per year (weighted by 1960 population). For twenty-nine, not counting India, the growth rate of population was 2.5 percent or less. Their population was 356 million in 1960, and their population-weighted average growth rate in per capita income was 2.1 percent per year. India, with a 1960 population of 432 million, had a growth rate of population of 2.3 percent per year and of per capita product of 1.1 percent. In the remaining thirty-seven countries, with a 1960 population of 413 million, the growth rate of population was more than 2.5 percent per year, and the population-weighted growth rate of per capita product was 2.9 percent per year. Thus, the association among the LDCs between the rate of population increase and the growth rate in per capita product was, if anything, positive rather than negative, reflecting in large part the difference in growth rates between Latin America and the other LDC regions. It would not be difficult to suggest specific explanations, but the finding is cited merely to indicate that over recent decades other factors tended to outweigh the high rates of population growth, at least among the LDCs.

Fourth, the acceleration in the rate of population increase in the LDCs has been marked because the rate of decline in the death rates was extremely high—about five times as fast in the two to three decades as the decline of mortality rates among the DCs in their comparable population-transition phase. And since the decline in birthrates has lagged behind that of death rates in the past experience of the currently developed countries, it is assumed that the lag in the case of the LDCs is only to be expected. But historical analogies may be misleading; unless there is a tested explanation and an indication of the operative mechanism, references to lags are just descriptions of still to be explained events. This comment is particularly relevant because in many LDCs in Latin America, long-term declines in death rates have been accompanying long-term rises in per capita product, and yet there has been no indication of a responsive fall in crude (or age-of-women standardized) birthrates.[14] One would expect that thirty to forty years of substantial decline in mortality, including that in infant and children's mortality, would lead to some contraction of birthrates, assuming that the high level of the latter in the past may have served in part to offset the deaths of infants and young children. The persistence of high birthrates, therefore, calls for an explanation.

Persistence of High LDC Birthrates: Hypotheses

Some tentative hypotheses to try to account for the persistence (and components) of high levels of fertility in the LDCs in recent decades have been presented elsewhere.[15] But they should be summarized here, if only because they interpret the pattern of demographic behavior as a reflection of economic and institutional conditions that have a major bearing on economic growth in the LDCs.

The relevant hypotheses were noted under three broad heads: (1) technology of birth control; (2) possibly lower costs of bearing and rearing children in the LDCs; and (3) possibly higher returns from larger numbers of children in the LDCs. The technology of birth control was viewed as affecting some segment of the population of the LDCs, the group that wishes to have fewer children. However, even for this group, a variety of birth control methods, which, in the long-term past, had led to control of population numbers (e.g., postponing the age of marriages of females), were still available. Since the group did *not* have to depend on the *modern* means, the significance of the technology factor is reduced. Nor is it clear that the desire for fewer children affects a substantial proportion of the population of the LDCs in their childbearing ages. The lower absolute costs of children in the LDCs are clearly recognized; but one may question whether these costs, relative to the economic level of the parental population, are so low, compared with their costs in the nuclear families of the developed countries. Furthermore, costs cannot be effectively discussed without consideration of returns, and it seemed warranted to place the burden of explanation on the returns from children. The implication, then, is that in the LDCs, families, in their own responses, and possibly reflecting the norms of blood-related collectives and societies wider than the family, view children as an investment—as a source of wealth, defined broadly as economic and social power—under the conditions determined by economic and social institutions within which they live.

Three aspects of this investment in children can be spelled out. "One is the economic, labor pool aspect, the desire for more children because under the rural or small family business conditions of the LDCs, children are a supply of labor at the disposal of the family that, after some years, provides economic savings and advance far greater than any that could be generated by the same family unit with fewer offspring."[16] The second aspect of investment in children may be designated the genetic pool aspect, relevant to those societies among the LDCs in which economic and social mobility is blocked by monopolization of economic and social power by a few families. Hence, limiting the number of children and giving them greater training or education is no assurance of future economic or social rise. "Under such conditions, advance for the offspring of the lowly is a matter of success based on personal characteristics or endowments, on a kind of genetic lottery that may turn up a dictatorial corporal or general, or a successful athlete, or the female consorts of either, so prevalent in many LDCs."[17] Here a rational calculation would call for as many children as will survive to maturity, as many more tickets in the genetic lottery.

The third, and perhaps most far-reaching, aspect of the investment in children is that of security—not merely or primarily the economic security of parents who, in their old age, have to rely on the help of surviving children, but much broader, encompassing protection against natural and social calamities, protection not provided by the government or other non-blood-related organs of society. The pressure in many preindustrial societies (e.g., for centuries in China) for larger families and a wider blood-tie group has been associated with the weakness of the government and the need to rely on family ties for security of the individual members. As long as governmental and other non-blood-related organizations remain weak in this respect, an adequate increase of those related by protective blood-ties will be a high priority goal, despite possible short-term disadvantages.

Rational Response and Returns Consideration Stressed

Two aspects of these tentative hypotheses advanced to explain the high fertility levels in the LDCs, and thus high rates of population growth, should be noted. One is that emphasis on returns from children as the main factor is corroborated by the structural characteristics of the high fertility rates in the LDCs. These characteristics are the entry of females into marriage at early ages; the continuation of childbearing to much more advanced ages of married women than in the DCs; the importance of high parity births; and the high proportion of children born to aged mothers and particularly to aged fathers (beyond forty years of age), despite the presence of a number of surviving siblings. All of this seems to suggest, although it does not prove, that the production of large numbers of children is a systematic and planned activity, rather than a reflection of impetuous and uncurbed passion or of blind adherence to some traditional and increasingly irrational pattern.

The second, and more important, aspect of the hypotheses is the emphasis on fertility rates as rational responses of the population to the economic and social conditions, implying that major declines in fertility are not likely until these conditions are changed.[18] The emphasis is then on economic and social structure, and the key factor suggested as setting limits to the economic growth of the LDCs is then the capacity of the societies for institutional innovations—for changing the existing economic and social institutions so as to take advantage of the potentials of modern (i.e., more advanced) technology. In their specific form, these potentials would differ from country to country depending on the historically conditioned endowments and the changing stock of available technology.

This implication is of particular relevance in the present connection. It may be amplified by suggesting that just as population growth cannot be treated as an exogenous variable determining growth rates in per capita product but must be viewed as the result of human decisions in roughly rational response to economic and social conditions, neither can we assume that there are some rigid technological constraints on the growth of the LDCs that would explain their limited achievements in the way of increased per capita product in the recent past. In particular, one must resist the tempting argument that because these LDCs are poor, they cannot generate sufficient savings to finance the capital formation necessary for higher growth rates. The proportional magnitude of material capital required for growth rates higher than those achieved would not be large even in economies with relatively low product per capita if a backlog exists in technological opportunities and effective utilization of productive factors is assumed. With flexibility of factor proportions, facilitated by choices in the rate of utilization of both capital and labor, relatively low capital-output ratios can be attained. Of course, an abundance of capital can be used in a trade-off for greater inefficiency; but this possibility does not justify the view that capital shortages are a key factor in limiting growth rates in the LDCs. That view is widely prevalent, despite the experience of not a few LDCs that managed to reach high levels of growth in per capita product with high rates of population growth and with adequate domestic savings proportions (low average incomes notwithstanding), and despite similar experiences in the past of a number of current DCs.

The Key Factor Limiting LDC growth

One must look, then, for the key factor in the capacity of LDCs to adjust their economic and institutional structure in order to provide optimal, or at least adequate, channels for growth. Such adjustments may easily be constrained for noneconomic reasons—for example, by resistance to the abandonment of wasteful practices that have assumed quasi-religious significance—and represent no special interest of any group. Or it may be that institutional changes adversely affect some groups while benefiting others, and the consensus for such changes is absent. Or it is possible that a higher rate of economic growth, with its disruptive (as well as productivity-raising) effects, would, if forced, upset the basic consensus and threaten the unity of the country, causing unavoidable delays in economic advance.

For this reference to innovations in economic and social institutions, and to the difficulties of sustaining them, to be more than a shift of focus to a rather vague concept of "capacity for modernization" calls for careful examination of individual LDCs. By this approach, those countries that have delayed the adjustment, that have adopted limited growth-promoting policies, that have not removed the obstacles to an effective program, and that have suffered breakdowns can be compared with others of apparent success and the specific antecedents to that success. Such an attempt would have to rely on the rapidly growing literature on the LDCs, whose diversity was emphasized earlier; and it is certainly beyond the scope of a brief summary. Even so, one may argue that, barring conditions of political subjection, a sovereign LDC, seen as a unit in a diversified world and with many technological opportunities, cannot properly be viewed as having the limits on its growth set, within reasonable magnitudes, by factors exogenous to its economic and social conditions—i.e., factors associated with either its genes, its demography, or some aspects of technology (with the possible exception of Eskimos in the Arctic wilderness, or nomads in the desert). And one can cite evidence from both recent and past history on the difficulties that the currently developed countries experienced in organizing themselves for modern economic growth by establishing a unified state that could channel such growth effectively. If one thinks of the rapid succession of internal conflicts in the two recent decades in Pakistan, Nigeria, the Congo, and Ethiopia, and if one reflects on the rapid changes in political regimes, frequently ending in military dictatorships or one-party governments, in many LDCs (including those in Latin America which have been politically sovereign for many years), one can see that setting and maintaining the basic conditions for economic growth is a demanding and never-ending task. The solutions to this task can vary greatly in terms of adherence to or sacrifice of principles highly prized by many societies (individual liberty, equality, or cooperation in loss and gain). It is the difficulty of easing this task that must be identified, in the first instance, as the proximate cause of the shortfalls in growth among the LDCs—shortfalls that may be viewed as avoidable.

The difficulty is exacerbated by two consequences of the low per capita product of the populous LDCs. One, already noted, is vulnerability to short-term calamities (whose frequent occurrence in LDCs is due to dependence upon less advanced agriculture and to greater difficulties in coping with natural disasters such as earthquakes, floods, etc.) because of lack of reserves to deal with emergencies and because of weakness of transport and other means of mobilization. The other consequence that deserves mention is the technological distance between the low-income and even middle-income LDCs and the developed countries from which they could borrow technology and secure assistance. The technological distance means that while, in general, there is a substantial backlog of accumulated technology that has not been exploited by LDCs, the current supply of technology and technological opportunities available in the DCs may be of little value to the LDCs. To illustrate, LDCs may need better small-scale transport or economical water pumps rather than complex computers, nuclear installations, or supersonic airplanes. The flexibility of choice of capital and labor apparently open to the LDCs may thus be limited by the nonavailability of a better technology that would suit their particular needs and the scarcity of technical talent to generate the adaptive uses of what can be selectively borrowed from the DCs.

These two consequences provide a partial explanation of the finding that the poorer LDCs in Asia and Sub-Saharan Africa, with their low per capita incomes, showed a lower growth rate of both total and per capita product than the richer LDCs, particularly in Latin America (excluding the oil-rich units from all groups). It is only a partial explanation, because so many LDCs in the Asian and African regions have only recently attained their political independence. Many of these faced particular difficulties in establishing a unified, and viable, new political entity, with an incidence of civil conflicts and political breakdowns; and in some of them, the resulting constraints upon economic performance and growth have continued. But even allowing for these major struggles in initial formative stages of a nation, it may still be true that the greater vulnerability of the lower-income LDCs and their greater technological distance from the DCs contributed to a lower growth rate in recent decades than was obtained in those LDCs whose higher initial per capita product and greater extent of industrialization reduced their vulnerability to short-term calamities and made adoption of modern technology easier.

Evaluation of, and Response to, Economic Growth

Changes in Expectations

Assume that, with the adjustments suggested earlier, the growth rate in per capita product of the LDCs over the last quarter century averages between 1.0 and 1.5 percent per year, which means a total rise over the period of between 28 and 45 percent. Consider also that an increase in real return per head is indicated by such evidence as the marked reduction in death rates over the period by between a quarter and a half, rising per capita consumption, and higher levels of education and health. Has an evaluation of, and response to, this undeniable economic advance of the LDCs, and for most of them after a long period of stagnation, been affected by changed expectations? And if so, why and how did expectations change?

In observing evaluation of economic growth in the DCs, three characteristics can be suggested, at least as related to modern economic growth. First, growth appears larger in prospect than in retrospect: quantity indexes weighted by beginning-of-period prices yield appreciably higher rates than the same indexes weighted by end-of-period prices. This difference is due to the fact that new, innovation-related products are priced much more highly in the earlier years—before their widespread and rapid growth and the associated improvement in production efficiency and reduction in costs—than in later years when these products become cheaper quasi–necessities. Second, all innovation-powered economic growth eventually generates problems of adjustment and undesirable externalities—many unforeseeable in the early stages because of inadequate knowledge of the properties of the technological innovation and of the social innovation that it may bring into being. This is an almost inevitable result of some "new" elements in an innovation, which by definition is a venture into the partly unknown. Third, since current events are always much more heavily weighted than past ones, the evaluation of economic growth tends to be biased downward, resulting in the deflation of the initially high values of the positive contribution of innovations and in the concentration on the current problems generated by them. The beneficiaries of electric power or of the internal combustion engine, for example, tend to take them for granted, while justifiably complaining of either pollution or failure of centralized sources of energy affecting millions of people. They forget the older days of confinement in equally or more polluted cities without a chance to escape to the suburbs, or of dependence on sources of light and energy far less efficient than centrally provided electric power. Similarly, in the field of health, the beneficiaries of reduced mortality in the younger ages are concerned about the degenerative diseases of older people and the prolongation of life to ages when it can be neither pleasant nor productive.

If tempered by consideration of the longer-term contribution of past economic growth, such emphasis on current problems (i.e., an implicit downward bias) may be justified. It becomes a necessary stimulus for overcoming the problems, or at least mitigating their effects. But the important point is the relevance of these observations to the view held by the LDCs of their economic attainments and growth in relation to their distance from the DCs. For with respect to the latter the LDCs are, in a way, like earlier versions of the DCs embodying the earlier generations who appraise growth in prospect rather than in retrospect; and the price weights of the LDCs are an analogue of the beginning-of-period prices used in weighting the quantity indexes. This analogy is confirmed by the recent study of comparative purchasing power on an international scale. To illustrate, when we compare consumption per capita in India and the United States, using Indian price weights, the ratio of quantities (India to

U.S.) is 1 to 22.2; whereas when we use the U.S. price weights, the ratio is 1 to 12.0.[19] Similar results can be found for the U.S.-Colombia and U.S.-Kenya binary comparisons. In other words, the LDCs, using their own standard to evaluate the levels of the DCs, appraise them more highly and find the distance to them greater than would the DCs, using their standard and appraising the distance to the LDCs. Likewise, one could suggest that not having fully experienced modern economic growth, the LDCs are much less aware of (or concerned about) some of the maladjustments and negative externalities that it brings in its wake. Thus, the LDCs would evaluate growth much more highly than the DCs. Furthermore, if in their evaluation of their own growth at least a part of the yardstick is formed by the attainments of the DCs, the distance to be at least partially reduced and the gap to be closed loom wide indeed.

We come now to the question of the bases of evaluation of economic growth in the LDCs—an evaluation within those countries as to the adequacy or shortfall of the growth attained. As already indicated, we deal here with intangibles, not susceptible of quantification or hard evidence (at least not at hand). Yet the judgment involved in an important factor in the response to economic growth that has already occurred, possibly inducing change-provoking action if growth is found to be significantly short of the minimum goals. In concluding this chapter, it would be tempting to speculate on the yardstick, the expectations that may be applied, and on the changes in such expectations that may have occurred in recent decades. But even such speculation involves review of various goals (greater output, more equity, minimum assurance of defense power in the divided and hostile world, adequate individual freedom, and so on). A review of such goals, some competing, some complementary, is beyond my scope and competence.

Some Aspects of Growth Perception

Instead, one may point out some aspects of the evaluation and possible response that are apparent from the discussion. First, if in evaluating economic growth the emphasis is not so much on the rise that may have been attained but on the distance to some minimum goal, the judgment will depend on the distance between the goal and the initial economic position of the country, as well as on the tolerance of interruptions and delays. To illustrate: if a country begins with a per capita product of $100, and has also previously suffered from short-term failures, the goal of growth may be set at $500 as a desirable level that would also act as protection from short-term disasters or, at least, minimize their impact. If, then, it is assumed that a fair target is to reach this level in fifty years (or thereabouts), an average growth rate in per capita product of about 3.3 percent per year is expected. If, over a twenty-five year period, growth has, in fact, raised per capita product by 50 percent, the movement was only an eighth of that necessary to cover the total distance—even with the target remaining fixed (and it is likely to move upward over time). For such a calculation, the comparison of the actual growth rates in the LDCs, either with those in their own past or those in the past records of the DCs, is not relevant, In the history of these LDCs, particularly those that were not free to plan their own destinies, such economic goals were overshadowed by the goal of political freedom and independence. And in the history of the current DCs, even of the follower countries, initial levels were much higher (except perhaps for Japan) and the distance between these levels and the goals set was narrower, so that the growth rates viewed as feasible and acceptable might have been distinctly below those that the recent post–World War II growth experience warranted.

Second, the same argument applies to distributive aspects of growth or to effects on inequality in the distribution of returns—which we did not touch upon partly for lack of space, but largely for lack of reliable data, despite prolific discussion in the recent literature. If the goal is to avoid, under given aggregate growth, deterioration of economic position of large, lower income groups, the requirement of some significant advance applies not only to the country as a whole but to subgroups of the population. The failure of crops affecting farmers, or unemployment and underemployment affecting large proportions of a labor force augmented by rapid population growth, represent shortfalls—even if the overall advance of the country may have been impressive by past standards.

Third, it may be realistically argued that the expectations, the yardsticks by which economic growth is evaluated, have changed in recent years. Goals are more ambitious, and delays are less well tolerated than probably was the case in the pre–World War II past. The increased technological power of man and the rapidity with which devastated countries recovered and forged ahead after World War II, the success in reducing and wiping out disease and ill health the world over, and the high rates of economic growth achieved by so many countries had an effect similar to that ushered in by modern economic growth when it emerged in the pioneer and early follower countries in the late eighteenth and the first half of the nineteenth century. The effect was to strengthen the view of man as master of his destiny. It served to create a vision of the vast potential power of man's advancing knowledge in providing economic abundance, once the needed adjustments of social structure were made. And through the widening ties of communication in the world, it had the further effect of spreading man's new view of himself to countries that had previously failed to exploit adequately the potentials of modern technology. These two views—of the dominant power and potential of modern technology (and of the stock of useful knowledge behind it) and its accessibility to any human society willing (and presumably capable) to make the needed adjustments in social and economic structure to channel this power properly—have certainly been strengthened and spread more widely in the world in the post–World War II decades, both by a denser network of communication and by examples of extraordinarily high economic performance bordering on miracles.

Fourth, the spread of political independence to so many national units in the world, which proceeded at such a phenomenally rapid rate after World War II and is still continuing, created many more foci of responsibility for economic growth. Accompanying the process was the tacit assumption (sometimes overt in the propaganda literature for political freedom) that the new sovereign powers would be capable of adequate response to the challenge of economic growth or would, at least, be more responsive than when they were colonies. In that sense, adequate economic growth was viewed as a promise, as a first priority task, by those many and populous LDCs that attained sovereignty only after World War II. So it has become for all states, with the recognition that what is crucial is the social response, not natural resource, not genetic endowments, not even the existing stock of material capital. In the case of the poorer LDCs, the challenge was, of course, much more acute, because they lacked reserves for ameliorating the effects of short-term relapses and of temporary stagnation.

Fifth, the multiplication of sovereign units represented, and naturally contributed to, the strengthening of nationalist tendencies and positions in the world—if only as a matter of establishing more firmly the new identities and developing a consensus on the basis of a feeling of common belonging. But this was also a divisive tendency; and in the newly established national units, there has often been room for strife within (among divergent ethnic, tribal, or religious groups) and conflict without. Economic growth was, consequently, sought to provide not only adequate economic returns to the population but also the sinews of strength in establishing viable unity within the country and in assuring an adequate defensive posture vis-à-vis the outside. The intensification of industrialization in many LDCs, particularly the larger ones, sometimes to the neglect of agriculture, was clearly motivated by the need for some minimum domestic supply of tools that, however useful in peace, were indispensable in the case of armed conflict. And this made judgment of adequacy of economic growth dependent not merely on progress toward peaceful goals but on its provision of the minimum power for self-protection in a divided and hostile world.

Conclusion

These brief comments, which could be elaborated by numerous illustrations taken from the record of events in the last few years, are sufficient to indicate that the evaluation of economic growth attainments in the LDCs, by the people involved (insofar as one can judge from the outside), may be in terms of high expectations—i.e., yardsticks that involve fairly ambitious goals. It is the application of such yardsticks that may explain the tension and strain and the search for modifications of national and international structures. This would be only a natural response to the judgment of inadequacy of the growth attained so far and in light of the dominant theory that potentials of modern technology and modern economic growth are accessible and available to all once the necessary modifications of economic and social structures, at home and abroad, are made.

Such a response is not without danger. If economic growth problems of the LDCs can effectively be met only by changes in internal social and economic structure (possibly requiring concurrent changes in the international framework that channels relations between the LDCs and the rest of the world), it is also true that each change or modification has its specific cost—short-term for the groups that are affected adversely and long-term for the whole society. And no calculus is available for measuring the balance of costs and gains, short-term and long-term, in order to provide guidance in seeking to maximize returns for the society or societies involved.

The difficulty is that economic analysis of economic growth, in terms of inputs and outputs, both the conventional and the more expanded (including inputs into human capital, valuation of leisure, etc.), is still too limited to encompass the costs and returns from modifying the economic institutions, let alone the social. How do we value the cost of shifting from the status of independent worker to that of employee, even if we can estimate the difference in average income? How do we measure the costs of displacement of rural population from the land and of the migration to the cities for a long period of acclimatization and adjustment to urban life? Or in the case of more violent modifications of social structures, how do we compare the costs of forceful reeducation campaigns (including concentration camps) with the additions of a fraction of a growth rate in GNP or in the product of heavy industry? The questions are not irrelevant, for these various alternatives have, in fact, been followed, with differing results in terms of conventional economic product; yet they obviously represent situations in which even the expanded economic calculation yields only a narrowly partial answer. And emphasizing such partial analyses, as something we can do, in the hope that they will shed some light on some aspects of the problems may mean a dangerous neglect of unmeasured major factors. We would, thereby, provide badly biased answers for situations in which the total costs are markedly different from those measured.

Since the widespread and far-reaching change in economic and social structures is a condition, part and parcel of modern economic growth, economic analysis of growth in its present state is severely limited. However, this is no argument either for neglecting the need, in a variety of situations, for such economic and social changes or for not pushing the study of economic growth toward a broader approach in which the application of quantitative analysis and direct consideration of the changes, past and present, in the institutional framework could be combined. Even if the combined measurement of economic costs and costs of social change may prove impossible, the very identification of changing aspects of social and economic institutions should be helpful both in refining the narrower economic analysis and in widening its use for aspects of economic growth neglected until now.

Notes

1. The figure for "centrally planned economies" is from the *World Bank Atlas: Population, Per Capita Product, and Growth Rates* (Washington: 1974), p. 8.

2. These estimates of per capita GNP in U.S. dollars are based on modified or unadjusted exchange rates and tend to exaggerate the contrast as compared with the results of detailed adjustments of local currency estimates for purchasing power parity. Yet one should not assume that such far-reaching adjustments reduce the gap to a narrow range. A recent elaborate study yields some illuminating results (Irving B. Kravis, Zoltan Kennessey, Alan Heston, and Robert Summers, *A System of International Comparisons of Gross Products and Purchasing Power,* published for the World Bank (Baltimore: The Johns Hopkins University Press, 1975). In a comparison of India and the United States, to take an extreme example, the conversion by exchange rates yields a ratio of per capita GDP of 2.04 to 100 (for 1970), while using per capita quantity indexes based on international prices yields a ratio of 7.12 to 100 (ibid., Table 1.3, p. 8). This is the largest proportional adjustment of the ratios ($3.5 = 7.12/2.04$). Similar results for Kenya and Colombia are 1.9 and 2.3, respectively. If we assume a proportional adjustment of about 2.5 for all low-income LDCs relative to all DCs, the ratio indicated in the *World Bank Atlas* ($110 to $3,670, or 0.029) would rise to 0.072, and the range

between the per capita product of the two groups of countries would still be 1 to 14. A range of this extent surely warrants consideration of the implications of the low per capita product of the LDCs for the vulnerability of their economies to short-term crises and for the meaning of even relatively high rates of growth in their per capita product.

3. The estimates for 1950–60 are from United Nations, *Yearbook of National Accounts Statistics,* 1969, Vol. II, *International Tables* (New York: 1970), Table 4b; those for 1960–72 are from United Nations, *Yearbook of National Accounts Statistics,* Vol. III, *International Tables* (New York: 1975), Table 4b. These volumes are referred to briefly as *YNAS,* 1969, II, and *YNAS,* 1973, III.

4. See Simon Kuznets, *Economic Growth of Nations* (Cambridge: Harvard University Press, 1971), Table 1, pp. 11–19.

5. The underlying annual indexes of gross domestic product at constant factor costs, total and per capita, and of output in the several sectors, particularly the A sector, are from Table 6b of *YNAS,* 1969, II and *YNAS,* 1973, III. The earlier volume is used to compute quinquennial arithmetic means of the indexes for 1950–54, 1955–59, and 1960–64, from which the growth rates for the first two quinquennial spans are derived. The later volume is used for 1960–64, 1965–69, and 1970–72, from which the growth rates for the quinquennium 1960–64 to 1965–69 and the four-year period from mid-1965–69 to mid-1970–72 are derived. The averages cited are the geometric means of the growth rates for the four intervals, with due regard to the shortness of the last interval.

6. See United States Department of Agriculture, Foreign Agricultural Economic Report, no. 98, *The World Food Situation and Prospects to 1985* (Washington: 1972), p. 12. The classification into the developing and developed groups is similar to that of the United Nations, but non-market economies (excepting Communist Asia) are included.

7. Several of the points raised here have been discussed in greater detail in my paper, "Problems in Comparing Recent Growth Rates for Developed and Less-Developed Countries," *Economic Development and Cultural Change* 20, no. 2 (January 1972): 184–209, reprinted in Simon Kuznets, *Population, Capital, and Growth: Selected Essays,* (New York: W. W. Norton, 1973), pp. 311–42.

8. Similarly significant differences are shown in ibid.

9. Illustrations are provided in ibid., particularly Section 4.

10. Ibid., Table 9.

11. For the sources and procedure in calculating the growth rates, see note 5.

12. For a convenient summary of the long-term population growth estimates see United Nations, Background Paper for the Bucharest World

Population Conference, *Demographic Trends in the World and Its Major Regions,* 1950–70 E/Conf. 60/CBP/14 (April 1974, mimeographed), Table 1, p. 5. The table shows world population estimates by John Durand back to 1950, linking after 1900 with those of the United Nations. Although nonmarket economies are included, and the distinction between less and more developed regions differs slightly from those used above, the results would not be changed even with adjustment to our classification and exclusion of communist countries.

13. Ibid., Tables 2 and 8, pp. 7 and 18.

14. A valuable collection of long-term series is found in O. Andrew Collver, *Birth Rates in Latin America: New Estimates of Historical Trends and Fluctuations,* Institute of International Studies, University of California, Research Series No. 7 (Berkeley: 1965). Two monographs by Eduardo Arriaga in the same research series provide valuable data and discussion on death rates and their declines. They are: *New Life Tables for Latin American Populations in the Nineteenth and Twentieth Centuries,* Research Series No. 3 (Berkeley: 1968); and *Mortality Decline and Its Demographic Effects in Latin America,* Research Series No. 6 (Berkeley: 1970).

15. See my paper, "Fertility Differentials Between Less Developed and Developed Regions," *Proceedings of the American Philosophical Society* 119, no. 5 (October 1975): 363–96.

16. Ibid., p. 394.

17. Ibid., p. 395.

18. Lest it be thought that continuation, for some time, of high rates of population growth proves impossible because of physical or technological limits, it should be noted that the United Nations population projections do envisage such trends for the remainder of this century. Yet these projections of population volumes are considered sustainable—barring, of course, catastrophes of the nuclear holocaust type—with declining death rates. The brief explanations of the assumptions in the two sources cited below clearly indicate the implications and the key roles particularly of those relating to the modernization of the economic and social structures.

The magnitudes projected should be noted, using the "medium" (of several) variants that can be viewed as more plausible than the others. In *World Population Prospects as Assessed in 1968* (New York: 1973), the population of less developed regions (defined again to include South Asia, Africa, and Latin America), which grew at the rate of 2.8 percent per year in 1965–70, would keep growing at roughly the same rate to 1985, and then the rate would gradually decline to 2.2 percent by the end of the century. For the developed regions (defined to include Europe, excluding Eastern Europe; North America; Japan; and Australia-New Zealand), the growth rate for 1965–70 of close to 1 percent would remain at that level to 1985 and then decline to 0.8 percent by the end of the century. The stability, at high levels, of the growth rate for LDCs through 1985 is the result of a decline in birthrates offset by an almost equal decline in crude death rates (e.g., for South Asia a decline in birthrates from 44 per thousand in 1965–70 to 37 per thousand in 1980–85, almost matched by a decline in death rates from 17 to 11 per thousand for the same two quinquennia, ibid., Table A.3.1, p. 68), with the further decline in birthrates outweighing the diminishing decline in death rates. For the DCs, the movements of crude birth and death rates are much slighter, as is the change in the absolute level of the low rate of population increase.

In *World Population Prospects, 1970–2000, as Assessed in 1973*, working paper, mimeographed, ESA/P/WP/.53 (New York: March 1975), the 1970 population totals have been revised slightly downward, and so have been the projected growth rates (due largely to unexpectedly sharp declines in fertility in the DCs and failure of death rates to decline as rapidly as projected earlier). However, the general patterns of persistence of high growth rates in the LDCs through 1985, and only moderate declines thereafter, and the contrast between these levels and those for the DCs (at about half to a third of those for the LDCs) remain (see, e.g., ibid., Table 1.1, p. 12).

This brief summary of UN population projections indicates that, even with substantial advance in modernization, a realistic prognosis suggests continuation of high rates of population growth in the LDCs, peaking in the decade 1975–85 but remaining at fairly high levels to the end of the century, and exceeding the population growth rates in the DCs by wide margins. The possible consequence for the difference in growth rates of per capita product between the LDCs and the DCs as well as the possible persistence and widening of the gap, is clear.

19. Kravis et al., op. cit., Table 13.5, p. 174.

Part II
Some Welfare Questions

4

The Scope of Consumer's Surplus Arguments

John S. Chipman
and James C. Moore

1. Introduction

The concept of consumer's surplus is one of the oldest in neoclassical economics, even predating the development of marginal utility theory; and it has proved to be one of the most durable. It has great intuitive appeal to the applied economist: for it promises to provide an objective money measure of a person's satisfaction, in terms of the amount of money he would, as proved by his actions, pay for a thing rather than go without it; and it enables one to calculate costs and benefits from empirical data with a minimum of subjective judgment, thus conferring the semblance of scientific objectivity to an operation that can have an important impact on the framing and outcome of policy decisions.

While the early contributions by Dupuit (1844, 1849, 1853) and Marshall (1867–72, 1879) recognized no distinction between a marginal utility curve and a demand curve, subsequent developments by Jevons (1879), Auspitz and Lieben (1889), and Marshall (1891) brought out the implicit assumption of "constancy" of the marginal utility of income, an assumption that, unfortunately, was open to a number of different interpretations. So strong was the appeal of the concept, however, that little difficulty was found in accepting this hypothesis, however interpreted. It was said that since a person's "expenditure on any one thing . . . is only a small part of his whole expenditure," it follows that changes in the marginal utility of income resulting from a price change would be "of the second order of smallness" and could therefore be safely neglected (Marshall 1890, pp. 740–1; 1920, p. 842). This was apparently enough to silence most critics.[1]

It was the major accomplishment of Pareto (1892) and Samuelson (1942) in this area to derive the empirical implications of "constancy" in the marginal utility of income, and to show that these implications were very stringent indeed. Nevertheless—and this is a most remarkable fact—their arguments have never been squarely met by defenders of the consumer's surplus concept, but have for the most part been evaded or entirely ignored. It has been held that results concerning the implications of exact constancy have no bearing on the question of approximate constancy—as if Marshall's own dictum, "natura non facit saltum," could be suspended in just this one case. Or, it has been held that the question of the constancy of the marginal utility of income is irrelevant, since one can always replace the demand function by an appropriately defined compensated demand function, in such a way that consumer's surplus will always correctly represent a person's preferences. The final line of retreat has been to maintain that consumer's surplus is not intended to measure a consumer's utility at all; but what it is supposed to measure we are not told (cf. Harberger 1971).

In this chapter our aim is to examine the validity of the consumer's surplus concept, considered (as originally proposed by Dupuit) as a measure of the consumer's utility. In a forthcoming paper we shall extend our analysis to a treatment of the closely related concept of "compensating variation" developed by Hicks (1939), Henderson (1941), and Hicks (1942, 1943, 1945–46, 1956). We shall reserve for a future occasion consideration of its validity as a measure of the welfare of a community—this latter entity having many possible alternative meanings, each of which introduces its own complication into the analysis. Obviously, a satisfactory analysis of the scope of consumer's surplus arguments in the one-consumer case is a precondition for a satisfactory analysis in the many-consumer case.

Instead of considering the question of "constancy of the marginal utility of income" directly, as has been the usual practice (cf. Pareto 1892, Samuelson 1942, Georgescu-Roegen 1968), we ask ourselves the general question: what properties must be satisfied by a vector-valued $((n + 1)$-component) function $f(p, I)$ of prices $p = (p_1, p_2, \ldots, p_n)$ and income I in order that the line integral of this function over the space of price-income pairs (p, I) connecting an initial point (p^0, I^0) and a terminal point (p^1, I^1), correctly measure the change in a consumer's utility as between these two situations? We then consider the question of whether one can choose as components of f the negatives of the demand functions for the n commodities.

Except for Section 4, which we include mainly in order to permit a comparison with the analysis of Hotelling and others in terms of inverse demand functions defined over the commodity space, our analysis is carried out in what may be called the "budget space," i.e., the space Ω of "budgets" or price-income pairs (p, I) which are assumed to have strictly positive components. We therefore deal in terms of direct demand functions, indirect preferences and indirect utility functions defined on this space. This permits a more general treatment than is possible if one deals instead with indirect demand functions, direct preferences, and direct utility functions on the commodity space; for the theory of line integrals then requires one to deal exclusively with twice differentiable utility functions defined in the interior of the commodity space. As Georgescu-Roegen (1968) has observed, this limits the analysis severely, requiring the restrictive assumption that the individual consumes all commodities in strictly positive amounts. On the other hand, not only does our analysis allow for corner solutions in the commodity space; it does not require assuming the indifference surfaces in the commodity space to be differentiable, since kinks and corners in the commodity space do not preclude differentiability in the budget space. In fact, as we show in an example following the proof of Lemma 3 in §2.1, we do not even require preferences in the commodity space to be continuous; our results are quite compatible with the case in which the consumer has a lexicographic ordering over the commodity space.

In Section 2 we show (§2.3) that if there is no restriction as to the choice of end-points (p^0, I^0), (p^1, I^1), it is never correct to choose the first n components of f to be the form $f^j(p, I) = -ah^j(p, I)$, where h^j is the consumer's demand function for commodity j and a is a positive constant. We show further (§2.4) that if the first n components of f are restricted to being functions of prices alone, the resulting line integral cannot be an acceptable measure of consumer's surplus (i.e., cannot correctly represent his preferences) unless preferences are homothetic, i.e., such that the preference between two bundles x^1 and x^0 is invariant with respect to multiplication of both by the same constant $\lambda > 0$; in this case, these components must be of the form $f^j(p, I) = -ah^j(p, 1)$ for some positive constant a. Likewise we show (in §2.5) that if the last n components of f are restricted to being functions of prices alone, the resulting line integral cannot be acceptable unless preferences are "parallel," i.e., such that the preference between two bundles x^1 and x^0 is invariant with respect to addition of a constant amount λ to the first component of each; in this case, the demand for commodities $2, 3, \ldots, n$ is independent of income, and the corresponding components of f must be of the form $f^j(p, I) = -(a/p_1)h^j(p, I) = -(a/p_1)\eta^j(p)$ for some $a > 0$. This latter case corresponds to that of Patinkin (1963), and underlies the analysis of Hicks (1939, pp. 38–41).

The results of Section 2 confirm and complete those of Samuelson (1942), showing that for the cases considered it is necessary for the marginal utility of income to be, in the first of the above cases (homothetic preferences), independent of prices, and in the second of the above cases (that of parallel preferences) independent of income and of all prices other than that of commodity 1, which can be taken as numéraire.

In Section 3 we take up the case of paths in the budget space that are restricted in the choice of end-points (p^0, I^0) and (p^1, I^1). We show that if attention is restricted to paths with the same initial and terminal income $I^0 = I^1 = \bar{I}$, then it is legitimate to choose $f^j(p, I) = -h^j(p, I)$, for $j = 1, 2, \ldots, n$, if and only if preferences are homothetic. Likewise, if attention is restricted to paths with end-points satisfying $p_1^0 = p_1^1 = \bar{p}_1$, i.e., such that the price of the numéraire is unchanged as between the two situations under comparison, then it is legitimate to choose $f^{n+1}(p, I) = 1$ and $f^j(p, I) = -h^j(p, I)$ for $j = 2, 3, \ldots, n$, if and only if preferences are parallel.

In Section 4 it is shown, among other things, that the well-known "integrability conditions" assumed by Hotelling (1932, 1938) in his analysis are precisely the necessary and sufficient conditions for preferences to be homothetic.

Our general conclusion thus confirms and extends those of Pareto and Samuelson: consumer's surplus arguments are severely limited in scope, being valid only when the consumer's preferences belong to one of two very special types. There is no avoiding the harsh truth that the validity of these methods becomes more and more questionable and uncertain the further the consumer's preferences depart from these stringent forms.

2. Analysis in the budget space: unrestricted paths

2.1 Preferences in the Budget Space

We start out by assuming that the individual consumer has a preference relation R defined over the nonnegative orthant of n-dimensional Euclidean space, E_+^n (the commodity space), which is a *weak order*;[a] "*xRy*" means "bundle x is preferred or indifferent to bundle y."

Letting $p = (p_1, p_2, \ldots, p_n)$ denote the price vector and letting I denote income, it will be convenient to define the sets

$$\Pi = \{p \in E^n : p > 0\}; \ \Omega = \{(p, I) \in E^{n+1} : p \in \Pi \ \& \ I > 0\}, \quad (2.1)$$

where $p > 0$ means that $p_j > 0$ for $j = 1, 2, \ldots, n$; thus, Π and Ω are the strictly positive orthants of E^n and E^{n+1}, respectively. We may refer to the elements (p, I) of Ω as *budgets*, and call Ω the *budget space*.

As usual, the *demand correspondence* for R is the set-valued function

$$h(p, I) = \{x \in E_+^n : p \cdot x \leq I, \ \& \ [y \in E_+^n, p \cdot y \leq I] \Rightarrow xRy\}$$

consisting of all bundles in the budget set which are preferred or indifferent to all other bundles in the budget set. We shall assume that $h(p, I)$ is a singleton set; this notation will therefore be used to denote the unique bundle preferred or indifferent to all other bundles in the budget set, i.e., a function $h: \Omega \to E_+^n$, with component functions denoted $h^j, j = 1, 2, \ldots, n$. We shall say that h is a *regular demand function for R* on an open

---

[a] I.e., it is transitive (*xRy*, *yRz* imply *xRz*) and total (for all x, y, either *xRy* or *yRx*).

subset Ω^* of Ω if it is continuously differentiable on Ω^* and satisfies the budget balance condition

$$(\forall(p, I) \in \Omega^*) : p \cdot h(p, I) \equiv \sum_{j=1}^{n} p_j h^j(p, I) = I. \qquad (2.2)$$

Throughout this section we shall assume that R *is a weak order and is such as to give rise to a regular demand function on some open subset* Ω^* $\subset \Omega$. In §§2.1-2.4 we shall take $\Omega^* = \Omega$; however, the results (in particular, Lemmas 1-3) remain valid when Ω is replaced by Ω^*.

Under the above assumptions, the relation R on $E_+{}^n$ induces a relation R^* on Ω (which is also a weak order) defined by

$$(p^1, I^1)R^*(p^0, I^0) \quad \text{if and only if} \quad h(p^1, I^1)Rh(p^0, I^0). \qquad (2.3)$$

We shall call R^* the *indirect preference relation*. We shall say that a real-valued function $V : \Omega \to E^1$ is an *indirect utility function*[b] *representing* R^* if and only if, for all (p^0, I^0), $(p^1, I^1) \in \Omega$,

$$V(p^1, I^1) \geq V(p^0, I^0) \quad \text{if and only if} \quad (p^1, I^1)R^*(p^0, I^0). \qquad (2.4)$$

Given that R^* is induced by R, we shall also say that V is an *indirect utility function representing* R.

The following lemma is immediate:

Lemma 1. Let R be a weak order, and let h be a regular demand function for R. If $V(p, I)$ is an indirect utility function representing R, then V must be positively homogeneous of degree 0 in (p, I), i.e.,

$$(\forall(p, I) \in \Omega)(\forall \lambda > 0) : V(\lambda p, \lambda I) = V(p, I). \qquad (2.5)$$

We shall also require the following:

Lemma 2. Let R be a weak order giving rise to a regular demand function h, and let $V : \Omega \to E^1$ be an indirect utility function representing R. Then V is a strictly increasing function of I.

Proof. Let $p \in \Pi$ be given and let $I^1 > I^0 > 0$. Since h is regular, $\bar{p} \cdot h(\bar{p}, I^1) = I^1 > I^0 = \bar{p} \cdot h(\bar{p}, I^0)$, and therefore $h(\bar{p}, I^1)$ is strictly preferred to $h(\bar{p}, I^0)$, i.e., $V(\bar{p}, I^1) > V(\bar{p}, I^0)$.

Q.E.D.

The conclusion of the following lemma goes back to Antonelli (1886), but it has been rediscovered several times, by Allen (1933, p. 190) and

---

[b]This terminology was introduced by Houthakker (1953), who also brought out the significance of the concept. The concept will be found, with varying degrees of explicitness, in the writings of Antonelli (1886), Hotelling (1932), Allen (1933), and Roy (1942, 1947).

Roy (1942, p. 21).[c] These authors all assumed that R was representable by a differentiable utility function defined on the interior of the commodity space E_+^n; however, as the proof of Lemma 3 and the example following it show, it is not even necessary to assume that R is continuous.

Lemma 3. Let R be a weak order, and let h be a regular demand function for R. If V is a differentiable indirect utility function representing R , we have, for all $(p, I) \in \Omega$,[d]

$$V_j(p, I) = -V_I(p, I)h^j(p, I) \quad \text{for} \quad j = 1, 2, \dots, n. \tag{2.6}$$

Proof. First we observe that, for any $(p^0, I^0) \in \Omega$,

$$(p^0, I^0) \text{ minimizes } p^0 \cdot h(p, I) \text{ subject to } V(p, I) \geq V(p^0, I^0). \tag{2.7}$$

For, (2.7) states that

$$h(p, I) \, Rh(p^0, I^0) \Rightarrow p^0 \cdot h(p, I) \geq p^0 \cdot h(p^0, I^0);$$

and this is an immediate consequence of the regularity of h.
Differentiating the Lagrangean expression

$$L(p, I; \lambda) = p^0 \cdot h(p, I) - \lambda[V(p, I) - V(p^0, I^0)]$$

with respect to p_j and I, and equating the results to zero at the value $(p, I) = (p^0, I^0)$, we obtain (2.6) at $(p, I) = (p^0, I^0)$, for all $(p^0, I^0) \in \Omega$.
Q.E.D.

Example. The following case of a lexicographic ordering (see, e.g., Debreu 1954, or Georgescu-Roegen 1954, pp. 518–20) shows that the validity of formula (2.6) in no way depends on the possibility of representing R by a real-valued, let alone differentiable or even continuous, utility function defined on the commodity space. Let R be defined on E_+^2 by (see Figure 4–1)

$$xRy \Leftrightarrow \begin{cases} x_1 > y_1 \text{ , or} \\ x_1 = y_1 \text{ and } x_2 \geq y_2 \text{ .} \end{cases}$$

Then $h(p, I) = (I/p_1, 0)$, so that R^* is given by

$$(p, I)R^*(p', I') \Leftrightarrow I/p_1 \geq I'/p'_1.$$

---

[c]It is usually attributed to Roy (1942); cf., e.g., Houthakker (1960), Lau (1969).

[d]Throughout this chapter, subscripts attached to real-valued functions of several variables denote partial derivatives; here, V_j and V_I ($= V_{n+1}$) denote $\partial V/\partial p_j$ and $\partial V/\partial I$, respectively, and similarly for other real valued functions defined on Ω or on E_+^n.

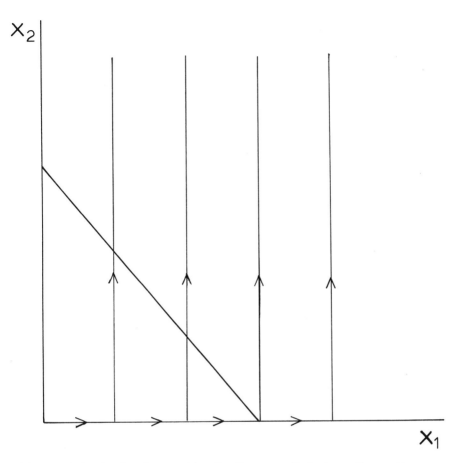

Figure 4–1. A Lexicographic Preference Ordering Generating an Infinitely Differentiable Indirect Utility Function.

Consequently, two analytic representations of R^* (indirect utility functions) are given by

$$V(p, I) = I/p_1,$$
$$F(p, I) = \log I - \log p_1.$$

These are infinitely continuously differentiable, and of course satisfy (2.6), even though no real-valued *direct* utility function exists, representing R on E_+^2.[e]

---

[e] On the other hand, there exists a real-valued function (namely, $U(x) = x_1$) representing R on the range of the demand function [see definition (2.35)], which in this case is the positive

2.2 Criterion for Consumer's Surplus Measure

As far as we are aware, in all existing formulations of the consumer's surplus concept the definition adopted of a change in consumer's surplus as between one situation and another (possibly hypothetical) one can be reduced to a certain line integral defined over either the commodity space or the budget space. Since in this section we are concerned with the budget space, we may formulate the matter as follows.

We consider a path, ω, connecting two points (p^0, I^0), (p^1, I^1) in Ω, defined parametrically as a function on the unit interval $[0, 1] \subset E^1$:

$$\omega : [0, 1] \to \Omega. \tag{2.8}$$

We shall say that ω *defines a polygonal path connecting* $(p^0, I^0) \in \Omega$ *and* $(p^1, I^1) \in \Omega$ if and only if

(1) ω is continuous on $[0, 1]$;
(2) $\omega(0) = (p^0, I^0)$; $\omega(1) = (p^1, I^1)$;
(3) the set

$$\omega([0, 1]) = \{\omega(t) : 0 \leq t \leq 1\}$$

can be expressed as the union of a finite number of line segments.

We shall let $\mathcal{P}$ denote the set of all paths (2.8) such that ω defines a polygonal path connecting two points of Ω. As will be apparent presently, condition (3) is not restrictive, as it might appear to be at first glance.

To define a line integral along a path ω , we introduce a continuously differentiable vector-valued function $f = (f^1, f^2, \ldots, f^{n+1})$ defined on Ω:

$$f : \Omega \to E^{n+1}. \tag{2.9}$$

The line integral of f with respect to ω, connecting $\omega(0) = (p^0, I^0)$ and $\omega(1) = (p^1, I^1)$, may be denoted (cf. Apostol 1957, pp. 276–77)[f]

$$\int_{\Gamma(\omega)} f \cdot d\omega = \int_0^1 f[\omega(t)] \cdot d\omega(t) = \sum_{j=1}^{n+1} \int_0^1 f^j[\omega(t)]d\omega_j(t), \tag{2.10}$$

---

horizontal axis; moreover, the same utility function defined on E_+^n generates the demand function of the example, although it does not represent preferences on E_+^n. See Hurwicz and Richter (1971, Ex. 3) for an example of a preference relation yielding a continuous demand function which cannot be generated by *any* lower semicontinuous utility function; it is an open question whether a similar example can be constructed with a differentiable demand function, however.

[f]Here and elsewhere, $\Gamma(\omega)$ denotes the "directed path" along $\omega([0, 1])$, which is defined formally as the equivalence class of vector-valued functions $\omega^* : [a, b] \to \Omega$ (where $a, b \in E^1$) for which there exists a continuous and strictly increasing real-valued function ϕ defined on the closed interval $[a, b]$ such that $\phi(a) = 0$, $\phi(b) = 1$, and $\omega^*(t) = \omega[\phi(t)]$ for $a \leq t \leq b$. Cf. Apostol 1957, pp. 171–74.

the third expression being valid whenever each Riemann-Stieltjes integral in the sum exists.

Formula (2.10) is presumably meant to provide an indicator of the change in a consumer's satisfaction or welfare as he passes from (p^0, I^0) to (p^1, I^1);[g] and our independent criterion of this is given by the indirect preference relation R^*. This motivates the following definition:

Definition. The function (2.9) will be said to furnish an *acceptable measure of consumer's surplus* if and only if f satisfies:

(1) for all $\omega, \omega^* \in \mathscr{P}$ satisfying

$$\omega(0) = \omega^*(0) = (p^0, I^0); \ \omega(1) = \omega^*(1) = (p^1, I^1) \qquad (2.11a)$$

we have

$$\int_0^1 f[\omega(t)] \cdot d\omega(t) = \int_0^1 f[\omega^*(t)] \cdot d\omega^*(t) \qquad (2.11b)$$

(*independence of path*); and

(2) for all $(p^0, I^0), (p^1, I^1) \in \Omega$ and for all $\omega \in \mathscr{P}$

satisfying

$$\omega(0) = (p^0, I^0); \ \omega(1) = (p^1, I^1), \qquad (2.12a)$$

we have

$$\int_0^1 f[\omega(t)] \cdot d\omega(t) \geqslant 0 \Leftrightarrow (p^1, I^1) \, R^* \, (p^0, I^0). \qquad (2.12b)$$

It is now clear why the polygonality assumption is not restrictive. If we require the conditions (2.11) and (2.12) to be satisfied for all piece-wise differentiable paths ω, then *a fortiori* they will be satisfied for polygonal paths. However, it is enough for them to be satisfied for polygonal paths in order to yield the following well-known result (cf. Apostol [1957], pp. 280-1, 293).

Let f furnish an acceptable measure of consumer's surplus. Then it follows from condition (1) of the preceding definition that there exists a twice differentiable real-valued function $F : \Omega \to E^1$, called a *potential function*, satisfying:

$$\int_0^1 f[\omega(t)] \cdot d\omega(t) = F(p^1, I^1) - F(p^0, I^0) \qquad (2.13)$$

---

[g]That consumer's surplus should provide a particular cardinal measure of a consumer's welfare seems obvious to us, in view of its use in making policy recommendations. But it should be pointed out that this point of view has been specifically rejected by Harberger (1971, pp. 788–79), apparently on the ground that there is something illegitimate about adopting a particular numerical utility index to measure satisfaction.

for all (p^0, I^0), (p^1, I^1) ϵ Ω and all ω ϵ $\mathscr{P}$ satisfying (2.12a); and

$$F_j(p, I) = f^j(p, I) \quad \text{for } j = 1, 2, \ldots, n; \; F_I(p, I) = f^{n+1}(p, I), \quad (2.14)$$

for all (p, I) ϵ Ω. Moreover, condition (2.13) holds for *any* piece-wise differentiable path ω. Furthermore, since F is twice differentiable, (2.14) yields the symmetry conditions

$$f^j_k(p, I) = f^k_j(p, I) \text{ for } j, k = 1, 2, \ldots, n + 1, \quad (2.15)$$

for all (p, I) ϵ Ω.

It follows at once from (2.13) and our definition of an acceptable measure of consumer's surplus that *F is an indirect utility function representing R^**.[h] Hence from Lemma 3 and (2.14) it follows immediately that f must satisfy

$$\begin{cases} f^j(p, I) = -F_I(p, I)h^j(p, I) \quad \text{for } j = 1, 2, \ldots, n; \\ f^{n+1}(p, I) = F_I(p, I), \end{cases} \quad (2.16)$$

for all (p, I) ϵ Ω. The function F_I is the well-known *marginal utility of income*.

It is of some interest to note in passing that we have proved that a necessary condition for the existence of an acceptable measure of consumer's surplus is that the indirect preference relation R^* be representable by a twice-differentiable indirect utility function. This means that the assumption that there exists an acceptable measure of consumer's surplus is a further assumption concerning the properties of the preference relation R, over and above the property of being a weak order which generates a regular demand function. Furthermore, upon applying the symmetry conditions (2.15) to (2.16) we obtain after a few straightforward substitutions the conditions

$$h^j_k(p, I) + h^j_I(p, I)h^k(p, I) = h^k_j(p, I) + h_I{}^k(p, I) \, h^j(p, I), \quad (2.17)$$

for $j, k = 1, 2, \ldots, n$ and all (p, I) ϵ Ω. These are precisely the Slutsky integrability conditions, which can also be deduced directly from (2.6) (see Lemma A.1 of Appendix 4A). Conversely, consider the total differential expression, or Pfaffian,

$$-\sum_{j=1}^{n} h^j(p, I)dp_j + dI. \quad (2.18)$$

---

[h] For the association of consumer's surplus with a change in indirect utility, see Katzner 1970, p. 152.

As is well known (cf., e.g., Wilson [1911], p. 255), the integrability conditions

$$h^j(h_l^k - h_k^l) + h^k(h_j^l - h_l^j) + h^l(h_k^j - h_j^k) = 0$$

$$(j, k, l = 1, 2, \ldots, n) \quad (2.19a)$$

and

$$h^j h_l^k - h^k h_l^j - (h_k^j - h_j^k) = 0$$

$$(j, k = 1, 2, \ldots, n) \quad (2.19b)$$

are necessary and sufficient for the existence of an integrating factor ι such that the product of $\iota(p, I)$ and (2.18) is an exact differential, i.e.,

$$dV(p, I) = \iota(p, I)[- \sum_{j=1}^{n} h^j(p, I)dp_j + dI] \quad (2.20)$$

for some function V. Now, it is easily seen that (2.19b) implies (2.19a); and (2.19b) is equivalent to (2.17). Thus, the Slutsky conditions (2.17) are necessary and sufficient for the existence of a twice-differentiable function $V(p, I)$ satisfying (2.6). If, further, the Slutsky matrix $[s_{jk}]$, where $s_{jk} = h_k^j + h_j^l h^k$, is negative semidefinite, then the argument of Hurwicz and Uzawa (1971) shows that, at least if a few additional technical assumptions are postulated,[i] there exists an integral V of (2.18) which is an indirect utility function representing R^* on Ω ; the corresponding integrating factor $\iota(p, I)$ is then precisely the marginal utility of income $V_I(p, I)$. As is clear from the example following the proof of Lemma 3 above, the Slutsky symmetry and negative semidefiniteness conditions are certainly not sufficient for the existence of a direct utility function $U(x)$ representing R on E_+^n.[j]

2.3 Impossibility of a Constant Marginal Utility of Income

It appears to be a fairly common procedure to choose the function f so that its first n components have the form (usually with $a = 1$)

$$f^j(p, I) = -ah^j(p, I) \quad (j = 1, 2, \ldots, n). \quad (2.21a)$$

---

[i]Namely, that h satisfy a local Lipschitzian property and that R be convex to the origin. It is our conjecture, however, that the statement in the text remains valid (under our assumptions) even without specifying these additional postulates.

[j]Nevertheless, the conditions of Hurwicz and Uzawa (1971) are sufficient for the existence of a direct utility function representing R on the range of the demand function. As shown in Appendix 4A, it is more natural to relate the Slutsky conditions to the indirect rather than to the direct utility function; the assumption of twice-differentiability of the direct utility function usually made in deriving the Slutsky equation (cf. Slutsky 1975, Hicks 1939, Samuelson 1947) can be dispensed with (cf. Hicks 1945–46, McKenzie (1957).

Now if f is to furnish an acceptable measure of consumer's surplus, its last component must be of the form

$$f^{n+1}(p, I) = a .$$ (2.21b)

For, since (2.21a) and (2.16) imply

$$-ah^j(p, I) = -F_I(p, I)h^j(p, I) \quad \text{for } j = 1, 2, \ldots, n$$

for all $(p, I) \in \Omega$, and since by our assumptions concerning h we must have, for all $(p, I) \in \Omega$, $h^j(p, I) > 0$ for some j, it necessarily follows that

$$F_I(p, I) = a \quad \text{for all } (p, I) \in \Omega ,$$ (2.22)

hence (2.21b) follows from (2.21a) by virtue of (2.16). Consequently, denoting

$$\omega(t) = (\pi(t), \chi(t)),$$ (2.23)

where $\pi_j(t) = \omega_j(t)$ for $j = 1, 2, \ldots, n$, and $\chi(t) = \omega_{n+1}(t)$, (2.10) becomes

$$\int_{\Gamma(\omega)} f \cdot d\omega = a\{I^1 - I^0 - \sum_{j=1}^{n} \int_0^1 h^j[\pi(t), \chi(t)]d\pi_j(t)\}$$ (2.24)

(cf., e.g., Foster & Neuburger 1974, p. 71).

In words, (2.22) states that the marginal utility of income is constant with respect to variation in all prices and income. It is an old, if seldom heeded, observation that this is impossible; this was shown by Samuelson (1942, p. 79; 1967, p. 191), and is an immediate consequence of Lemmas 1 and 2. For Lemma 1 implies that F_I is homogeneous of degree -1, whence (2.22) yields

$$a = F_I(\lambda p, \lambda I) = \lambda^{-1}F(p, I) = \lambda^{-1}a$$

for all $\lambda > 0$, which is impossible unless $a = 0$. But this would violate Lemma 2.

Assuming (2.22) to hold amounts to treating the expression (2.18) as if it were an exact differential. We have just shown that it cannot be. It is thus inevitable that if f is chosen to be of the form (2.21), the value of the line integral (2.10) will not be independent of the path of integration. Indeed, this fact seems to be acknowledged and even accepted by some authors (e.g., Burns 1973, p. 342), who justify the choice of (2.21) on the grounds that the difference in the value of the integral (2.10) along different paths is likely to be "small" (a claim that is unfortunately seldom substantiated,[k] and that in practice there will in any case be errors of measurement—as if the existence of error were a reason for compounding it with more error. What these discussions seem to overlook is the fact that so long as the Slutsky integrability conditions (2.17) are fulfilled (combined with the negative semidefiniteness of the Slutsky matrix and possibly some additional technical assumptions—see footnote i), an integrating factor will always exist, making it possible to construct a line integral which is path-independent and which always represents the change in the consumer's welfare. No additional empirical data are needed in order to find this integrating factor; all that is needed is the demand function h, satisfying all the Hurwicz-Uzawa (1971) integrability conditions. And if h fails to satisfy these conditions, one can hardly justify consumer's surplus at all.

2.4 Invariance of Marginal Utility of Income with Respect to Price Changes, and Homothetic Preferences

Instead of trying to require f to have the form (2.21), one might inquire whether it would be possible for its first n components to have the form

$$f^j(p, I) = -\gamma(I)h^j(p, I) \qquad (j = 1, 2, \ldots, n), \qquad (2.25)$$

where γ is a function of income alone. Owing to (2.2) and (2.16) this would clearly imply

$$f^{n+1}(p, I) = F_I(p, I) = \gamma(I), \qquad (2.26)$$

i.e., that the marginal utility of income is independent of prices. According to both Pareto (June 1892) and Samuelson (1942), such an assumption was implicitly made by Marshall (1890); accordingly it has come to be known as the assumption of "Marshallian constancy" of the marginal utility of income (cf. Katzner 1967), although this interpretation is still controversial.[2]

Another possible specification of f can also be seen to lead to (2.26). Suppose the first n components of f are required to be functions of prices alone, i.e.,

$$f^j(p, I) = g^j(p) \qquad \text{for } j = 1, 2, \ldots, n.$$

---

[k]The only study we have been able to find in the published literature which attempts to tackle this problem directly is that of Barone (September 1894), but his analysis was unfortunately marred by the slipping in of a tacit assumption (p. 222; 1936, p. 73) that the marginal utility of income was constant—thus assuming what had to be proved.

It then follows from (2.15) and (2.14) that

$$0 = f_I^j(p, I) = f_j^{n+1}(p, I) = \frac{\partial}{\partial p_j} F_I(p, I) \quad \text{for } j = 1, 2, \ldots, n, \quad (2.27)$$

identically in $(p, I) \in \Omega$.

The following result goes back to Samuelson (1942). Alternative proofs have been presented by Wilson (1946) and Katzner (1967). We present here a simple, self-contained proof.

Lemma 4. Let R be a weak order defined on the commodity space E_+^n, and let $h : \Omega \to E_+^n$ be a regular demand function for R. Let R^* be the indirect preference relation induced by R and h, and let $F: \Omega \to E^1$ be a twice-differentiable indirect utility function representing R^* on Ω. Finally, let $F_I(p, I)$ be independent of p. Then
   (1) the marginal utility of income is given by

$$F_I(p, I) = \frac{a}{I} \quad \text{for some constant } a > 0, \quad (2.28)$$

hence the indirect utility function is given by

$$F(p, I) = a \log I + G(p) \quad (2.29)$$

for some function $G: \Pi \to E^1$; and
   (2) the demand function is positively homogeneous of degree 1 in income, i.e.,

$$h(p, \lambda I) = \lambda h(p, I) \quad \text{for} \quad \lambda > 0, (p, I) \in \Omega. \quad (2.30)$$

Proof. By Lemma 3 we have

$$F_j(p, I) + h^j(p, I)F_I(p, I) = 0 \quad (j = 1, 2, \ldots, n). \quad (2.31)$$

Differentiating (2.31) with respect to I and taking account of the hypothesis that F_I is differentiable and independent of p, we obtain

$$h^j(p, I)F_{II}(p, I) + h_I^j(p, I) F_I(p, I) = 0 \quad (j = 1, 2, \ldots, n). \quad (2.32)$$

Since F_I is homogeneous of degree -1 (by Lemma 1), and independent of p, it is homogeneous of degree -1 in I, whence by Euler's theorem

$$F_I(p, I) = -F_{II}(p, I)I > 0 . \quad (2.33)$$

Now since F_{II} is homogeneous of degree -2 in I, and independent of p, (2.33) becomes

$$F_I(p, I) = -F_{II}(p, I)I = -\frac{F_{II}(p, 1)}{I} \equiv \frac{a}{I}$$

where we define the constant $a = -F_{II}(p, 1)$. This establishes (2.28); integrating (2.28) one obtains (2.29), establishing (1).

Conclusion (2) follows upon substituting (2.33) in (2.32), to obtain

$$h^j(p, I) = h^j_1(p, I)I \qquad (j = 1, 2, \ldots, n) , \qquad (2.34)$$

yielding (2.30) by Euler's theorem.

Q.E.D.

We shall denote the *range of the demand function h* by

$$X = \{h(p, I): (p, I) \in \Omega\} . \qquad (2.35)$$

We may now determine the precise implications the hypotheses of Lemma 4 have for the direct preference relation R over X. The substance of the following result was already conjectured by Samuelson in 1942.[3]

Theorem 1. Suppose $R, F(p, I)$ satisfy the hypotheses of Lemma 4, so that F can be expressed in the form (2.29). Then there exists a function U: $X \to E^1_+$ which is positively homogeneous of degree 1, and represents R on X. Moreover, given any function $U: X \to E^1$ which is positively homogeneous of degree 1 and which represents R on X, there exists a constant b such that

$$F(p, I) = a \log U[h(p, I)] + b . \qquad (2.36)$$

Proof. Define $F^*(p, I)$ by

$$F^*(p, I) = \frac{1}{a} F(p, I) = \log I + \frac{1}{a} G(p) \equiv \log I + G^*(p) . \quad (2.37)$$

Define the correspondence ψ from X to the power set of Ω (the *inverse demand correspondence*) by

$$\psi(x) = \{(p, I) \in \Omega: x = h(p, I)\} . \qquad (2.38)$$

It follows at once from the definition of R^* that

$$(\forall x \in X)(\forall (p, I), (p', I') \in \psi(x)): F^*(p, I) = F^*(p', I').$$

Hence we can define the function $U^*: X \rightarrow E_+^1$ by

$$U^*(x) = \exp \{F^*(p, I)\} \quad \text{for} \quad (p, I) \epsilon \psi(x) .$$

Since $F^*(p, I) \geq F^*(p', I')$ if and only if $(p, I)R^*(p', I')$, it is clear that U^* represents R on X, and satisfies whatever continuity and differentiability properties are satisfied by $F(p, I)$.

To show that U^* is positively homogeneous of degree 1 on X, let $x \epsilon X$ and $\lambda > 0$. Then by Lemma 4(2), if $(p, I) \epsilon \psi(x)$, then $(p, \lambda I) \epsilon \psi(\lambda x)$. Hence

$$U^*(\lambda x) = \exp\{F^*(p, \lambda I)\} = \exp\{\log \lambda I + G^*(p)\}$$
$$= \lambda I \exp \{G^*(p)\} = \lambda[\exp\{\log I + G^*(p)\}] = \lambda U^*(x).$$

Let $U: X \rightarrow E^1$ be any other function representing R on X, which is positively homogeneous of degree 1 on X (note that X is a cone.[1]) Then it is shown in Chipman and Moore (1976, Lemma A.5) that there exists a constant $\beta > 0$ such that

$$(\forall x \epsilon X) : U(x) = \beta U^*(x).$$

But then

$$\log U[h(p, I)] = \log \{\beta U^*[h(p, I)]\} = \log [\beta \exp\{F^*(p, I)\}]$$
$$= \log \beta + F^*(p, I).$$

Putting $b = -a \log \beta$, (2.36) now follows from (2.37).

Q.E.D.

Another way of stating this result is that if there exists an indirect utility function F for R of the form (2.29), then preferences on the set $X \subseteq E_+^n$ are homothetic, and representable by a utility function U which is positively homogeneous of degree one; and given any such U, there exists a constant b such that, defining the utility function $\Phi: X \rightarrow E^1$ by

$$\phi(x) = a \log U(x) + b , \tag{2.39}$$

the indirect utility function satisfies

$$F(p, I) = \Phi[h(p, I)]. \tag{2.40}$$

It remains to consider the implications of (2.36) for the form of the consumer's surplus integral. Suppose we start with the assumption that R is representable on X by a positively homogeneous of degree 1, differen-

---

[1] An "unpointed cone," since the origin is excluded. The treatment in Chipman and Moore (1976) covers the extended case allowing $I = 0$, for which $h(p, 0)$ is the origin of E^n.

tiable function $U : X \to E_1^+$. Choosing any constants $a > 0$ and b, let the indirect utility function $F : \Omega \to E_+^1$ be defined by (2.36). Since R is homothetic we have, as is well known (e.g., Chipman 1974),

$$h(p, I) = Ih(p, 1) , \tag{2.41}$$

where $h(p, 1)$ is positively homogeneous of degree -1 in p. Since U is positively homogeneous of degree 1, we have

$$U[h(p, I)] = U[Ih(p, 1)] = IU[h(p, 1)] \tag{2.42}$$

hence (2.36) can be written in the form (2.29), where we define

$$G(p) = a \log U[h(p, 1)] + b . \tag{2.43}$$

Since $F(p, I)$ is a strictly increasing and differentiable transformation of $U[h(p, I)]$, it is a differentiable indirect utility function representing R^*, hence it satisfies (2.31) (by Lemma 3). Substituting

$$F_I(p, I) = a/I \tag{2.44a}$$

from (2.29) in (2.31) together with (2.41), we obtain

$$(\forall(p, I) \in \Omega): F_j\, (p, 1) = -ah^j(p, 1)$$
$$\text{for } j = 1, 2, \ldots, n. \tag{2.44b}$$

Now, (2.41) implies (2.34), so that the Slutsky conditions (2.17) yield

$$h_k^j(p, 1) = h_j^k(p, 1) \quad \text{for all } p \in \Pi, j, k = 1, 2, \ldots, n. \tag{2.45}$$

It follows therefore from (2.44) and (2.14) that the function $f: \Omega \to E^{n+1}$ defined by

$$\begin{cases} f^j(p, I) = -ah^j(p, 1) & \text{for } j = 1, 2, \ldots, n ; \\ f^{n+1}(p, I) = a/I , \end{cases} \tag{2.46}$$

furnishes an acceptable measure of consumer's surplus when (2.36) holds, where U represents R on X and is differentiable and positively homogeneous of degree 1, and $a > 0$ and b are chosen arbitrarily. This yields for the consumer's surplus integral (2.10) the particularly simple form (cf. Katzner 1970, p. 153; Rader 1975)

$$\int_{\Gamma(\omega)} f \cdot d\omega = a\{\log I^1 - \log I^0 - \sum_{j=1}^{n} \int_0^1 h^j[\pi(t), 1]d\pi_j(t)\} . \tag{2.47}$$

It is interesting to contrast this with the (illegitimate) form (2.24).

2.5 Invariance of Marginal Utility of Income with Respect to Changes in Income and Nonnuméraire Prices, and Parallel Preferences

Analogously to (2.5) one might wish to inquire whether and under what conditions it would be possible for f to be such that its first n components were of the form

$$f^j(p, I) = -\gamma(p_1)h^j(p, I) \qquad (j = 1, 2, \ldots, n) \tag{2.48}$$

for all (p, I) in some open subset Ω' of Ω, where γ is a function of the price of commodity 1 alone, commodity 1 being some distinguished commodity taken to be the numéraire, or "money." Again, from (2.2) and (2.16), (2.48) clearly implies that

$$f^{n+1}(p, I) = F_I(p, I) = \gamma(p_1), \tag{2.49}$$

i.e., that the marginal utility of income is independent of income and of the prices of the remaining $n - 1$ commodities. This assumption was, in effect, adopted by Hicks (1939, pp. 36–41), and explicitly by Wilson (1939); in fact, it goes back to Auspitz and Lieben (1889) who, however, interpreted commodity 1 literally as "money," which they included in the individual's utility function.[4]

Analogously to the case considered in §2.4, another possible specification of f also leads to (2.49). Suppose the last n components of f are required to be functions of prices alone, i.e.,

$$f^j(p, I) = g^j(p) \quad \text{for} \quad j = 2, 3, \ldots, n + 1 . \tag{2.50}$$

It then follows from (2.15) and (2.14) that

$$0 = f_j^1(p, I) = f_j^{n+1}(p, I) = \frac{\partial}{\partial p_j} F_I(p, I) \quad \text{for} \quad j = 2, 3, \ldots, n ,$$

and

$$0 = f_I^{n+1}(p, I) = \frac{\partial}{\partial I} F_I(p, I),$$

identically in $(p, I) \epsilon \Omega'$.

The following result is due to Samuelson (1942, pp. 84–6). For convenience, we include a self-contained proof.

Lemma 5. Let R be a weak order on E_+^n giving rise to a regular demand function $h : \Omega' \to E_+^n$ on some open subset Ω' of Ω. Let R^* be the

indirect preference relation induced by R and h, and let $F : \Omega' \to E^1$ be a twice-differentiable indirect utility function representing R^* on Ω'. Finally, let $F_I(p, I)$ be independent of $p_2, p_3, \ldots, p_n, I$ on Ω'. Then
(1) the marginal utility of income is given, for all $(p, I) \in \Omega'$, by

$$F_I(p, I) = \frac{a}{p_1} \quad \text{for some constant } a > 0, \tag{2.51}$$

hence the indirect utility function is given by

$$F(p, I) = \frac{aI}{p_1} + G(p) \tag{2.52}$$

for some function $G : \Pi \to E^1$, homogeneous of degree 0;
(2) the demand function has the form

$$h^j(p, I) = \eta^j(p) \quad \text{for} \quad j = 2, 3, \ldots, n; \tag{2.53a}$$

$$h^1(p, I) = \frac{I}{p_1} - \sum_{i=2}^{n} \frac{p_i}{p_1} \eta^i(p) , \tag{2.53b}$$

on Ω', and Ω' is a subset of the set[m]

$$\Omega_\eta = \{(p, I) \in \Omega : I \geq \sum_{i=2}^{n} p_i \eta^i(p)\} , \tag{2.54}$$

where the η^j are homogeneous of degree 0 and satisfy

$$\eta_k^j(p) = \eta_j^k(p) \quad \text{for} \quad j = 2, 3, \ldots, n . \tag{2.55}$$

Proof. As in Samuelson (1942), (2.51) follows immediately from the fact that, by Lemma 1, $F_I(p, I) = \gamma(p_1)$ is homogeneous of degree -1, hence

$$F_I(p, I) = p_1^{-1} F_1(p_1^{-1} p_1^{-1} I) = p_1^{-1} \gamma(1),$$

yielding (2.51) where $a \equiv \gamma(1)$, which must be positive by virtue of Lemma 2. Integrating (2.51) we obtain (2.52), the homogeneity of G following from Lemma 1.

By Lemma 3, F satisfies (2.31). Differentiating (2.31) with respect to I and taking account of (2.49) we obtain, for all $(p, I) \in \Omega'$ and some $\Omega' \subseteq \Omega$,

$$h_I^j(p, I) F_I(p, I) = 0 \quad \text{for} \quad j = 2, 3, \ldots, n . \tag{2.56}$$

Now if, for any $j = 2, 3, \ldots, n$, $h_I^j(p^0, I^0) > 0$ for some $(p^0, I^0) \in \Omega'$, then by the continuity of h_I^j we must have, for some neighborhood Ω_0 of $(p^0,$

---

[m]The possibility $\Omega' = \Omega_\eta = \Omega$ is not ruled out, as shown by the example following the proof of Lemma 3.

I^0), $h_1^j(p, I) > 0$ for all $(p, I) \in \Omega_0$; (2.56) would then imply $F_I(p, I) = 0$ for all $(p, I) \in \Omega_0$, which is impossible on account of Lemma 2. Therefore, $h_1^j(p, I) = 0$ for all $(p, I) \in \Omega'$ and all $j = 2, 3, \ldots, n$, hence (2.53a) holds, and $\Omega' \subseteq \Omega_\eta$ for some system of functions η^j satisfying (2.55). (2.53b) follows by the budget equation (2.2). The symmetry conditions (2.55) are simply the Slutsky conditions (2.17) as applied to (2.53a).

Q.E.D.

The substance of the following result was contained in Samuelson (1942).

Theorem 2. Suppose that R and $F: \Omega_\eta \to E^1$ satisfy the hypotheses of Lemma 5 for some η^j satisfying (2.55) and Ω_η given by (2.54), so that F can be expressed in the form (2.52). Then there exists a function $U: X \to E^1$ of the form

$$U(x_1, x_2, \ldots, x_n) = x_1 + W(x_2, \ldots, x_n) \qquad (2.57)$$

which represents R on X. Moreover, given any function U of the form (2.57) which represents R on X, there exists a constant b such that

$$F(p, I) = a \, U[h(p, I)] + b. \qquad (2.58)$$

Proof. Define $F^*(p, I)$ by

$$F^*(p, I) = \frac{1}{a} F(p, I) = \frac{I}{p_1} + \frac{1}{a} G(p) \equiv \frac{I}{p_1} + G^*(p). \quad (2.59)$$

Define the correspondence ψ as in (2.38); then we may define the function $U^*: X \to E^1$ by

$$U^*(x) = F^*(p, I) \quad \text{for} \quad (p, I) \in \psi(x). \qquad (2.60)$$

Clearly, U^* represents R on X.

Now, from Lemma 5 (2) we verify that for any $\lambda \geq - h^1(p, I)$,

$$(p, I) \in \psi(x) \Rightarrow (p, I + \lambda p_1) \in \psi(\lambda + x_1, x_2, \ldots, x_n),$$

hence from (2.59),

$$U^*(\lambda + x_1, x_2, \ldots, x_n) = F^*(p, I + \lambda p_1) = \lambda + F^*(p, I)$$
$$= \lambda + U^*(x_1, x_2, \ldots, x_n).$$

Now this functional equation

$$U^*(\lambda + x_1, x_2, \ldots, x_n) = \lambda + U^*(x_1, x_2, \ldots, x_n) \qquad (2.61)$$

implies in particular that

$$U^*(\lambda, x_2, \ldots, x_n) = \lambda + U^*(0, x_2, \ldots, x_n). \qquad (2.62)$$

(Note from (2.53) that X is a cylinder, containing with every $(x_1, x_2, \ldots, x_n)$ the elements $(\lambda + x_1, x_2, \ldots, x_n)$ for all $\lambda \geq -x_1$.) Defining

$$W^*(x_2, \ldots, x_n) = U^*(0, x_2, \ldots, x_n), \qquad (2.63)$$

(2.62) yields

$$U^*(x_1, x_2, \ldots, x_n) = x_1 + W^*(x_2, \ldots, x_n). \qquad (2.64)$$

Conversely, with U^* defined by (2.64), it is clear that U^* satisfies (2.61).

Now, if $U: X \to E^1$ is any function satisfying (2.57) and representing R on X, it must be an increasing transformation T of U^*, hence

$$x_1 + W(x_2, \ldots, x_n) = T[x_1 + W^*(x_2, \ldots, x_n)]. \qquad (2.65)$$

Since the left side of (2.65) is differentiable with respect to x_1, the right side must be, hence $T'(u) = 1$ and thus $T(u) = u + c$ for some constant c. We therefore have from (2.57), (2.60), and (2.59),

$$U[h(p, I)] = T\{U^*[h(p, I)]\} = U^*[h(p, I)] + c$$
$$= F^*(p, I) + c = \frac{1}{a} F(p, I) + c,$$

whence (2.58) follows upon setting $b = -ac$.

Q.E.D.

The result may also be expressed as follows. Given F satisfying (2.52), R is representable on X by a utility function of the form (2.57); given any such utility function U, there exists a constant b such that, defining

$$\Phi(x) = a \, U(x) + b = b + ax_1 + aW(x_2, \ldots, x_n), \qquad (2.66)$$

the given indirect utility function satisfies

$$F(p, I) = \Phi[h(p, I)]. \qquad (2.67)$$

Combining (2.48), (2.49), (2.51), and (2.53) we now have

$$\begin{cases} f^1(p, I) = -\dfrac{a}{p_1} \left[\dfrac{I}{p_1} - \sum_{i=2}^{n} \dfrac{p_i}{p_1} \eta^i(p) \right]; \\[4mm] f^j(p, I) = -\dfrac{a}{p_1} \eta^j(p) \quad \text{for} \quad j = 2, 3, \ldots, n; \\[4mm] f^{n+1}(p, I) = \dfrac{a}{p_1}. \end{cases} \qquad (2.68)$$

Unlike the case (2.46) examined in §2.4, this does not yield a pleasant expression for the consumer's surplus integral analogous to (2.47), *unless p_1 happens to be constant*. We take this case up in §3.3.

The indifference surfaces $U(x)$ = constant given by the utility functions of the form (2.57) give rise to income-expansion paths which are straight lines parallel to the axis of commodity 1, as is clear from (2.54). These surfaces are therefore sometimes described as being themselves "parallel" to one another (cf. Boulding [1945], Samuelson [1947, p. 194], [1964]; Mansfield [1970, p. 68]); "homothetic to $(-\infty, 0, \ldots, 0)$" might be an alternative description. For convenience we may characterize preferences as "parallel" if they are representable by a utility function of the form (2.57). We may express this formally as follows. Define the vector $e_1 \in E^n$ as the coordinate vector

$$e_1 = (1, 0, 0, \ldots, 0). \tag{2.69}$$

Then it is clear from (2.57) that a parallel preference relation R is characterized by the property that, for all $x^0, x^1 \in E_+^n$ and all $\lambda > \max\{-x_1^0, -x_1^1\}$,

$$x^1 R x^0 \Leftrightarrow x^1 + \lambda e_1 R x^0 + \lambda e_1. \tag{2.70}$$

The case $n = 2$ is illustrated in Figure 4–2. Such preferences have the strange property that, at any fixed set of prices, any increase in income is spent entirely on commodity 1. This becomes stranger still if commodity 1 is literally interpreted as "money"; for this means that all increases in income are hoarded and left unspent. The most plausible interpretation—which is apparently that of Hicks (1939)—is that commodity 1 is a composite commodity, the prices of whose components remain unchanged, and on which the bulk of any increment to income (strictly speaking, all of it) is spent.

One often finds the argument put forward that the marginal utility of income will not be appreciably affected by a change in the price of a commodity if that commodity absorbs only a small proportion of total expenditure (cf. Jevons [1957], p. 114; Marshall [1920], pp. 335, 842; Pigou [1932], p. 785; Hicks [1941], p. 109; Patinkin [1963], p. 104). This proposition was the subject of detailed discussion on the part of Friedman (1935) and Georgescu-Roegen (May 1936); as the latter has more recently observed (1968, p. 177) it is not logically correct. Indeed, suppose one takes $n = 2$, and chooses commodity 2 rather than commodity 1 to be the numéraire, while retaining the utility function (2.66) in the specific form $\Phi(x) = U(x) = x_1 + 2\sqrt{(x_2)}$. The demand functions (2.53) then become

$$h^1(p, I) = \frac{I}{p_1} - \frac{p_1}{p_2}, \quad h^2(p, I) = \left(\frac{p_1}{p_2}\right)^2,$$

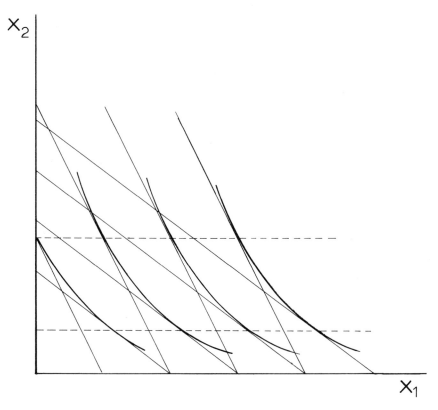

Figure 4–2. Parallel Preferences and the Corresponding Horizontal Income-Expansion Paths.

for $I > p_1^2/p_2$. Choosing the values

$$p_1 = \frac{1}{\sqrt{(M)}}, \quad p_2 = 1, \quad I = \frac{1}{(1 - \epsilon)M},$$

where $M > 0$ and $0 < \epsilon < 1$, at these values the share of commodity 1 in total expenditure is ϵ, which can be arbitrarily small; and yet from (2.51) we have, at these same prices and income, $|F_{Ip_1}| = 1/p_1^2 = M$, i.e., the effect of a small change in the price of commodity 1 on the marginal utility of income can be arbitrarily great. In short, the assumption that marginal utility of income is independent of nonnuméraire prices and income is an assumption about preferences, and nothing can be inferred concerning preferences from the fact that a particular commodity under consideration absorbs a negligible proportion of the consumer's income, other than that fact itself.

3. Analysis in the Budget Space: Restricted and Normalized Paths

3.1 Paths with Unchanged Income

In the preceding section we considered paths ω whose initial and terminal points $\omega(0) = (p^0, I^0)$ and $\omega(1) = (p^1, I^1)$ were absolutely unrestricted (subject only to having positive components). Possibly this is too strong an assumption, since in a number of applications it seems to be implicitly assumed that changes in income are "small" and can therefore be disregarded. (Cf., e.g., Harberger [1971], esp. pp. 788–92.) It is therefore worth considering in place of the set $\mathscr{P}$ of §2.2, consisting of all polygonal paths connecting two points (p^0, I^0) and (p^1, I^1) of Ω, the proper subset $\mathscr{P}_{n+1}$ of $\mathscr{P}$ consisting of paths ω for which $I^1 = \omega_{n+1}(1) = \omega_{n+1}(0) = I^0$. Any requirements that are to be imposed on these paths must, of course, be satisfied in particular by paths ω for which $\omega_{n+1}(0) = \omega_{n+1}(1) = \overline{I}$, where $\overline{I}$ is some fixed level of income chosen in advance. Moreover, since we are going to require that the value of the line integral between two points $(p^0, \overline{I})$ and $(p^1, \overline{I})$ be independent of the path between them, we might as well restrict ourselves to paths with constant income, i.e., paths ω such that $\omega_{n+1}(t) = \overline{I}$ for $0 \leqslant t \leqslant 1$.

Given $\overline{I} > 0$, let the twice-differentiable mapping

$$f|\overline{I}: \Pi \to E^n \tag{3.1}$$

be related to (2.9) by $(f|\overline{I})^j(p) = f^j(p, \overline{I})$ for $j = 1, 2, \ldots, n$. Furthermore, denote $\pi_j(t) = \omega_j(t)$ for $j = 1, 2, \ldots, n$, and $\chi(t) = \omega_{n+1}(t)$, as in (2.23), and consider the set $\mathscr{R}$ of polygonal paths

$$\pi: [0, 1] \to \Pi \tag{3.2}$$

connecting two points $\pi(0) = p^0$ and $\pi(1) = p^1$ of Π. The line integral of $f|\overline{I}$ with respect to π may be denoted

$$\int_{\Gamma(\pi)} f|\overline{I} \cdot d\pi = \int_0^1 (f|\overline{I})[\pi(t)] \cdot d\pi(t) = \sum_{j=1}^n \int_0^1 f^j[\pi(t), \overline{I}]d\pi_j(t), \tag{3.3}$$

where $\Gamma(\pi)$ is the directed path along $\pi([0, 1])$, the third expression of (3.3) being valid whenever each Riemann-Stieljes integral in the sum exists.

Now it is clear that for any path $\omega = (\pi, \chi)$ for which $\chi(t) = \overline{I}$ for $0 \leqslant t \leqslant 1$, the line integral of f with respect to ω is the same as the line integral of $f|\overline{I}$ with respect to π.

Given $\overline{I} > 0$, let the conditional indirect preference relation S_i^* be defined by (see Figure 4–3)

$$p^1 S_i^* p^0 \quad \text{if and only if} \quad h(p^1, \overline{I}) \ R \ h(p^0, \overline{I}), \tag{3.4}$$

for any $p^0, p^1 \in \Pi$. We shall say that (3.1) *furnishes an acceptable measure of consumer's surplus for income-restricted paths* ω *with* $\omega_{n+1}(t) = \overline{I}, 0 \leqslant t \leqslant 1$, if and only if it satisfies
  (1) for all $\pi, \pi^* \in \mathscr{R}$ such that

$$\pi(0) = \pi^*(0) = p^0, \quad \pi(1) = \pi^*(1) = p^1,$$

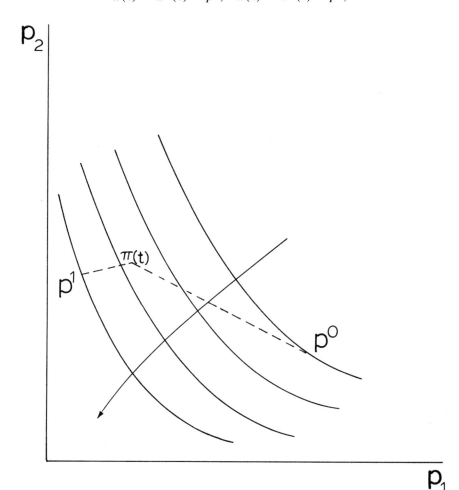

Figure 4–3. A Polygonal Path in the Budget Space, and the Corresponding Indirect Indifference Curves, with Income Constant.

we have

$$\int_0^1 (f|\,\overline{I})[\pi(t)] \cdot d\pi(t) = \int_0^1 (f|\,\overline{I})[\pi^*(t)] \cdot d\pi^*(t)$$

(*independence of path*); and

(2) for all $p^0, p^1 \in \Pi$ and all $\pi \in \mathscr{R}$ such that

$$\pi(0) = p^0, \qquad \pi(1) = p^1 , \tag{3.5a}$$

we have

$$\int_0^1 (f|\overline{I})[\pi(t)] \cdot d\pi(t) \geq 0 \Leftrightarrow p^1 S_i^* p^0. \tag{3.5b}$$

The reasoning now proceeds just as it did in the preceding section. If $f|\overline{I}$ furnishes an acceptable measure of consumer's surplus for income-restricted paths ω with $\omega_{n+1}(t) = I$, $0 \leq t \leq 1$, there exists a twice-differentiable function $F|\overline{I}: \Pi \to E^1$, where $(F|\overline{I})(p) = F(p, \overline{I})$, such that, for all $p^0, p^1 \in \Pi$ and all $\pi \in \mathscr{R}$,

$$\int_0^1 (f|\overline{I})[\pi(t)] \cdot d\pi(t) = F(p^1, \overline{I}) - F(p^0, \overline{I}) \tag{3.6}$$

and

$$F_j(p, \overline{I}) = f^j(p, \overline{I}) \quad \text{for} \quad j = 1, 2, \ldots, n. \tag{3.7}$$

From (3.7) it then follows that

$$f_k^j(p, \overline{I}) = f_j^k(p, \overline{I}) \quad \text{for} \quad j, k = 1, 2, \ldots, n. \tag{3.8}$$

We may now ask: under what conditions on the individual's preferences R does it hold that an acceptable measure of consumer's surplus for paths with constant income $\overline{I}$ is furnished by a function $f|\overline{I} = f(\cdot, \overline{I})$ of the form

$$f^j(p, \overline{I}) = -\gamma(\overline{I})h^j(p, \overline{I}) \quad \text{for} \quad j = 1, 2, \ldots, n, \tag{3.9}$$

where γ is some positive-valued function (not excluding the constant function $\gamma(I) \equiv 1$)?

From (3.8) it is immediate that a necessary condition for this is that, for the given $\overline{I} > 0$,

$$h_k^j(p, \overline{I}) = h_j^k(p, \overline{I}) \quad \text{for} \quad p \in \Pi, \; j, k = 1, 2, \ldots, n. \tag{3.10}$$

As pointed out by Silberberg (1972, p. 946), this in turn implies that preferences must be homothetic.[n] This is a consequence of the following lemma, which was stated without proof by Samuelson (1942, p. 81n), and employed by Silberberg; since a proof does not seem to be available in the literature, we present one here. It may be noted that the converse of Lemma 6 was already derived in §2.4, in showing that (2.41) implied (2.45).

Lemma 6. Condition (3.10) implies that the demand function h is homogeneous of degree 1 in income, i.e., that (2.30) holds.

Proof. First we note that since the functions h_k^j and h_j^k are homogeneous of degree -1 in (p, I), for any $I' > 0$ it follows from (3.10) that, defining $p' = pI'/I$,

$$h_k^j(p', I') = h_j^k(p', I') \quad \text{for} \quad p' \in \Pi, \quad j, k = 1, 2, \ldots, n; \quad (3.11)$$

(3.11) therefore holds for all $(p', I') \in \Omega$. Dropping the primes and substituting (3.11) in the Slutsky equations (2.17), we obtain

$$h_I^j(p, I)h^k(p, I) = h_I^k(p, I)h^j(p, I) \quad (j, k = 1, 2, \ldots, n)$$

for all $(p, I) \in \Omega$. Together with (2.2) this implies

$$h^j(p, I) = \sum_{k=1}^{n} p_k h_I^k(p, I)h^j(p, I) = \sum_{k=1}^{n} p_k h_I^j(p, I)h^k(p, I) = Ih_I^j(p, I),$$

yielding the result by Euler's theorem.

Q.E.D.

It follows from Lemma 6 and our assumptions concerning R and h that in order for (3.9) to furnish an acceptable measure of consumer's surplus for paths ω with constant income $\bar{I}$, it is necessary for preferences to be homothetic on the range X of h (cf. Chipman 1974). It follows that in (3.4) we have

$$\bar{I}h(p^1, 1) \, R \, \bar{I}h(p^0, 1) \Leftrightarrow h(p^1, 1) \, R \, h(p^0, 1).$$

Thus, the relation S_i^* is independent of $\bar{I}$. From (3.5b) and (3.6) it follows that $F(p^1, \bar{I}) - F(p^0, \bar{I})$ is independent of $\bar{I}$, hence F must be of the form

$$F(p, I) = \gamma(I) + G(p). \quad (3.12)$$

---

[n]The symmetry condition (3.10) was stated by Pfouts (1953, p. 326) to hold "if the consumer is rational." It was also arrived at by Foster and Neuberger (1974, p. 74) who deduced from it the consequence that "the income elasticity for all goods is the same," but not the further consequence that it must be unitary.

Now, (3.12) need not be an indirect utility function; however, if it is an indirect utility function then, since F_I is independent of p, it must have the form (2.29) given by Lemma 4, and the function γ of (3.9) and (3.12) must have the form $\gamma(I) = a/I$. If, as seems to be the common practice, one instead takes $\gamma(\bar{I}) = 1$ in (3.9), then (3.12) cannot be an indirect utility function. Nevertheless, so long as preferences are homothetic, the function $F|\bar{I} = F(\cdot, \bar{I})$ is a conditional indirect utility function which can be validly used for comparing $(p^0, \bar{I})$ and $(p^1, \bar{I})$, for any $\bar{I} > 0$; and in this case, γ in (3.9) can be any positive-valued function, including the function $\gamma(I) = 1$ for all $I > 0$. In general, the consumer's surplus integral (3.3) will have the form

$$\int_{\Gamma(\pi)} f|\bar{I} \cdot d\pi = -\bar{I}\gamma(\bar{I}) \sum_{j=1}^{n} \int_0^1 h^j[\pi(t), 1] \cdot d\pi_j(t), \qquad (3.13)$$

which coincides with (2.47) when $\gamma(\bar{I}) = a/\bar{I}$.

3.2 Normalization by Income

Since, by Lemma 1, indirect utility functions are homogeneous of degree 0, i.e., constant along any ray from the origin in the budget space Ω, it is natural to consider a normalization so that the paths under consideration are contained in an n-dimensional space. One simple way to do this is to express all prices relative to income. Thus we may define the function $\hat{r}: \Omega \rightarrow \Pi$ by

$$r = \hat{r}(p, I) = p/I. \qquad (3.14)$$

We define the relation R^*_{n+1} over Π by

$$r^1 R^*_{n+1} r^0 \quad \text{if and only if} \quad h(r^1, 1)Rh(r^0, 1). \qquad (3.15)$$

We consider a twice-differentiable mapping

$$g: \Pi \rightarrow E^n, \qquad (3.16)$$

and the set $\mathcal{R}$ of polygonal paths (3.2) connecting two points of Π. The line integral of g with respect to π is then

$$\int_{\Gamma(\pi)} g \cdot d\pi = \int_0^1 g[\pi(t)] \cdot d\pi(t) = \sum_{j=1}^{n} \int_0^1 g^j[\pi(t)]d\pi_j(t). \qquad (3.17)$$

We say that g furnishes an acceptable measure of consumer's surplus for income-normalized paths if and only if (3.17) is path-independent and satisfies, for all $r^0, r^1 \epsilon \Pi$ and $\pi \epsilon \mathcal{R}$ such that $\pi(0) = r^0$ and $\pi(1) = r^1$,

$$\int_0^1 g[\pi(t)] \cdot d\pi(t) \geq 0 \Leftrightarrow r^1 R^*_{n+1} r^0. \tag{3.18}$$

If g fulfills these conditions then there exists a twice-differentiable potential function $G: \Pi \to E^1$ such that

$$\int_0^1 g[\pi(t)] \cdot d\pi(t) = G(r^1) - G(r^0) \tag{3.19}$$

and

$$G_j(r) = g^j(r) \quad \text{for } j = 1, 2, \ldots, n. \tag{3.20}$$

This yields the symmetry conditions

$$g_k{}^j(r) = g_j{}^k(r) \text{ for } j, k = 1, 2, \ldots, n. \tag{3.21}$$

From (3.19) and (3.14) it is clear that the function $F: \Omega \to E^1$ defined by

$$F(p, I) = G[\hat{r}(p, I)] = G(p/I) \tag{3.22}$$

is an indirect utility function for R, and is differentiable. By Lemma 3 it then follows that, using (3.20) and (3.14),

$$g^j(r) = r \cdot g(r)h^j(r, 1). \tag{3.23}$$

We find also that

$$\hat{r}(p, I) \cdot g[\hat{r}(p, I)] = -IF_I(p, I),$$

hence a necessary and sufficient condition for an acceptable g to have the form

$$g^j(r) = -ah^j(r, 1) \quad (j = 1, 2, \ldots, n) \qquad \text{-} \tag{3.24}$$

is that (2.28) hold. The conclusions of Theorem 1 follow as before.

3.3 Paths with Unchanged Price of the Numéraire

In many applications of consumer's surplus analysis, it is quite inappropriate to assume unchanged income, since the problem may involve a comparison of the price and income effects of a certain policy measure such as a tax (an illustration will be given later). In such circumstances it may nevertheless be appropriate to assume that the price of a certain commodity remains unchanged as between the two situations under comparison.° It is therefore of interest to consider, instead of the set $\mathcal{P}$ of all polygonal paths connecting any two points of Ω, the proper subset $\mathcal{P}_1$ of $\mathcal{P}$ consisting of paths ω for which the price of commodity 1, say, remains unchanged as between the two situations, i.e., $p_1^1 = \omega_1(1) = \omega_1(0) = p_1^0$. By the previous argument it is clear that it is enough, in order to obtain necessary conditions that must be satisfied by a consumer's surplus measure, to consider for any fixed $\bar{p}_1 > 0$ only those paths ω for which $\omega_1(t) = \bar{p}_1$ for $0 \leqslant t \leqslant 1$.

Denoting $q_j = p_{j+1}$ for $j = 1, 2, \ldots, n - 1$, and $q_n = I$, let

$$\Theta = \{q = (p_2, p_3, \ldots, p_n, I) > 0\}, \tag{3.25}$$

and let $\mathcal{Q}$ be the set of polygonal paths

$$\theta : [0, 1] \to \Theta \tag{3.26}$$

connecting two points of Θ. Given $\bar{p}_1 > 0$, let the twice-differentiable mapping

$$f|\bar{p}_1 : \Theta \to E^n \tag{3.27}$$

be related to (2.9) by $(f|\bar{p}_1)^j(q) = f^{j+1}(\bar{p}_1, q)$ for $j = 1, 2, \ldots, n$. Then, for paths ω for which $\omega_1(t) = \bar{p}_1$ for $0 \leqslant t \leqslant 1$, the line integral of f with respect to ω is clearly the same as the line integral of $f|\bar{p}_1$ with respect to θ:

$$\int_{\Gamma(\theta)} f|\bar{p}_1 \cdot d\theta = \int_0^1 (f|\bar{p}_1)[\theta(t)] \cdot d\theta(t) = \sum_{j=2}^{n+1} \int_0^1 f^j[\bar{p}_1, \theta(t)] \, d\theta_j(t). \tag{3.28}$$

Let the relation $Q^*_{p_1}$ be defined by (see Figure 4–4)

$$q^1 \, Q^*_{p_1} \, q^0 \quad \text{if and only if} \quad h(\bar{p}_1, q^1) \, R \, h(\bar{p}_1, q^0), \tag{3.29}$$

for any $q^0, q^1 \in \Theta$. We shall say that (3.27) *furnishes an acceptable measure of consumer's surplus for paths with unchanged price of commodity 1* if and only if (3.28) is path-independent and satisfies, for all $q^0, q^1 \in \Theta$ such that $\theta(0) = q^0$ and $\theta(1) = q^1$,

$$\int_0^1 (f|\bar{p}_1)[\theta(t)] \cdot d\theta(t) \geqslant 0 \Leftrightarrow q^1 \, Q^*_{p_1} \, q^0. \tag{3.30}$$

°This type of assumption is implicit in the diagrammatic arguments employed by Hicks (1939, 1942). On the other hand, it appears to be the case that absolute rather than normalized prices are usually used in applications.

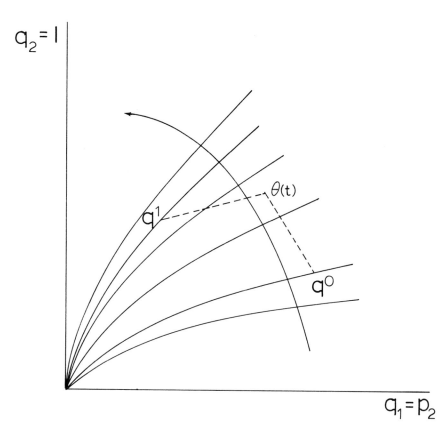

Figure 4–4. A Polygonal Path in the Budget Space, and the Corresponding Indirect Indifference Curves, with the Price of Commodity 1 Held Constant.

As before, if $f|\bar{p}_1$ is acceptable in this sense, there exists a twice-differentiable function $F|\bar{p}_1 : \Theta \to E^1$, where $(F|\bar{p}_1)(q) = F(\bar{p}_1, q)$, such that, for all q^0, $q^1 \in \Theta$ and all $\theta \in \mathcal{Q}$,

$$\int_0^1 (f|\bar{p}_1)[\theta(t)] \cdot d\theta(t) = F(\bar{p}_1, q^1) - F(\bar{p}_1, q^0) \tag{3.31}$$

and

$$F_j(\bar{p}_1, q) = (F|\bar{p}_1)_{j-1}(q) = (f|\bar{p}_1)^{j-1}(q) = f^j(\bar{p}_1, q) \tag{3.32}$$
$$\text{for} \quad j = 2, 3, \ldots, n + 1.$$

From (3.32) it then follows that

$$f_k^j(\bar{p}_1, q) = f_j^k(\bar{p}_1, q) \quad \text{for} \quad j, k = 2, 3, \ldots, n + 1. \tag{3.33}$$

We may now ask: under what conditions on the consumer's preferences R does it hold that an acceptable measure of consumer's surplus for paths with a constant price of the numéraire is furnished by a function $f|\bar{p}_1$ of the form [as in (2.49) and (2.50)]

$$(f|\bar{p}_1)^j(q) = f^{j+1}(\bar{p}_1, q) = -\gamma(\bar{p}_1)h^{j+1}(\bar{p}_1, q) \quad \text{for} \quad j = 1, 2, \ldots, n - 1;$$
$$(f|\bar{p}_1)^n(q) = f^{n+1}(\bar{p}_1, q) = \gamma(\bar{p}_1) \tag{3.34}$$

where γ is some positive-valued function of p_1, not excluding the constant function $\gamma(p_1) \equiv 1$?

From (3.33) it is immediate that a necessary condition for this is that, for given $\bar{p}_1 > 0$,

$$h_k^j(\bar{p}_1, q) = h_j^k(\bar{p}_1, q) \quad \text{for} \quad j, k = 2, 3, \ldots, n \tag{3.35}$$

and

$$h_1^j(\bar{p}_1, q) = 0 \quad \text{for} \quad j = 2, 3, \ldots, n. \tag{3.36}$$

It follows that the demand function has the form (2.53) of Lemma 5. Moreover, the last equations of (3.32) and (3.34) respectively imply that $F_I(\bar{p}_1, q) = \gamma(\bar{p}_1)$, hence F must be of the form

$$F(\bar{p}_1, q) = \gamma(\bar{p}_1)I + G(\bar{p}_1, p_2, \ldots, p_n). \tag{3.37}$$

This need not be an indirect utility function for R; however, if it is an indirect utility function then from Lemma 5 we must have $\gamma(p_1) = a/p_1$ for some $a > 0$, and F must be given by (2.52).

The line integral of (3.34) with respect to θ, connecting $\theta(0) = q^0$ and $\theta(1) = q^1$, is

$$\int_{\Gamma(\theta)} f|\bar{p}_1 \cdot d\theta = \gamma(\bar{p}_1)\{I^1 - I^0 - \sum_{j=2}^{n} h^j[\bar{p}_1, \theta(t)]d\pi_j(t)\}, \tag{3.38}$$

where $h^j[\bar{p}_1, \theta(t)] = \eta^j[\bar{p}_1, \pi_2(t), \ldots, \pi_n(t)]$. Given the assumption of parallel preferences, (3.38) correctly measures the welfare change from (p^0, I^0) to (p^1, I^1) provided $p_1^0 = p_1^1 = \bar{p}_1$.

An illustration is given in Figure 4–5 of the case $\gamma(\bar{p}_1) = 1$ and $n = 2$, in which the consumer's surplus integral (3.38) reduces to

$$I^1 - I^0 - \int_0^1 \eta^2[\bar{p}_1, \pi_2(t)]d\pi_2(t). \tag{3.39}$$

Suppose that in period 0 the demand for commodity 2, which is supplied at constant unit cost p_2^0, is $x_2^0 = \eta^2(\bar{p}_1, p_2^0)$, and that in period 1 a tax is levied on commodity 2 to the amount of $p_2^1 - p_2^0$ per unit, so that the

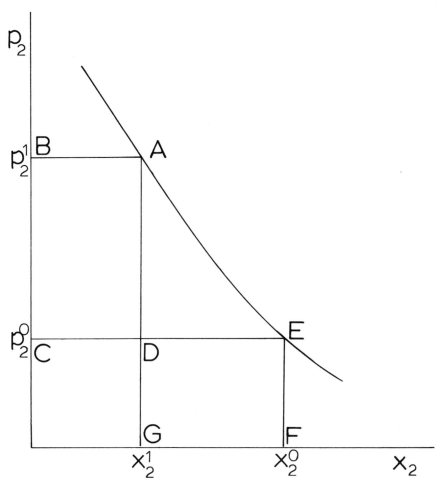

Figure 4–5. The Deadweight Loss *ADE*, or Negative Consumer's Surplus, Resulting from the Imposition of an Excise Tax of *BC* on Commodity 2, the Proceeds *ABCD* of Which Are Spent Entirely on Commodity 1.

demand is $x_2^1 = \eta^2(\bar{p}_1, p_2^1)$; and that the proceeds $(p_2^1 - p_2^0)x_2^1$ of the tax are paid out to the consumer and added to his income, so that $I^1 - I^0 = (p_2^1 - p_2^0) x_2^1$. The tax proceeds, which are spent entirely on commodity 1, are represented by the rectangle *ABCD* in the figure, and the remaining term of (3.39) is the area *ABCE*; expression (3.39) thus gives the famous triangle *ADE*, representing the "deadweight loss" to the consumer of the excise tax.[p]

---

[p]This diagram is as old as consumer's surplus analysis itself; cf. Dupuit (1844), Plate 75; (1969), pp. 280–83; Marshall (1879), pp. 25–28; Whitaker (1975), II, pp. 219–23.

3.4 Normalization by the Price of a Numéraire

A more usual, although less symmetrical, kind of normalization than that treated in §3.2 is obtained by expressing income and all but one of the prices relative to the remaining price. Accordingly, taking commodity 1 as numéraire and denoting by $\Theta = E_+^n$ the set of vectors of these normalized prices and income, let the function $\hat{q}: \Omega \to \Theta$ be defined by

$$q = \hat{q}(p, I) = \frac{1}{p_1} (p_2, p_3, \ldots, p_n, I), \qquad (3.40)$$

and let $\mathcal{Q}$ be the set of polygonal paths

$$\theta: [0, 1] \to \Theta \qquad (3.41)$$

connecting two points of Θ. We define the relation R^*_1 over Θ by

$$q^1 R^*_1 q^0 \quad \text{if and only if} \quad h(1, q^1) R h(1, q^0), \qquad (3.42)$$

Given a twice-differentiable mapping

$$g: \Theta \to E^n, \qquad (3.43)$$

the line integral of g with respect to θ is

$$\int_{\Gamma(\theta)} g \cdot d\theta = \int_0^1 g[\theta(t)] \cdot d\theta(t) = \sum_{j=1}^n \int_0^1 g^j[\theta(t)]d\theta_j(t). \qquad (3.44)$$

We say that g furnishes an acceptable measure of consumer's surplus for paths normalized by the price of commodity 1 if and only if (3.44) is path-independent and satisfies, for all $q^0, q^1 \in \Theta$ and all $\theta \in \mathcal{Q}$ such that $\theta(0) = q^0$ and $\theta(1) = q^1$,

$$\int_0^1 g[\theta(t)] \cdot d\theta(t) \geq 0 \Leftrightarrow q^1 R^*_1 q^0. \qquad (3.45)$$

If g fulfills these conditions, there exists a twice-differentiable function $G: \Theta \to E^n$ such that

$$\int_0^1 g[\theta(t)] \cdot d\theta(t) = G(q^1) - G(q^0) \qquad (3.46)$$

and

$$G_j(q) = g^j(q) \quad \text{for} \quad j = 1, 2, \ldots, n, \qquad (3.47)$$

hence g satisfies

$$g_k{}^j(q) = g_j{}^k(q) \quad \text{for} \quad j, k = 1, 2, \ldots, n. \tag{3.48}$$

In view of (3.46) and (3.45) the function $F: \Omega \to E^1$ defined by

$$F(p, I) = G[\hat{q}(p, I)] \tag{3.49}$$

is an indirect utility function for R, and is differentiable. We verify from (3.49), (3.40), and (3.47) that $F_j = g^{j-1}/p_1$ for $j = 2, 3, \ldots, n$, and $F_I = g^n/p_1$, hence from Lemma 3 we have

$$g^j(q) = -g^n(q)h^{j+1}(1, q) \quad \text{for} \quad j = 1, 2, \ldots, n - 1. \tag{3.50}$$

It follows from (3.50) that if an acceptable g has as its first $n - 1$ components

$$g^j(q) = -ah^{j+1}(1, q) \quad (j = 1, 2, \ldots, n - 1) \tag{3.51a}$$

then its nth component must necessarily be

$$g^n(q) = a. \tag{3.51b}$$

But (3.51) implies, together with (3.48),

$$h_1^j(1, q) = 0 \quad \text{for} \quad j = 2, 3, \ldots, n, \tag{3.52}$$

and

$$h_k{}^j(1, q) = h_j{}^k(1, q) \quad (j, k = 2, 3, \ldots, n) \tag{3.53}$$

as before.

4. Analysis in the Commodity Space

4.1 Normalization by Income

In many formulations of the consumer's surplus concept it is customary to consider paths in the commodity space rather than in the budget space. To relate our results to these formulations it will therefore be instructive to carry out the analogous analysis in terms of the formal framework developed in the preceding sections.

In place of the demand function $h(p, I)$ defined on Ω, it will now be necessary instead to work with the inverse demand correspondence $\psi(x)$

of (2.38), defined on X [see (2.35)]. However, this is very awkward to work with, and it will be more convenient to employ a normalization. First we take up the case in which ψ is redefined by

$$\psi(x) = \{r \in \Pi : x = h(r, 1)\} \quad \text{for} \quad x \in X. \tag{4.1}$$

We shall assume that X is open in E^n and that $\psi(x)$ is a singleton for each $x \in X$; this implies that the indifference surfaces are differentiable for all $x \in X$, and that the elements of X have strictly positive components—a restrictive assumption indeed, and one which was not needed in our anlaysis in the budget space.[a] The same symbol $\psi(x)$ will be used to denote the unique vector $r = p/I \in \Pi$ belonging in the set (4.1) for given x.

Throughout this section we shall assume that R is represented on X by a differentiable utility function $U: X \to E^1$, and that the budget balance condition (2.2) holds. Accordingly, $\psi : X \to E^n$ is given by

$$\psi^j(x) = \frac{U_j(x)}{\displaystyle\sum_{i=1}^{n} U_i(x)x_i} \quad (j = 1, 2, \ldots, n). \tag{4.2}$$

These equations are the counterpart to equations (2.6) over the budget space.

We now consider the set $\mathscr{X}$ of polygonal paths

$$\xi : [0, 1] \to X \tag{4.3}$$

connecting two points of X, and a continuously differentiable vector-valued function $\phi = (\phi^1, \phi^2, \ldots, \phi^n)$ defined on X:

$$\phi : X \to E^n. \tag{4.4}$$

The line integral of ϕ with respect to ξ is then

$$\int_{\Gamma(\xi)} \phi \cdot d\xi = \int_0^1 \phi[\xi(t)] \cdot d\xi(t) = \sum_{j=1}^{n} \int_0^1 \phi^j[\xi(t)]d\xi_j(t). \tag{4.5}$$

We say that ϕ furnishes an acceptable measure of consumer's surplus if and only if (4.5) is independent of the path ξ connecting any two given points, and for all $x^0, x^1 \in X$ and all $\xi \in \mathscr{X}$ satisfying $\xi(0) = x^0$ and $\xi(1) = x^1$,

---

[a] In particular, indifference surfaces must not cut the axes except possibly with tangent contact. And a case such as in the example following Lemma 3 could not be handled by the methods of this section.

$$\int_0^1 \phi[\xi(t)] \cdot d\xi(t) \geq 0 \Leftrightarrow x^1 R x^0. \tag{4.6}$$

If ϕ is acceptable then there exists a twice-differentiable real-valued function $\Phi : X \to E^1$ (a potential function), satisfying

$$\int_0^1 \phi[\xi(t)] \cdot d\xi(t) = \Phi(x^1) - \Phi(x^0) \tag{4.7}$$

for all $x^0, x^1 \epsilon X$ and all $\xi \epsilon \mathscr{X}$ such that $\xi(0) = x^0$, $\xi(1) = x^1$; and

$$\Phi_j(x) = \phi^j(x) \quad \text{for} \quad j = 1, 2, \ldots, n, \tag{4.8}$$

(where $\Phi_j(x) \equiv \partial\Phi(x)/\partial x_j$). Obviously, Φ is a utility function representing R on X, so we have incidentally shown that for ϕ to furnish an acceptable measure of consumer's surplus, R must be representable by a twice differentiable utility function. From (4.8) we have the symmetry conditions

$$\phi_k^j(x) = \phi_j^k(x) \quad \text{for} \quad j, k = 1, 2, \ldots, n. \tag{4.9}$$

From (4.8) and the fact that (4.2) holds for Φ, we have

$$\phi^j(x) = \sum_{i=1}^n \Phi_i(x)x_i\psi^j(x) \quad (j = 1, 2, \ldots, n). \tag{4.10}$$

From (4.10) and (4.8) it follows that the function

$$\nu(x) = \sum_{i=1}^n \Phi_i(x)x_i, \tag{4.11}$$

which is equal to income multiplied by the marginal utility of income, is an integrating factor for the total differential expression

$$d\Phi(x) = \nu(x) \sum_{j=1}^n \psi^j(x)dx_j, \tag{4.12}$$

hence ψ must satisfy the well-known integrability conditions [cf. Wilson (1911), p. 255; Allen (1932), p. 223n]

$$\psi^j(x)[\psi_l^k(x) - \psi_k^l(x)] + \psi^k(x)[\psi_j^l(x) - \psi_l^j(x)]$$
$$+ \psi^l(x)[\psi_k^j(x) - \psi_j^k(x)] = 0 \tag{4.13}$$
$$(j, k, l = 1, 2, \ldots, n).$$

As shown in Appendix 4A (Lemma A.2), an equivalent set of conditions is

$$\psi_k^j(x) - \psi^k(x) \sum_{i=1}^{n} \psi_i^j(x)x_i = \psi_j^k(x) - \psi^j(x) \sum_{i=1}^{n} \psi_i^k(x)x_i \qquad (4.14)$$
$$(j, k = 1, 2, \ldots, n).$$

Conditions (4.13) were obtained by Hotelling (1932, p. 592) who, however, adopted the more stringent set of conditions (4.18) below.

Hotelling (1932, p. 590) interpreted the values of the functions ψ^j to be prices p_j rather than price-income ratios $r_j = p_j/I$—a procedure which is obviously not legitimate unless income is assumed to be constant. Moreover, the set $\phi^j = \psi^j$, so that $\nu(x) \equiv 1$ and the expression following $\nu(x)$ in (4.12) is an exact differential.[5] Slightly more generally, we may ask: under what conditions is it possible for ϕ to have the form

$$\phi^j(x) = a\,\psi^j(x) \quad (j = 1, 2, \ldots, n) \qquad (4.15)$$

for some $a > 0$?

From (4.10), condition (4.15) is equivalent to the assumption that the integrating factor ν of (4.11) is equal to a constant, $a > 0$.[6] From the argument in Katzner (1967) it follows that R must be homothetic and that Φ must have the form (2.39).[r] A simple, direct proof of this is given in the following lemma.

Lemma 7. Let X be an open subset of E_+^n. A differentiable function Φ : $X \rightarrow E^1$ satisfies

$$\sum_{i=1}^{n} \Phi_i(x)x_i = a > 0 \quad \text{for all } x \in X \qquad (4.16)$$

if and only if there exists a constant b, and a function $U : X \rightarrow E_+^1$ which is positively homogeneous of degree 1, such that Φ is given by (2.39).

Proof. Let (4.16) hold. For any $B > 0$, define

$$U(x) = Be^{\Phi(x)/a}. \qquad (4.17)$$

Then $\sum_{i=1}^{n} U_i(x)x_i = U(x)$ hence U is homogeneous of degree 1. Defining $b = -a \log B$, (2.39) follows directly from (4.17). The converse is immediate.

Q.E.D.

---

[r]Katzner omitted the constant term b, but his argument is easily amended to yield the result of Lemma 7, although in a less direct fashion.

From (4.15) and (4.9) we immediately deduce Hotelling's conditions

$$\psi_k^j(x) = \psi_j^k(x) \quad (j, k = 1, 2, \ldots, n), \tag{4.18}$$

which he adopted in place of what he called the "looser conditions" (4.13).[s] Clearly, (4.18) is equivalent to (4.15), given (4.9). Differentiating the budget identity

$$\sum_{k=1}^{n} \psi^k(x)x_k = 1$$

with respect to x_j, to obtain

$$\psi^j(x) + \sum_{k=1}^{n} \psi_j^k(x)x_k = 0,$$

and substituting (4.18), we conclude that

$$\sum_{k=1}^{n} \psi_k^j(x)x_k = -\psi^j(x),$$

i.e., that ψ^j is homogeneous of degree -1, for $j = 1, 2, \ldots, n$.

Hotelling (1932, pp. 590–91) justified (4.18) by assuming that the consumer was a middleman, maximizing not utility but net money revenue defined as $S(x) - \sum_{i=1}^{n} r_i x_i$, where $S(x)$ represents gross sales as a function of amounts purchased and the r_i are treated as parameters by the consumer.[7] Subsequently Hotelling (1935) attempted to justify (4.18) on empirical grounds, appealing to econometric results obtained by Schultz (1933) [see also Hotelling (1938), pp. 246–47]. Schultz himself (1933, p. 474) adopted (4.18), and explicitly recognized that it implied "constancy" of the marginal utility of income (actually, independence of prices, since the integrating factor (4.11) is equal to the product of income and the marginal utility of income).[8] It was not recognized by either of these authors, however, that if ψ is generated by preference maximization, (4.18) implies that preferences are homothetic. This result also falls right out of our analysis in §§2.4 and 3.2, as follows.

By its definition, ψ satisfies $\psi[h(r, 1)] = r$ and $h[\psi(x), 1] = x$, i.e., $h(r, 1) = \psi^{-1}(r)$ for $r \in \Pi$, and thus ψ is homogeneous of degree -1 if and only if $h(r, 1)$ is homogeneous of degree -1 in r, i.e., if and only if $h(p, I)$ is homogeneous of degree 1 in I. The conclusions of Theorem 1 follow

---

[s] See also the recent discussion in Pressman (1970, pp. 306–10), where Hotelling's rationale is followed closely.

immediately. It may be noted also that the Jacobian matrix $[\psi_k^j(x)]$ is the inverse of $[h_k^j(r, 1)]$, so that the symmetry conditions (4.18) are equivalent to (3.10) (for $\bar{I} = 1$).

4.2 Normalization by the Price of a Numéraire

In integrability theory (cf. Antonelli [1886], Allen [1932], Georgescu-Roegen [August 1936], Samuelson [1950], Hurwicz [1971]) it is more customary to adopt the less symmetric procedure of normalizing by the price of a numéraire, say commodity 1. In place of (4.1) we may therefore define

$$\psi(x) = \{q \in \Theta : x = h(1, q)\} \quad \text{for} \quad x \in X, \qquad (4.19)$$

and assuming $\psi(x)$ to be a singleton, denote also by $\psi(x)$ the unique $q = (p_2/p_1, p_3/p_1, \ldots, p_n/p_1, I/p_1) \in \psi(x)$ for each x. For convenience we shall denote the components of $\psi(x)$ by

$$\psi(x) = (\psi^2(x), \psi^3(x), \ldots, \psi^{n+1}(x)), \qquad (4.20)$$

Accordingly, if U is a differentiable utility function representing R on X, we have

$$\begin{cases} \psi^j(x) = U_j(x)/U_1(x) \quad \text{for} \quad j = 2, \ldots, n; \\ \psi^{n+1}(x) = x_1 + \sum_{i=1}^{n} \dfrac{U_i(x)x_i}{U_1(x)} = x_1 + \sum_{i=1}^{n} \psi^i(x)x_i. \end{cases} \qquad (4.21)$$

We proceed exactly as before, with the set $\mathscr{X}$ of polygonal paths (4.3) and the line integral (4.5) of (4.4) with respect to ξ. Conditions (4.6) through (4.9) go through without change. In place of (4.10), however, we have

$$\begin{cases} \phi^1(x) = \Phi_1(x), \\ \phi^j(x) = \Phi_1(x)\psi^j(x) \quad \text{for} \quad j = 2, \ldots, n. \end{cases} \qquad (4.22)$$

The function $\Phi_1(x)$ is now the corresponding integrating factor for the differential expression

$$d\Phi(x) = \Phi_1(x) \left[dx_1 + \sum_{j=2}^{n} \psi^j(x)dx_j\right], \qquad (4.23)$$

and thus the integrability conditions corresponding to (4.13) are

$$\psi^j(x)\psi_1^k(x) - \psi^k(x)\psi_1^j(x + \psi^1(x)[\psi_k^j(x) - \psi_j^k(x)] = 0, \qquad (4.24)$$

which are the well-known Antonelli (1886) conditions [see also Hicks and Allen (1934), p. 211n; Georgescu-Roegen, (August 1936), p. 593; and Samuelson (1950)].

We may now ask: under what conditions is it possible to take ϕ to be of the form

$$\begin{cases} \phi^1(x) = a \\ \phi^j(x) = a\,\psi^j(x) \quad \text{for} \quad j = 2, 3, \ldots, n, \end{cases} \qquad (4.25)$$

where a is a positive constant?

From (4.22), condition (4.25) is equivalent to the assumption that

$$\Phi_1(x) = a > 0 \quad \text{for all} \quad x \in X, \qquad (4.26)$$

i.e., the marginal utility of commodity 1 is a positive constant. This immediately implies that Φ has the form (2.66) of §2.5. This result goes back to Edgeworth (1891, p. 237n; 1925, II, p. 317n); see also Berry (1891, p. 550) and Marshall (1891, p. 756; 1961, I, p. 845).[1] Its relation to the results of §§2.5 and 3.4 may be simply indicated, as follows.

We have by the definition of ψ, $\psi[h(1, q)] = q$ and $h[1, \psi(x)] = x$, so $h(1, q) = \psi^{-1}(q)$. Denoting $\psi^{n+1} = \psi^1$ and rewriting $\psi = (\psi^1, \psi^2, \ldots, \psi^n)$ for convenience, we see that the Jacobian matrix of ψ has the form

$$\frac{\partial \psi}{\partial x} = \begin{bmatrix} 1 & \psi_2^1 & \psi_3^1 & \cdots & \psi_n^1 \\ 0 & \psi_2^2 & \psi_3^2 & \cdots & \psi_n^2 \\ 0 & \psi_2^3 & \psi_3^3 & \cdots & \psi_n^3 \\ \cdot & \cdot & \cdot & & \cdot \\ \cdot & \cdot & \cdot & & \cdot \\ \cdot & \cdot & \cdot & & \cdot \\ 0 & \psi_2^n & \psi_3^n & \cdots & \psi_n^n \end{bmatrix}, \qquad (4.27)$$

where the bottom right matrix of order $n - 1$ is symmetric. Therefore that of $h(1, q)$, which (upon permuting the arguments $p_1 = 1$ and $I = q_{n+1}$) is the inverse of (4.27), must have the same form, i.e., $h_1^j = 0$ for $j = 2, \ldots, n$, and $h_k^j = h_j^k$ as in (3.35) and (3.36). The conclusions of Theorem 2 therefore follow immediately.

The example at the end of §3.3 may be used to illustrate this case as well. Taking $\Phi_2(x) = a = 1$, $p_1 = 1$, and $n = 2$, we have $\psi^1(x) = \phi^1(x) = $

---

[1] See also Patinkin (1963), who also draws attention to the common error of assuming that (4.26) follows from the assumption $\Phi_{11}(x) \equiv 0$ alone.

$\Phi_1(x) = 1$ and $\psi^2(x) = \phi^2(x) = \Phi_2(x) = W_2(x_2)$ [from (4.25), (4.8), and (2.66)], hence the line integral (4.5) connecting $\xi(0) = x^0$ and $\xi(1) = x^1$ becomes

$$\sum_{j=1}^{2} \int_0^1 \psi^j[\xi(t)]d\xi_j(t) = x_1^1 - x_1^0 + \int_{x_2^0}^{x_2^1} W_2(\xi_2)d\xi_2. \qquad (4.28)$$

Since by hypothesis the consumer's income rises by the amount of the tax revenue, we have

$$I^1 - I^0 = x_1^1 + p_2^1 x_2^1 - x_1^0 - p_2^0 x_2^0 = (p_2^1 - p_2^0)x_2^1, \qquad (4.29)$$

hence

$$x_1^1 - x_1^0 = p_2^0(x_2^0 - x_2^1). \qquad (4.30)$$

In Figure 4-5, (4.30) corresponds to the area of the rectangle $DEFG$, whereas the remaining term on the right in (4.28) corresponds to the area $AGFE$; accordingly, (4.28) gives the triangular region ADE. This may be related to formula (3.39) by substituting the demand function (2.53a) for commodity 2 for ξ_2 in (4.28), performing a transformation of variables, and integrating by parts, to obtain

$$\int_{x_2^0}^{x_2^1} W_2(\xi_2)d\xi_2 = \int_{p_2^0}^{p_2^1} W_2[\eta^2(1, \pi_2)]d\eta^2(1, \pi_2)$$

$$= \int_{p_2^0}^{p_2^1} \pi_2 \eta_2^2(1, \pi_2)d\pi_2$$

$$= p_2^1 x_2^1 - p_2^0 x_2^0 - \int_{p_2^0}^{p_2^1} \eta^2(1, \pi_2)d\pi_2. \qquad (4.31)$$

Substituting (4.31) in (4.28) and making use of (4.29), we obtain (3.39) back again.

We take up briefly the "integrability conditions" for the direct demand
function h of §2.1, and the indirect or inverse demand functions ψ of §§4.1
and 4.2. We shall be concerned only with what Hurwicz (1971) calls
"mathematical integrability," i.e., conditions for the existence of solutions of the partial differential equations (2.6), (4.2), and (4.21), respectively. As is now well known (cf. Allen [1932], Georgescu-Roegen [Au-
gust 1936], for early discussions of this point), these are not sufficient for
the solution function to be economically meaningful, and interpretable as
a utility function; for this one needs also to consider negative
semidefiniteness, leading to "economic integrability" in Hurwicz's terminology. It will be seen from the following development that the natural
approach is to proceed from the direct demand function $h(p, I)$ and the
Antonelli equations (2.6) (usually called "Roy's identity"—cf. Lau
[1969]) to the indirect utility function $V(p, I)$; and likewise, from the
indirect demand function $\psi(x)$ of §4.1 and the equations (4.2), or alternatively the indirect demand function $\psi(x)$ of §4.2 and the Jevons-Walras-
Antonelli equations (4.21), to the direct utility function $U(x)$. The appropriate integrability conditions in solving for $V(p, I)$ from $h(p, I)$ are the
Slutsky conditions, whereas the appropriate integrability conditions in
solving for $U(x)$ from $\psi(x)$ are the Antonelli conditions and their variants.

Lemma A.1. A necessary condition for the existence of a solution V
to the system of partial differential equations (2.6) of Lemma 3 is that h
satisfy the Slutsky conditions (2.17).

Proof. Denote the partial differential operator S_j (the Slutsky
operator), operating on $V(p, I)$ by

$$S_j = \frac{\partial}{\partial p_j} + h^j \frac{\partial}{\partial I}. \tag{A.1}$$

Then (cf. Chester [1971], pp. 319–20; Goursat [1959], pp. 269–71) a
necessary condition for the existence of a solution V to the system of
partial differential equations

$$S_j V(p, I) = 0 \quad (j = 1, 2, \ldots, n - 1) \tag{A.2}$$

[which corresponds to (2.6)] is that (A.2) be a Jacobian system, i.e., that
the equations

$$(S_j S_k - S_k S_j) V(p, I) = 0 \tag{A.3}$$

be satisfied for $j, k = 1, 2, \ldots, n - 1$.

We readily compute

$$S_k S_j V = V_{jk} + h_k^j V_I + h^j V_{Ik} + h^k [V_{jI} + h_j^j V_I + h^j V_{II}].$$

Accordingly,

$$(S_k S_j - S_j S_k)V = [h_k^j + h^k h_I^j - h_j^k - h^j h_I^k]V_I.$$

Equating this to zero and noting (from Lemma 2) that V_I cannot vanish on any open set, (2.17) follows immediately.

Q.E.D.

The Slutsky conditions can be restated for the case in which prices are normalized by income and we define the normalized demand functions η^j [not to be confused with (2.53a) with which, however, they coincide for $j = 2, \ldots, n$ when the assumptions of Lemma 5 hold] by

$$\eta^j(r) = h^j(r, 1) \quad (j = 1, 2, \ldots, n). \tag{A.4}$$

Since h is homogeneous of degree zero in (p, I), by Euler's theorem we have

$$h_I^j(r, 1) = -\sum_{i=1}^n h_i^j(r, 1)r_i = -\sum_{i=1}^n \eta_i^j(r)r_i,$$

whence, defining the unnormalized and normalized Slutksy functions by

$$s_{jk}(p, I) = h_k^j(p, I) + h^k(p, I)h_I^j(p, I) \tag{A.5}$$

and

$$\sigma_{jk}(r) = s_{jk}(r, 1) \tag{A.6}$$

respectively, we have

$$\sigma_{jk}(r) = \eta_k^j(r) - \eta^k(r)\sum_{i=1}^n \eta_i^j(r)r_i.$$

Accordingly, the Slutsky symmetry conditions reduce to

$$\eta_k^j(r) - \eta^k(r)\sum_{i=1}^n \eta_i^j(r)r_i = \eta_j^k(r) - \eta^j(r)\sum_{i=1}^n \eta_i^k(r)r_i. \tag{A.7}$$

Lemma A.2. A necessary condition for the existence of a solution U to the system of partial differential equations (4.2) is that ψ satisfy the conditions (4.14). An equivalent set of conditions is given by (4.13).

Proof. Define the partial differential operator X_j, operating on $U(x)$, by

$$X_j = \frac{\partial}{\partial x_j} - \psi^j \sum_{i=1}^n x_i \frac{\partial}{\partial x_i}, \tag{A.8}$$

so that

$$X_j U(x) = U_j(x) - \psi^j(x) \sum_{i=1}^n U_i(x) x_i. \tag{A.9}$$

Then a necessary condition for the existence of a solution U to the system of partial differential equations

$$X_j U(x) = 0 \quad (j = 1, 2, \ldots, n-1) \tag{A.10}$$

is that (A.10) be a Jacobian system, i.e., that

$$(X_j X_k - X_k X_j) U(x) = 0 \quad \text{for} \quad j, k = 1, 2, \ldots, n-1. \tag{A.11}$$

We find after considerable computation that

$$(X_j X_k - X_k X_j) U = [\psi_k^j - \psi_j^k + \sum_{i=1}^n x_i(\psi^j \psi_i^k - \psi^k \psi_i^j)]\iota \tag{A.12}$$

where

$$\iota(x) = \sum_{i=1}^n U_i(x) x_i \tag{A.13}$$

[compare (4.11)]. Since ι does not vanish on any open set, (4.14) follows.

We verify that (A.12) may also be written in the form

$$(X_j X_k - X_k X_j) U = (\psi_k^j - \psi_j^k)\iota + \psi^j \iota_k - \psi^k \iota_j. \tag{A.14}$$

Forming the analogous commutators $(X_k X_l - X_l X_k)U$, $(X_l X_j - X_j X_l)U$, multiplying the three expressions by ψ^l, ψ^j, ψ^k respectively, and summing and equating to zero, we obtain (4.13).

Q.E.D.

The formal identify of (A.7) and (4.14) should be noted.

Analysis of (4.21) proceeds in exactly the same way, in terms of the Antonelli operator

$$A_j = \psi^j \frac{\partial}{\partial x_1} - \frac{\partial}{\partial x_j}, \tag{A.15}$$

exactly as in Antonelli's original memoir (1886).

Notes

1. This type of argument goes back at least to Jevons (1879, p. 123; 1957, p. 114). One finds it again espoused by Edgeworth (1894) in the course of his dispute with Nicholson (1893, 1894), as well as by Lieben (1894, p. 718) who stated: "We therefore have assumed that the [marginal] utility of money does not vary, an hypothesis practically admissible only as long as the alterations in the amount of expenditure are small." Nicholson objected to Marshall's application of his argument to a commodity like coals—a necessity; Marshall responded (1895, p. 795) by changing "coals" to "tea." There is thus some justice in Georgescu-Roegen's conclusion (1968, p. 181) that "as far as demand theory is concerned, Marshall's is bourgeois, perhaps even petit bourgeois economics." Nicholson (1894, p. 346) was less charitable: "It is only applicable to a few careless millionaires."

The modern proponent of the Jevons-Marshall argument is Hicks, who has stated (1941, p. 109): "Whenever the commodity in question is one on which the consumer is likely to be spending a small proportion only of his total income, the assumption of 'constant marginal utility of money' can usually be granted; and it can still be granted, even if this condition is not fulfilled, provided the particular change does not involve a large *net* change in real incomes." While this argument has been repeated for about a century, we show at the end of § 2.5 that it is simply incorrect.

2. The alternative interpretation is that the marginal utility of income is independent of income and of all prices save that of the numéraire (see §2.5). This latter interpretation identifies "money" with a numéraire which enters the (direct) utility function, and the "marginal utility of money" with the "marginal utility of the numéraire." The former identifies it with money income (Pareto's *bene instrumentale*), which has no direct utility of its own (cf. Pareto, June 1892, p. 490; Pareto 1960, I, pp. 374-9). As was pointed out by Samuelson (1942), and is immediate from (2.28) and (2.51), the former is consistent with Marshall's espousal (1920, p. 95) of the principle of diminishing marginal utility, but the latter is not. Friedman (1953, p. 82n) interpreted Marshall's statement that "a per-

son's material resources being unchanged, the marginal utility of money to him is a fixed quantity" to be "merely a verbal statement of an identity (if income is unchanged, so is marginal utility of money)", apparently taking for granted that the marginal utility of income would be independent of prices; and yet he adopted the second interpretation rather than the first. Pareto, in the *Cours* (1896, I, pp. 36-7n), and with reference to the controversy between Walras (1890) and Auspitz and Lieben (1890), discussed the second interpretation, which he described as constancy of the "elementary ophelimity of the commodity which serves as money," to distinguish it from the first interpretation (p. 35n), which was his initial interpretation of Auspitz and Lieben's (1889) assumption (cf. Pareto, March 1892); later, in the *Manuel* (1909, Appendix, §§56-65, pp. 585-95) he discussed both approaches. The two approaches were subsequently analyzed by Friedman (1935), Samuelson (1942, 1947), and Georgescu-Roegen (1968). Hicks (1939, pp. 38-41) adopted the second interpretation exclusively, without taking the first into consideration; in this he has been followed by Patinkin (1963). Stigler's (1950, p. 390) assessment is compatible with either interpretation. We find the Pareto (1892) and Samuelson (1942) interpretations persuasive, among other reasons because they are compatible with Marshall's applications of consumer's surplus arguments to tax-and-bounty schemes involving several commodities, as has been shown in Chipman (1970).

3. A particular case of this result, also arrived at by Samuelson (1942), goes back to Pareto (June 1892, pp. 493-94); namely, that is the utility function (2.39) is assumed to be additively separable, it must be log-linear (see the discussion in Chipman 1976). A subsequent alternative proof of this same result by Pareto (August 1892, p. 123) was repeated by Barone (May 1894, p. 434; 1936, p. 48), but without reference to Pareto.

4. See Auspitz and Lieben (1889), formula (6) on p. 465 (1914, p. 305) and pp. 470-78 (1914, pp. 308-15). They obtained a function of the form (2.66) (1899, p. 471; 1914, p. 310), but it was a hybrid utility function, containing consumption, production, stocks, prices, and cash balances as arguments, the latter being identified with "money." However, after being confronted by sharp criticism on the part of Walras (1890)—who had previously (1889, 41ᵉ Leçon, pp. 493–505; 1954, pp. 434–46) furnished a similar criticism of Dupuit's work—Auspitz and Lieben (1890, p. 602) made explicit their assumption that they regarded the marginal utility of the numéraire as constant. This was subsequently taken up by Edgeworth (1891, p. 237n), who derived (2.66) and showed how the Auspitz-Lieben diagrams involved the implicit assumption of parallel preferences; see also Berry (1891) and Marshall (1891, p. 756; 1920, p. 845), Pareto (1896, p. 37), Wilson (1939), Samuelson (1942, p. 85; 1974, p. 1279), and Georgescu-Roegen (1968).

5. In doing so, Hotelling was following Edgeworth (1897, p. 20n; 1925, I, p. 117n): "I assume, notwithstanding the objections raised by some distinguished economists, in particular Prof. V. Pareto . . . and Prof. Irving Fisher . . . , that for every system of quantities . . . there is for each individual a money measure of the total utility which he derives from the consumption of assigned quantities . . . , a measure represented by a function of those quantities." The reference to Fisher is surprising, since the latter accepted the consumer's surplus concept; but the page in Fisher (1892, p. 89) referred to by Edgeworth deals not with consumer's surplus but with the integrability problem. Thus it seems that Edgeworth fell into the same confusion as did Pareto himself (1906) in not distinguishing between integrability conditions and conditions for a differential form to be exact. Pareto's confusion consisted in trying to define an "ophelimity index" in terms of a line integral (4.5) when the conditions (4.9) failed to hold, where the ϕ^j's were the intuitively defined "elementary ophelimities." It seems that in citing Pareto, Edgeworth was referring to his discussions of integrability rather than to Pareto's objections to the assumption of constancy of the marginal utility of income (Pareto, June 1892). Edgeworth's 1897 discussion provoked Pareto in a letter to Pantaleoni dated September 15, 1907 (cf. Pareto 1960, III, p. 63) to describe the Marshall-Edgeworth assumption as "asinine."

6. This result may also be arrived at via another route. Fisher (1892, p. 19) introduced a definition of "gain or consumer's rent" which we can interpret as

$$\Gamma(x) = \sum_{i=1}^{n} \int_0^1 \Phi_i[\xi(t)]d\xi_i(t) \quad - \sum_{i=1}^{n} \Phi_i(x)x_i,$$

where the Φ_i are partial derivatives of a utility function Φ and the path ξ connects $\xi(0) = 0$ and $\xi(1) = x$. Since this definition is equivalent to $\Gamma(x) = \Phi(x) - \Phi(0) - \sum_{i=1}^{n} \Phi_i(x)x_i$, in order for $\Gamma(x^1) - \Gamma(x^0)$ to coincide with $\Phi(x^1) - \Phi(x^0)$ for any two bundles x^0 and x^1 it is clearly necessary for the function (4.11) to be a constant. Barone (September 1894) followed Fisher in adopting this definition, without being aware of its consequences; and without apparent justification, he attributed this concept of gain to Walras (1892).

7. This justification agrees with the second of the following two explanations put forward by Marshall (1890, 1891, p. 393; 1920, p. 335): "When a person buys anything for his own consumption, he generally spends on it a small part of his total resources; while when he buys it for the purposes of trade, he looks to re-selling it, and therefore his potential resources are not diminished. In either case the marginal utility of money to him is not appreciably changed."

8. Schultz followed the first of the alternative explanations provided by Marshall in the passage cited in the previous note.

117

Bibliography

Allen R. G. D. "The Foundations of a Mathematical Theory of Exchange." *Economica* 12 (May 1932): 197–226.

————. "The Marginal Utility of Money and Its Application." *Economica* 13 (May 1933): 186–209.

Antonelli, G. B. *Sulla teoria matematica della economia politica.* Pisa: nella Tipografia del Folchetto, 1886. Reprinted in the *Giornale degli Economisti e Annali di Economia,* N.S., 10 (May-June 1951): 233–63. English translation: "On the Mathematical Theory of Political Economy," in Chipman, Hurwicz, Richter, and Sonnenschein (1971), 332–64.

Apostol, Tom M. *Mathematical Analysis.* Reading, Mass.: Addison-Wesley Publishing Company, Inc., 1957.

Auspitz, Rudolf, and Lieben, Richard. *Untersuchungen über die Theorie des Preises.* Leipzig: Duncker und Humblot, 1889. French translation: *Recherches sur la théorie du prix,* in two volumes (Texte, Album). Paris: M. Giard & É. Brière, 1914.

————. "Correspondance." *Revue d'économie politique* 4 (November-December 1890): 599–605.

Barone, Enrico. "A proposito delle indagini del Fisher." *Giornale degli Economisti* [2], 8 (May 1894): 413–39. Reprinted in Barone (1936), pp. 18–55.

————. "Sulla 'consumers' rent.'" *Giornale degli Economisti* [2], 9 (September 1894): 211–24. Reprinted in Barone (1936), pp. 57–76.

————. *Le opere economiche* (in three volumes), Vol. I. Bologna: Nicole Zanichelli Editore, 1936.

Berry, Arthur. "Alcune brevi parole sulla teoria del baratto di A. Marshall." *Giornale degli Economisti* [2], 2 (June 1891): 549–53.

Boulding, Kenneth E. "The Concept of Economic Surplus." *American Economic Review* 35 (December 1945): 851–69.

Burns, Michael E. "A Note on the Concept and Measure of Consumer's Surplus." *American Economic Review* 53 (June 1973): 335–44.

Chester, Clive R. *Techniques in Partial Differential Equations.* New York: McGraw-Hill Book Company, 1971.

Chipman, John S. "External Economies of Scale and Competitive Equilibrium." *Quarterly Journal of Economics* 84 (August 1970): 347–85.

————. "Homothetic Preferences and Aggregation." *Journal of Economic Theory* 8 (May 1974): 26–38.

————. "The Paretian Heritage." *Cahiers Vilfredo Pareto: Revue européenne des sciences sociales* 14, no. 37 (1976): 65–171.

Chipman, John S., Leonid Hurwicz, Marcel K. Richter, and Hugo Sonnenschein, *Preferences, Utility, and Demand*. New York: Harcourt Brace Jovanovich, Inc., 1971.

Chipman, John S., and Moore, James C. "Aggregation and Real National Income with Homothetic Preferences and a Fixed Distribution of Income." Working paper, 1976.

Debreu, Gerard. "Representation of a Preference Ordering by a Numerical Function." In *Decision Processes*. Edited by R. M. Thrall, C. H. Coombs, and R. L. Davis. New York: John Wiley & Sons, Inc., 1954, pp. 159–65.

Dupuit, Jules. "De la mesure de l'utilité des travaux publics." *Annales des Ponts et Chaussées, Mémoires et documents relatifs à l'art des constructions et au service de l'ingénieur* [2], 8 (2e semestre, 1844): 332–75. English translation: "On the Measurement of the Utility of Public Works." In *Readings in Welfare Economics*. Edited by Kenneth J. Arrow and Tibor Scitovsky. Homewood, Ill.: Richard B. Irwin, Inc., 1969, 255–83.

———. "De l'influence des péages sur l'utilité des voies de communication." *Annales des Ponts et Chaussées, Mémoires et documents* [2], 17 (1er semestre, 1849): 170–248.

———. "De l'utilité et de sa mesure. De l'utilité publique." *Journal des Economistes* 36 (July 1853): 1–27.

Edgeworth, F. Y. "Osservazioni sulla teoria matematica dell'economia politica con riguardo speciale ai principi di economia di Alfredo Marshall." *Giornale degle Economisti* [2], 2 (March 1891): 233–45. "Ancora a proposito della teoria del baratto." Ibid. 3 (October 1891): 316–18. Abridged English translation: "On the Determinateness of Economic Equilibrium." In Edgeworth (1925), II, pp. 313–19.

———. "Professor J. S. Nicholson on Consumer's Rent." *Economic Journal* 4 (March 1894): 151–58. "The Measurement of Utility by Money." Ibid. 4 (June 1894): 347–48.

———. "La teoria pura del monopolio." *Giornale degli Economisti* [2], 15 (July, October, November 1897): 13–31, 307–20, 405–14. English translation: "The Pure Theory of Monopoly." In Edgeworth (1925), I, pp. 111–42.

———. *Papers Relating to Political Economy* (in three volumes). London: Macmillan and Co., Limited, 1925.

Fisher, Irving. "Mathematical Investigations in the Theory of Value and Prices." *Transactions of the Connecticut Academy* 9 (July 1892): 1–124. Reprinted, New York: Augustus M. Kelley, 1961.

Foster, C. D., and Neuberger, H. L. I. "The Ambiguity of the Consumer's Surplus Measure of Welfare Change.'' *Oxford Economic Papers*, N.S., 26 (March 1974): 66–77.

Friedman, Milton. ''Professor Pigou's Method for Measuring Elasticities of Demand from Budgetary Data.'' *Quarterly Journal of Economics* 50 (November 1935): 151–63.

——. ''The Marshallian Demand Curve.'' *Journal of Political Economy* 51 (December 1949): 463–95. Reprinted in Friedman, Milton. *Essays in Positive Economics*. Chicago: The University of Chicago Press, 1953, pp. 47–99.

Georgescu-Roegen, Nicholas. ''Marginal Utility of Money and Elasticities of Demand.'' *Quarterly Journal of Economics* 50 (May 1936): 533–39.

——. ''The Pure Theory of Consumer's Behavior.'' *Quarterly Journal of Economics* 50 (August 1936): 545–93. Reprinted in Georgescu-Roegen (1966): 133–70.

——. ''Choice, Expectations, and Measurability.'' *Quarterly Journal of Economics* 58 (November 1954): 503–34. Reprinted in Georgescu-Roegen (1966): 184–215.

——. *Analytical Economics*. Cambridge, Mass.: Harvard University Press, 1966.

——. ''Revisiting Marshall's Constancy of Marginal Utility of Money.'' *Southern Economic Journal* 35 (October 1968): 176–81.

Goursat, Édouard. *A Course in Mathematical Analysis*, Vol. II, Part 2, *Differential Equations*. New York: Dover Publications, Inc., 1959.

Harberger, Arnold C. ''The Measurement of Waste.'' *American Economic Review, Papers and Proceedings* 54 (May 1964): 58–76.

——. ''Three Basic Postulates for Applied Welfare Economics: An Interpretive Essay.'' *Journal of Economic Literature* 9 (September 1971): 785–97.

Henderson, A. ''Consumer's Surplus and the Compensating Variation.'' *Review of Economic Studies* 8 (February 1941): 117–21.

Hicks, J. R. *Value and Capital*. Oxford: Clarendon Press, 1939. 2nd ed., 1946.

——. ''The Rehabilitation of Consumers' Surplus.'' *Review of Economic Studies* 8 (February 1941): 108–16.

——. ''Consumers' Surplus and Index-Numbers.'' *Review of Economic Studies* 9 (Summer 1942): 126–37.

——. ''The Four Consumer's Surpluses.'' *Review of Economic Studies* 11 (Winter 1943): 31–41.

——. ''The Generalized Theory of Consumer's Surplus.'' *Review of Economic Studies* 8 (1945–46): 68–74.

Hicks, J. R. *A Revision of Demand Theory*. Oxford: Clarendon Press, 1956.

Hicks, J. R., and Allen, R. G. D. "A Reconsideration of the Theory of Value." *Economica*, N.S., 1 (February, May 1934): 52–76, 196–219.

Hotelling, Harold. "Edgeworth's Taxation Paradox and the Nature of Demand and Supply Functions." *Journal of Political Economy* 40 (October 1932): 577–616.

————. "Demand Functions with Limited Budgets." *Econometrica* 3 (January 1935): 66–78.

————. "The General Welfare in Relation to Problems of Taxation and of Railway and Utility Rates." *Econometrica* 6 (July 1938): 242–69.

Houthakker, H. S. "Compensated Changes in Quantities and Qualities Consumed." *Review of Economic Studies* 19 (1953): 155–64.

————. "Additive Preferences." *Econometrica* 28 (April 1960): 244–57.

Hurwicz, Leonid. "On the Problem of Integrability of Demand Functions." In Chipman, Hurwicz, Richter, and Sonnenschein (1971), pp. 174–214.

Hurwicz, Leonid, and Richter, Marcel K. "Revealed Preference Without Demand Continuity Assumptions." In Chipman, Hurwicz, Richter, and Sonnenschein (1971), pp. 59–76.

Hurwicz, Leonid, and Uzawa, Hirofumi. "On the Integrability of Demand Functions." In Chipman, Hurwicz, Richter, and Sonnenschein (1971), pp. 114–48.

Jevons, W. Stanley. *The Theory of Political Economy*. London and New York: Macmillan and Co., 1871. 2nd ed., 1879. 3rd ed., 1888. 5th ed., New York: Kelley & Millman, Inc., 1957.

Katzner, Donald W. "A Note on the Constancy of the Marginal Utility of Income." *International Economic Review* 8 (February 1967): 128–30.

————. *Static Demand Theory*. New York: The Macmillan Company, 1970.

Lau, Lawrence J. "Duality and the Structure of Utility Functions." *Journal of Economic Theory* 1 (December 1969): 374–96.

Lieben, Richard. "On Consumer's Rent." *Economic Journal* 4 (December 1894): 716–19.

McKenzie, Lionel W. "Demand Theory without a Utility Index." *Review of Economic Studies* 24 (June 1957): 185–89.

Mansfield, Edwin. *Microeconomics*. New York: W. W. Norton & Company, Inc., 1970. 2nd ed., 1975.

Marshall, Alfred. "Influence of Taxation," and "Tolls (and Railway Fares)" (c. 1867–72). In Whitaker (1975), II, pp. 279–83.

————. *The Pure Theory of Domestic Values*. London: privately printed, 1879. Reprinted in Alfred Marshall. *The Pure Theory of Foreign Trade, The Pure Theory of Domestic Values*. London: London School of Economics and Political Science, 1949. Also in Whitaker (1975), II, pp. 186–236.

————. *Principles of Economics*. London: Macmillan and Co., 1890. 2nd ed., 1891. 3rd ed., 1895. 4th ed., 1898, 5th ed., 1907. 6th ed., 1910. 7th ed., 1916. 8th ed., 1920. 9th (variorum) ed., in two volumes, 1961.

Nicholson, J. Shield. *Principles of Political Economy*, Vol. I. London: Adam and Charles Black, 1893.

————. "The Measurement of Utility by Money." *Economic Journal* 4 (June 1894): 342–47.

Pareto, Vilfredo. "La teoria dei prezzi dei Signori Auspitz e Lieben e le osservazioni del professore Walras." *Giornale degli Economisti* [2], 4 (March 1892): 201–39.

————. "Considerazioni sui principii fondamentali dell'economia politica pura," Part 2. *Giornale degli Economisti* [2], 4 (June 1892): 485–512; Part 3, ibid., 5 (August 1892): 119–57.

————. *Cours d'économie politique* (in two volumes). Lausanne: F. Rouge, 1896, 1897.

————. "L'ofelimità nei cicli non chiusi." *Giornale degli Economisti* 2, 33 (July 1906): 15–30. English translation: "Ophelimity in Non-Closed Cycles." In Chipman, Hurwicz, Richter, and Sonnenschein (1971), pp. 370–85.

————. *Manuel d'économie politique*. Paris: V. Giard et E. Brière, 1909.

————. *Lettere a Maffeo Pantaleoni*. Edited by Gabriele de Rosa (in three volumes). Rome: Banca Nazionale del Lavoro, 1960.

Patinkin, Don. "Demand Curves and Consumer's Surplus." In Christ, Carl F., et al. *Measurement in Economics, Studies in Mathematical Economics and Econometrics in Memory of Yehuda Grunfeld*. Stanford, California: Stanford University Press, 1963, pp. 83–112.

Pfouts, R. W. "A Critique of Some Recent Contributions to the Theory of Consumers' Surplus." *Southern Economic Journal* 19 (January 1953): 315–33.

Pigou, A. C. *The Economics of Welfare*. London: Macmillan and Co. Ltd., 1920. 2nd ed., 1924. 3rd ed., 1929. 4th ed., 1932.

Pressman, Israel. "A Mathematical Formulation of the Peak-Load Pricing Problem." *The Bell Journal of Economics and Management Science* 1 (Autumn 1970): 304–26.

Rader, Trout. "Equivalence of Consumer Surplus, the Divisia Index of

Output, and Eisenberg's Addilog Social Utility." Unpublished manuscript, 1975.

Roy, René. *De l'utilité. Contribution à la théorie des choix.* Paris: Hermann & Cie, Éditeurs, 1942.

—. "La distribution du revenu entre les divers biens." *Econometrica* 15 (July 1947): 205–25.

Samuelson, Paul A. "Constancy of the Marginal Utility of Income." In *Studies in Mathematical Economics and Econometrics, In Memory of Henry Schultz,* edited by Oscar Lange, Francis McIntyre, and Theodore O. Yntema. Chicago: University of Chicago Press, 1942, pp. 75–91.

—. *Foundations of Economic Analysis.* Cambridge, Mass.: Harvard University Press, 1947.

—. "The Problem of Integrability in Utility Theory." *Economica,* N.S., 17 (November 1950): 355–85.

—. "Principles of Efficiency—Discussion." *American Economic Review, Papers and Proceedings* 54 (May 1964): 93–96.

—. "Complementarity. An Essay on the 40th Anniversary of the Hicks-Allen Revolution in Demand Theory." *Journal of Economic Literature* 12 (December 1974): 1255–89.

Schultz, Henry. "Interrelations of Demand." *Journal of Political Economy* 41 (August 1933): 468–512.

Silberberg, Eugene. "Duality and the Many Consumer's Surpluses." *American Economic Review* 62 (December 1972): 942–52.

Slutsky, Eugenio. "Sulla teoria del bilancio del consumatore." *Giornale degli Economisti e Rivista di Statistica* [3], 51 (July 1915): 1–26. English translation: "On the Theory of the Budget of the Consumer." In *Readings in Price Theory,* edited by George J. Stigler and Kenneth E. Boulding. Homewood, Ill.: Richard D. Irwin, Inc., 1952, pp. 27–56.

Stigler, George J. "The Development of Utility Theory." *Journal of Political Economy* 58 (August, October 1950): 307–27, 373–96. Reprinted in Stigler, George J. *Essays in the History of Economics.* Chicago: The University of Chicago Press, 1965, pp. 66–155.

Walras, Léon. *Élements d'économie politique pure.* Lausanne: Imprimerie L. Corbaz et Cie, 1874, 1877. 2nd ed., Lausanne: F. Rouge, 1889.

—. "Observations sur le principe de la théorie du prix de MM. Auspitz et Lieben." *Revue d'économie politique* 4 (May-June 1890): 320–23. Reprinted in Walras (1896), pp. 481–84. English translation in Walras (1954), pp. 483–88.

————. "Geometrical Theory of the Determination of Prices." *Annals of the American Academy of Political and Social Science* 3 (July 1892): 45–64. Retranslated in Walras (1954), pp. 461–82.

————. *Élements d'économie politique pure,* 3rd ed. Lausanne: F. Rouge, Éditeur, 1896. English translation of 4th ("definitive") edition: *Elements of Pure Economics.* London: George Allen and Unwin Ltd., 1954.

Whitaker, J. K. *The Early Economic Writings of Alfred Marshall, 1867– 1890,* in two volumes. London and Basingstoke: The Macmillan Press, 1975.

Wilson, Edwin B. *Advanced Calculus.* New York: Ginn and Company, 1911.

————. "Pareto versus Marshall." *Quarterly Journal of Economics* 53 (August 1939): 645–50.

————. "Notes on Utility Theory and Demand Equations." *Quarterly Journal of Economics* 60 (May 1946): 453–60.

5 Equitable Income Distribution: Another Experiment

Jan Tinbergen

Essence of Proposed Definition

In an earlier article,[1] I defined equity in income distribution as equality of welfare between social groups. This implies that it is possible to measure welfare. In what I called an interdisciplinary approach, I started from the idea that a utility or welfare function contains three types of elements: variables, parameters, and coefficients.[2] Variables represent factors affecting the individual's choices—for example, a salary scale and a job chosen on that scale. Parameters indicate personal characteristics, such as IQ or, as a proxy, years of schooling completed. Coefficients are equal for all members of a community and characterize that community (the Netherlands in my first example). Variables and some parameters were measured by de Wolff and van Slijpe[3] on evidence derived from a Swedish sample due to Husen. In a first experiment with my definition, I took only two variables, income after income tax (x) and schooling required for the job held (h), one parameter (h'), actual schooling achieved, and two coefficients (c_0 and c_2) in a welfare function

$$w_i = f\left\{ x_i - c_0 h_i - \frac{1}{2} c_2 (h_i - h_i')^2 \right\}, \qquad (5.1)$$

where i indicates an individual (or a homogeneous group), w_i his welfare, and f the welfare function. The two terms following x_i can be considered as corrections to compensate for labor disutility. The first term, $-c_0 h_i$, stands for dissatisfaction (or satisfaction if $c_0 < 0$) connected with job h. The second term represents the dissatisfaction (or tension) of having a job whose educational requirement, h_i, does not correspond with the schooling h_i' achieved. The use of the difference $h - h'$ implies commensurability of these two figures. In the first experiment, h was assumed to be the upper quartile of all observed h' among those who held the job in 1960. The way in which $h - h'$ is established in the present experiment will be discussed below.

The term h' is not introduced separately in the function on grounds that only the difference between h and h' is relevant as an adjustment to take account of dissatisfaction. To have a term in h' is to suggest that

Some of the materials presented in this Chapter are included in *Income Distribution: Analysis and Policies* (Amsterdam: North-Holland Publishing Company, 1975).

125

native capabilities (of which h' is a surrogate) should be allowed income correction. The absence can also be interpreted as the impossibility to compare welfare of two persons with different innate abilities.

Some other elements are absent in formula (5.1) which could have been introduced without much trouble—for instance, size of family or health. They have been left out because their differences between the groups considered are not important. They become important as soon as subgroups of households with different size or health are considered. The same applies to differences in working hours.

For the estimation of the coefficients c_0 and c_2, we need data on incomes earned by persons having the same education but different jobs.

Indirect Estimation of Two-Entry Table

Unfortunately, a two-entry classification indicating incomes by education and jobs (occupations) is not published in the U.S. census volumes. Therefore, an indirect method was devised in order to estimate the figures in the cells most relevent in a two-entry table. Using the levels of education and the categories of occupations as distinguished by Dougherty,[4] and arranging both in the order of increasing incomes, our data only indicate the column (education) and row (occupation) averages of incomes and the total numbers of people in each column and row. The classification of the occupational groups is shown in the last column of Table 5–1; those for the educational groups have been expressed in years of schooling. More precisely, the figures are employment figures in the experienced civilian labor force in 1959, expressed in equivalent males. Using the state of Illinois for this experiment, we first found that the grand total by education exceeded the grand total by occupation by 441,000 persons. In order to arrive at identical grand totals, those 441,000 with unknown occupations were distributed proportionately over the occupation classes. Thus, the sums in Table 5–1 were reconciled. In order to fill in the cells of the table, the northwest-corner rule was applied, well known from the "Hitchcock problem."[5,6] The method may be interpreted as an optimum use of the available manpower in the various occupation classes, where the optimum means the cheapest way of having the jobs done, in the sense of using people with the lowest education available first and only adding people with higher education if manpower is still insufficient. As could be expected, only a number of cells around the main diagonal are non-empty but enough of them exist to make possible vertical comparisons—that is comparisons of groups with the same education but in different occupations.

The next step is to estimate the incomes for the non-empty cells.

Table 5–1
Estimated Employment, Illinois, 1959
(*In Thousands of Male Equivalents*)

h	h'								Total	Denomination
	0	3	6	8	10	12	14	18		
0	54	155	.	.	.	.	.	.	209	Laborers
3	.	12	87	.	.	.	.	.	299	Service workers
6	.	.	127	638	.	.	.	.	765	Operatives
8	.	.	.	90	455	.	.	.	545	Clerical workers
10	.	.	.	.	198	439	.	.	637	Craftsmen
12	.	.	.	.	.	233	.	.	233	Sales workers
14	.	.	.	.	.	88	286	.	374	Professionals, technicians
18	.	.	.	.	.	.	15	304	319	Administrators, proprietors
Total	54	167	414	728	653	760	301	304	3381	

Using mean earnings by occupational and educational categories supplied in Dougherty's Tables 12 and 13, as modified by the adjustment discussed in the previous paragraph, we obtained the average of these means. This procedure yields the estimated income for each cell. Thus, for cell (1;1) we take the average of 2.8 (mean earnings of $2,837 of laborers having no schooling) and 3.9 (mean earnings of $3,868 of all persons classified as laborers) and round to 3.4, and so on. This produces the body of Table 5–2. The last row and column give weighted averages of the cells in the body of the table. The true averages, from Dougherty's tables, are shown in parentheses, and it will be seen that the deviations between our estimated and the observed average incomes are not large.

The units chosen for h' are, as already said, years of schooling; in order to attain a crude degree of commensurability between h and h', the eight occupation classes have been numbered in the same way, suggesting that these figures represent the education required for each of the occupation classes.

Since income after tax appears in our welfare function, Table 5–3 has been calculated from Table 5–2 by the deduction of personal income taxes prevailing in 1959.

Estimation of Welfare Function as Proposed

As announced, the estimation of coefficients c_0 and c_2 will be based on the comparison of vertical variations in Table 5–3, since these refer to groups with the same parameter h'. We exclude from the seven cases involved

Table 5–2
Average Earnings, Illinois, 1959
(*In Thousands of Dollars*)

h	0	3	6	8	10	12	14	18	*Average*
				h'					
0	3.4	3.6							3.5 (3.9)
3		3.7	4.1						4.1 (4.0)
6			4.6	5.1					5.0 (5.1)
8				5.1	5.7				5.6 (5.2)
10					6.4	6.9			6.7 (6.6)
12						7.5			7.5 (7.8)
14						8.2	9.0		8.7 (9.3)
18							9.7	11.1	11.0 (10.8)
Average	3.4	3.6	4.2	5.1	5.9	7.2	9.0	11.1	
	(2.8)	(3.3)	(4.2)	(5.0)	(6.2)	(7.1)	(8.6)	(11.3)	

the lower one in column $h' = 12$, since $h = 12$ (sales workers) and $h = 14$ (professional and technical workers) professions differ not only in h value but also in the degree of independence needed for the two groups of professions.

For each pair of observations, we assume that their welfare figures are equal, since free mobility between the two is possible. Hence:

$$x_1 - c_0 h_1 - \frac{1}{2} c_2 (h_1 - h')^2 = x_2 - c_0 h_2 - \frac{1}{2} c_2 (h_2 - h')^2, \quad (5.2)$$

where subscript 1 refers to the lower and subscript 2 to the higher h in the pairs.

Equation (5.2) reduces to:

$$x_1 - x_2 = c_0 h_1 - h_2) + \frac{1}{2} c_2 \left\{ h_1^2 - h_2^2 - 2 h' (h_1 - h_2) \right\}. \quad (5.3)$$

Table 5–3
Incomes After Personal Income Tax

h	0	3	6	8	10	12	14	18
					h'			
0	3.1	3.3						
3		3.4	3.7					
6			4.2	4.6				
8				4.6	5.1			
10					5.7	6.2		
12						6.7		
14						7.2	7.8	
18							8.4	9 5

Replacing the left side by x, the expression in parentheses on the right side by h, and the expression in brackets by z, equation 5.3 reduces to:

$$x = c_0 h + \frac{1}{2} c_2 z. \qquad (5.4)$$

For the six pairs of observations contained in Table 5–3, this equation can be tested, assuming that no constant term appears on the right-hand side. Writing $\bar{x}$ for the average and x' for $x - \bar{x}$, and similarly for h and z, the assumption can be written:

$$\bar{x} - \gamma_0 \bar{h} - \frac{1}{2} \gamma_2 \bar{z} = 0, \qquad (5.5)$$

where γ_0 and γ_2 are the estimates of c_0 and c_2. Assumption 5.5 links γ_0 and γ_2 and reduces our regression to a single regression because:

$$\gamma_2 = -0.33 + 2.29 \gamma_0. \qquad (5.6)$$

The dependent variable is $X = x' + 0.164z'$, and the independent one is $H = h' + 1.14z'$, for the first regression. For it we find

$$X = 0.144H \quad (R = 0.98), \qquad (5.7)$$

and for the second regression,

$$X = 0.149H. \qquad (5.8)$$

Transformed back into the original variables, we find for the two regressions,

$$x = 0.144h + 0.00z, \qquad (5.9)$$

and

$$x = 0.149h + 0.007z, \qquad (5.10)$$

respectively, meaning that in Frisch's[7] bunch-map-analysis way, $c_0 = 0.147 \pm 0.003$ and $c_2 = 0.003 \pm 0.003$.

Tentative Conclusion

The conclusion to be drawn from this experiment, with all the assumptions it is based upon (and they are numerous), is that for the groups on the diagonal (where $z = 0$), equity in income distribution implies a difference between the lowest and the highest income after tax of $0.146 \times 18 = 2.6$ as against an observed difference of 6.4 (9.5 − 3.1). Leaving out the two upper strata, since they require more independence, the "equitable" difference would amount to $0.146 \times 12 = 1.75$ as against an observed difference of 3.6 (6.7 − 3.1). Although the first-mentioned experiment, for the Netherlands, used a different method of estimating h, the conclusion reached there—namely, that an equitable income distribution would show half the differences observed in reality—seems to be supported by this second experiment for Illinois.

Can an Equitable Income Distribution Be Attained?

A definition and possible quantitative estimation of an equitable income distribution, even if accepted by the profession of economics, does not imply that such an income distribution can also be attained with the instruments of socioeconomic policy now at our command. Something may be said about the impact of one rather important instrument, however: the probable impact of extended education.

Elsewhere[8,9] I have tried to show that a generalized Cobb-Douglas production function with capital and five types of labor can be used as a basis for the demand for these production factors by the organizers of production. More particularly, I have tried to show that the unitary elasticity of substitution of the demand for university-trained labor in comparison to all other labor can be considered as a realistic estimate. For the other types of labor, a different demand elasticity of substitution is obtained, in line with research by Dougherty[10] and others. For university-trained labor, the corresponding exponent ρ_3 then indicates the share of national income to be allocated to that type of labor.

The next step in using the production function was to assume that technological development expresses itself in an upward trend of ρ_3, with rising income per capita y of the economy studied. Expressing y in 1960 dollars, I found two regression equations for ρ_3 on y: one based on a time series for 1900–1963, and one based on a cross-section of four countries. The former runs:

$$\rho_3' = 0.046 + 18\,y \cdot 10^{-6} \qquad\qquad (R = 0.83), \qquad\qquad (5.11)$$
$$(5)$$

and the latter is:

$$\rho_3'' = 0.016 + 26\,y \cdot 10^{-6} \qquad\qquad (R = 0.86). \qquad\qquad (5.12)$$
$$(8.2)$$

In order to extrapolate values for ρ_3 for 1980 and 1990, I assumed a 3 percent annual growth in income per capita in constant prices for 1970–80 and, alternatively, a 3 percent (high) and a 2 percent (low) rate of growth $(\dot{y})$ for 1980–90.

From the U.S. Bureau of the Census, extrapolated figures of the total population twenty-five years of age and older,[11] as well as of those among them with four years college or more, were used to estimate the portion x_3 of the latter in the former.

The ratio of incomes of university-trained labor to average income can then be estimated by calculating ρ_3/x_3. All the figures just enumerated are shown in Table 5–4.

The absolute figures of the income ratio are lower than some would expect because capital income is included in average income but not in labor income of university-trained persons. Since capital income represents 20 percent of national income, leaving out capital income would raise the ratio by 25 percent, which would make the figures more realistic in a way.

The main feature to be emphasized for our purpose, however, is the systematic fall in the ratio between 1960 and 1990, amounting, in our four alternatives, to 30, 38, 13, and 24 percent, respectively. The answer to the question put at the beginning of this section is, according to these figures, that increased education will not by 1990 produce an equitable income distribution between academics and other groups, but it will make a substantial contribution to it.

In order to fully attain an equitable income distribution—as tentatively estimated in this chapter—supplementary measures, presumably in the field of taxes, will be required.

Table 5–4
Values of Income Share of University-Trained Labor

	1960	1970	1980	1990 (high)	1990 (low)
Income share of academics ρ_3'	0.096	0.114	0.138	0.169	0.158
Income share of academics ρ_3''	0.088	0.115	0.149	0.194	0.178
Portion of academics in pop. ≥ 25, x_3	0.077	0.110	0.148[a]	0.205	0.181
Income ratios academics					
ρ_3'/x_3	1.25	1.04	0.94	0.87	0.77
ρ_3''/x_3	1.14	1.04	1.01	0.99	0.87

[a] Average of two estimates by Bureau of the Census.

132

Notes

1. J. Tinbergen, *An Interdisciplinary Approach to the Measurement of Utility* (Dublin: The Economic and Social Research Institute, Fifth Geary Lecture, 1972).

2. For a fuller discussion of the quantitative specification of utility or welfare, see Tinbergen, *Income Distribution: Analysis and Policies,* pp. 57–61.

3. P. de Wolff and A. R. D. van Slijpe, *The Relations Between Income, Intelligence, Education and Social Background* (Amsterdam: University of Amsterdam, Institute of Actuarial Science and Econometrics, 1972).

4. C. R. S. Dougherty, *Estimates of Labour Aggregation Functions,* Project for Quantitative Research in Economic Development, Economic Development Report No. 190 (Cambridge, Mass.: The Center for International Affairs, 1971), esp. Tables 12, 13, 14, and 15.

5. F. L. Hitchcock, "The Distribution of a Product from Several Sources to Numerous Localities," *J. Math. Phys.* 20 (1941): 224.

6. L. B. M. Mennes, Jan Tinbergen, and J. George Waardenburg, *The Element of Space in Development Planning* (Amsterdam/London: 1969), p. 38 ff.

7. R. Frisch, *Confluence Analysis* (Oslo: 1934).

8. J. Tinbergen, "Substitution Between Types of Labour in Production," to be published in a volume in honor of Professor Del Vecchio.

9. J. Tinbergen, "Substitution of Graduate by Other Labour," *Kyklos* 27 (1974): 217.

10. Dougherty, *op. cit.*

11. U.S. Bureau of the Census, *Current Population Reports,* Series P-25, no. 476, and Series P-20, no. 229, as quoted in *Statistical Abstract of the U.S.A.* (1972), p. 111.

**Part III
The Element of Time**

Some Questions of Time in Economics

Sir John R. Hicks

Two years ago I published a book called *Capital and Time*. You might reasonably expect that in the present essay I should just be going on with what I did in that book. This is in fact one of the things to which I shall be coming; but such continuation is only one of the things which I have in mind. My subject here is much broader. It concerns a principle which has come up, in several ways, in the work of Professor Georgescu; so it should be a suitable topic for a chapter that is being written for him. It has also come up, sometimes in similar ways, more often in different ways, in much of my own work. I have not always been faithful to it; but when I have departed from it I have found myself coming back to it. It is clearly his principle; but I think I can claim that on the whole it has been mine as well.

It is a very simple principle: the irreversibility of time. In space we can move either way, or any way; but time just goes on, never goes back. We represent time on our diagrams by a spatial coordinate; but that representation is never a complete representation; it always leaves something out. And it is not only in simple diagrams that we represent time by space; there are highly sophisticated models which, in effect, do the same thing. It is quite hard to get away, in any part of our thinking, from the spatial representation. We represent time by a "trend variable"; but that is again the same thing; it does not fully show time going on.

One of the principal consequences of the irreversibility of time is that past and future are different. Not just different as front and back are different; you cannot turn past into future, or future into past, as by turning round you can turn back into front. The past is past, over and done with; it is there and cannot be changed. "Not heaven itself upon the past hath power"—the line of Dryden which I was already quoting, on nearly the first occasion when I came to grips with the issue, in *Value and Capital* (1939).[1] The past, however, has this virtue that we can have knowledge of it, knowledge of fact. The knowledge that we have, or can have, of the past is different in kind from what we can know of the future; for the latter, at best, is no more than a knowledge of probabilities. This may happen, or that may happen. But it is something quite definite which *has* happened.

It is true that our knowledge of the past is incomplete. All we know is what has been remembered, or recorded; or perhaps it has left some mark upon the present world from which we can deduce what happened,

135

probably what happened. Thus even our knowledge of the past is largely a matter of probabilities. But these probabilities are different from probabilities about the future. Past populations, for instance, are recorded at census dates; if we want a figure for population between census dates we have to estimate it. Yet the estimation of population in 1885, when populations in 1880 and in 1890 alone are recorded, is a matter of getting as near as we can to a *right* figure. The country did have a population in 1885; by using more and more of relevant information available to us now we can in this (no doubt favourable) case be fairly sure that we cannot be far wrong. With estimates of the future, the situation is quite different. There is no *right* figure for population in 2000, no right figure *now*. There will be a right figure when 2000 comes, but only when that date is passing into the past.

It is already apparent from this simple example how complicated these time-relations can be; how easy it is to slip into ways of thinking which treat past and future alike. How easy it is to forget, when we contemplate the past, that much of what is now past was then future. Action is always directed toward the future; but past actions, when we contemplate them in their places in the stream of past events, lose that orientation toward the future which they undoubtedly possessed at the time when they were taken. We arrange past data in time-series, but our time-series are not fully in time. The relation of year 9 to year 10 looks like its relation to year 8; but in year 9 year 10 was future while year 8 was past. The actions of year 9 were based, or could be based, upon knowledge of year 8; but not on knowledge of year 10, only on guesses about year 10. For in year 9 the knowledge that we have about year 10 did not yet exist.

What I have been saying, so far, must sound very obvious. But its consequences for economics are quite far reaching.

One application, which I shall do no more than mention, is to Social Accounting. We are tempted to say that the net investment of a year is the difference between opening and closing stock—the difference between the value of the capital stock at the end of the year and at the beginning. We know that we must correct, for inflation or deflation, changes in the value of money which may have occurred within the year. But this does not get to the root of the matter. The value that is set upon the opening stock depends in part upon the value which is expected, at the beginning of the year, for the closing stock; but that was then future, while at the end of the year it is already present (or past). There may be things which were included in the opening stock because, in the light of information then available, they seemed to be valuable; but at the end of the year it is clear that they are not valuable, so they have to be excluded. Such revisions, due to new information, may occur at any time. Suppose that information comes in during year 2 which makes it clear that the capital stock at the end of year 1 was over-valued. This may well mean that the net investment of year 1, calculated at the end of year 1, was over-valued—at least it seems to be over-valued from the standpoint of the end of year 2. It needs to be written down for its mistakes—mistakes which only in the course of time have become revealed.[2]

I leave that on one side, and pass to other applications, of which the first is a simple application to consumer theory. The point is very simple; yet it is one which in most presentations (including some for which I have been personally responsible) gets most blatantly left out. It is immensely convenient, in economics, to suppose that "the consumer" (as we call him) has a fully formed scale of preferences, by which all the choices that are available to him on the market can be ordered. I am still of the opinion that there are many purposes (including, very probably, the most important purposes) for which that assumption can be justified. But it is itself a very odd assumption; to take it, as many economists do, as being justifiable for all purposes, must, I now believe, be wrong.

The picture which is called to mind by this conventional assumption is that of the consumer (or his wife) paying a weekly visit to the super-market, having been given just so much to spend out of the family income. She picks up goods from the shelves; then, as she adds up the cost in her mind, she finds that it comes to more than her allowance. So she has to give up some of the things she wanted to buy, or has to substitute something cheaper. She juggles things about until she finds the collection which is within her budget and which suits her best.

Such a consumer I would agree, "reveals her preferences." But consider the case of another consumer decision, a decision of what car to buy, or whether to buy a new car. If it is asked how that decision is made it is surely a matter of deciding *what one can afford*. I can afford this; I cannot afford that. But what is meant by not being able to afford it? The conventional answer, by the economist, is to say that if the car is acquired, something else will have to be given up; and that "something else" is more desired than the car. That is to say, the consumer is supposed to re-think his whole budget, identifying the collection of goods which would have to be given up if the car was purchased. Now it may sometimes happen that a consumer proceeds in that way, but it seems unlikely that it will often happen. It seems much more likely that he proceeds with some idea, based upon previous experience, of what he can afford. He judges whether or not to buy the car, not by re-thinking his whole budget, but by a single test.

From this point of view the replacement of the old consumer theory—the marginal utility theory—by the modern theory of ordinal preferences (a replacement in which I myself have played a part) was not so clear an advance as is usually supposed. Marshall's consumer, who decides on his purchases by comparing the marginal utility of what is to be bought with the marginal utility of the money he will have to pay for it, is more like an actual consumer, at least so far as some important purchases are concerned, than Samuelson's consumer, who "reveals his preferences." The marginal utility of money, on which Marshall relies, is much more than the mere Lagrange multiplier, the role to which it has been degraded. It is the means by which the consumer is enabled to make his separate decisions, and to make them fairly rationally, without being obliged to take the trouble to weigh all conceivable alternatives. It is the means by which he decides *what he can afford*.

But his estimate of the marginal utility of money, to him, is based upon his past experience. It is by experience that he learns the standard by which his desires for the things he would like to buy are to be judged. In static conditions, when income is steady (or fairly steady) and prices are steady (or fairly steady), it is a reliable standard; and it was of course in terms of such conditions that Marshall's theory was originally set out. But when income is changing (or when many prices are changing) it becomes less reliable. It is based on the past; when the present is seriously unlike the past it becomes a less reliable guide. The *lags* with which consumption responds to a change in real income, though they are partly a matter of constraints set by commitments (including as commitments the possession of durable goods), must also be a matter of the time which is taken for the marginal utility of money, as it appears to the consumer, to respond to the change. To make fully rational decisions in fundamentally new conditions is by no means easy.

The matter is probably of greater importance in times of inflation than it is in more settled conditions. I believe that we miss the point about inflation when we look at it, as we so usually do, ·in terms of index-numbers. In terms of index-numbers there has always been some inflation (or deflation); an index-number of prices hardly ever stays quite constant from year to year. Yet there have been conditions in which there has been no inflation, in a highly significant sense. This is when there are many prices which are not changing, or changing very little. So long as that condition holds, the standard which the consumer makes for himself, out of his past experience, is a reliable standard; so he can make his decisions, deciding what he can afford fairly rationally. This is to be contrasted with the condition that is now being experienced in so many countries, when all prices, or nearly all prices, have broken loose from their moorings. That is true inflation; apart from its other costs (which are more familiar) there is this other cost—that rational decisions, even within the field of consumption, become so much harder to make.

That is all I have to say on this particular matter. I turn to wider questions. The parts of economics where the distinction with which I began is of greatest importance are the theory of capital and (as we shall see) the theory of markets.

As far as capital theory is concerned, the story goes back a long way. It appears, very strikingly, in the history of the Austrian school, a group of economists who (as everyone knows) were particularly concerned about the relations of capital and time. The two progenitors of the Austrian school were Menger and Böhm-Bawerk (Wieser, at this time of day, seems very secondary; while Schumpeter and Hayek belong to later generations). At a casual reading, Menger and Böhm appear to be saying much the same thing; so it is something of a shock when one discovers that in the view of Menger (as recorded by Schumpeter)[3] Böhm-Bawerk's theory was "one of the greatest errors ever committed." What was it in Böhm that so annoyed Menger? I believe it is simply that in Menger time is uni-directional. Menger's theory is an economics *in* time but Böhm's is an economics *of* time, in which time is no more than a mathematical parameter—a parameter of what we should now call capital-intensity. (Of course there are passages in which Böhm gets closer to Menger than he does in the structure of his theory; but to say that in Böhm time is just a parameter of capital-intensity is not so far wrong.) In Menger time is much more than that.

I do not suppose that Menger ever read Wicksell; but if he had read Wicksell's version of Böhm's theory (the version which has become more familiar to most economists) he would have found that his judgment was amply confirmed. For he would have found that in the hands of Wicksell the theory became no more than a theory of a stationary state, no more than that. In a stationary state one moment of time is just like another. The stationary state is out of time; time has stood still. In Menger, time never stood still.

I do not claim that Menger had more than the beginnings of a theory of an economy *in* time. But he did have that; a clear indication is his theory of liquidity.[4] What Menger had to say on liquidity is deeper than what was said by anyone else before Keynes; indeed I think it is deeper than what is in Keynes. I know that I had to go on thinking about liquidity for many years after Keynes before I realised that I had got to a point which Menger had reached, in effect, nearly a hundred years before. For Menger had grasped, already, that the holding of liquid reserves, in money or near-money, is only one aspect (though no doubt the most important aspect) of a much more general kind of behaviour. It is a matter of provision against an uncertain future—not passive provision (like insurance) but active provision, providing oneself with the ability to take action to meet emergencies which may arise in the future, and which are such that their particular shape cannot be accurately foreseen. Obviously, then, there can be no question of liquidity, in either the wide or the narrow sense, in a stationary state. Liquidity is a problem of the economy *in* time.

I have begun with this old story because it presents the issue so sharply. In later work, it has been thoroughly muddled. The man who began the muddling was Keynes.

Keynes's theory has one leg which is *in* time, but another which is not. It is a hybrid. I am not blaming him for this; he was looking for a theory which would be effective, and he found it. I am quite prepared to believe that effective theories always will be hybrids—they cannot afford to bother about difficulties which are not important for the problem in hand. Complications (and for a simple theory the flow of time is a complication) must be allowed for when they have to be allowed for; but if there is any place where we can avoid them, avoid them we will. In facing the world that may well be good policy; but when a hybrid theory is subjected to classroom criticism, places are bound to be exposed which are not easy to defend.

There are many passages—many famous passages—in which Keynes proclaims his theory to be *in* time; he makes quite a fuss about it. "The dark forces of time and ignorance which envelop our future"[5]—everyone knows them. Take these passages at their face value, as they are so often taken, and one would suppose that Keynes was acutally producing a full theory of economics *in* time—the theory which Menger had adumbrated but had certainly not carried through. Yet that is not so; there is only a part of the Keynes theory which is *in* time. He has (very skillfully) divided his theory into two parts. There is one, that concerned with the Marginal Efficiency of Capital and with Liquidity Preference, which is unquestionably *in* time; it is basically forward-looking; time and uncertainty are written all over it. But there is another, the multiplier theory (and indeed the whole theory of production and prices which is—somehow—wrapped up in the multiplier theory) which is out of time. It runs in terms of demand curves, and supply curves and cost curves—just the old tools of equilibrium economics. A state of equilibrium, by definition, is a state in which something, something relevant, is *not* changing; so the use of an equilibrium concept is a signal that time, in some respect at least, has been put to one side.

For Keynes's own purpose, I have insisted, this was justifiable; but what a muddle he made for his successors! The "Keynesian revolution" went off at half-cock; so the line, which I believe to be a vital line, was smudged over. The equilibrists, therefore, did not know that they were beaten; or rather (for I am not claiming that they had been altogether beaten) they did not know that they had been challenged. They thought that what Keynes had said could be absorbed into their equilibrium systems; all that was needed was that the scope of their equilibrium systems should be extended. As we know, there has been a lot of extension, a vast amount of extension; what I am saying is that it has never quite got to the point.[6]

I shall make no attempt in what follows to work through the whole of what has happened; that would be a vast job, and I much doubt if I am capable of doing it. What I can do, and am perhaps well fitted to do, is to look over my own work, since 1935, and to show how some aspects of the struggle, and the muddle, are reflected in it. I can at least explain how it has been that, in one way after another, I have found myself facing the issue, and (very often) being baffled by it.

I begin (as I am sure you will want me to begin) with the old ISLM (or SILL) diagram, which appeared in a paper I gave to the Econometric Society within a few months of the publication of the *General Theory*.[7] The letter which Keynes wrote me about that paper has now been published.[8] I think I am justified in concluding from that letter that Keynes did not wholly disapprove of what I had made of him. All the same, I must say that that diagram is now much less popular with me than I think it still is with many other people. It reduces the *General Theory* to equilibrium economics; it is not really *in* time. That, of course, is why it has done so well.

Much more to the point is *Value and Capital* (1939). A good deal of that book was written before I saw the *General Theory*; though Keynes came in at the end, even the so-called "dynamic" part was begun under the influence of Lindahl. Lindahl, it is surely fair to say, was most decidedly *not* an equilibrist; the distinction between past and future (*ex ante* and *ex post*) was at the centre of his work. Thus, even before I read Keynes, I was finding myself confronted with a parallel problem: how to build a bridge between equilibrium economics and an economics which should be securely *in* time. (Since the first part of my book was very thoroughgoing, quite static, equilibrium economics, the problem came up in my work even more sharply than it did in Keynes's.) I built a kind of a bridge, but, as I now see very well, it was a very imperfect bridge, not so very unlike the imperfect bridge that had been built by Keynes. My theory also was divided; there was a part that was *in* time and a part that was not. But we did not divide in the same place. While Keynes had relegated the whole theory of production and prices to equilibrium economics, I tried to keep production *in* time, just leaving *prices* to be determined in an equilibrium manner. I wanted, that is, to go further than Keynes, keeping closer to Lindahl. But I could only do so by an artificial device, my "week," which was such that all prices could be fixed up in what would now be called a "neo-Walrasian" or "neo-classical" manner, on the "Monday"; then, on the basis of these predetermined prices, production *in* time could proceed. It was quite an interesting exercise; it did bring out some points—even some practically important points—fairly well; but I have become abundantly conscious how artificial it was. Much too much had to happen on that "Monday"! And, even if that was overlooked (as it should not have been overlooked) I was really at a loss how to deal with the futher problem of how to string my "weeks" and my "Mondays" together.

In *Value and Capital* terms, there were these two problems left over; they correspond fairly well, though not precisely, with what could be expressed in Keynesian (or Marshallian) language. Keynes (he would no doubt have admitted) had been mainly concerned with constructing a general theory of Marshall's *short period*. All he had said about the things included in Marshall's long period had been pretty sketchy; and, except in relation to financial markets, the things with which Marshall had been concerned in his theory of exchange (or barter) had got quite left out. Whether one prefers that statement, or my statement (as just given), does not much matter. What does matter is that the Keynes theory and the *Value and Capital* theory were weak in corresponding ways. They both lacked, at one end, a satisfactory theory of *markets*; and at the other end, they lacked a satisfactory theory of *growth*.

Since these deficiencies were so different, it is scarcely surprising that what has come out of them has been very different. I shall have to take them quite separately.

Growth theory, say since Harrod and Domar (or perhaps since von Neumann), has been the scene of a tremendous come-back of equilibrism. Trying to push on beyond Keynes it has slipped back behind him. What made this possible was the discovery of the Regularly Progressive Economy, or "steady state." A stationary state, as found in the Classics or in Wicksell, was a very poor instrument for the study of saving and investment, even in the long run; for in a Stationary State both net saving and net investment must by definition equal zero. The Steady State, with its constant growth rate, admitted positive saving, so it looked much better. It could be tidied up, on equilibrium lines, just as well as the Stationary State; for though the quantities of inputs and outputs did not remain unchanged over time, their ratios did. In ratio terms, the Steady State was still quite stationary. Thus, so long as attention was fixed on ratios (and the growth rate itself is a ratio) the Steady State could be absorbed into full-blown equilibrium economics, in which one point of time is just like another. It was just as much "out of time" as the Stationary State itself.

I shall not say much about Steady State economics; for in spite of all that it has meant for the economics of the fifties and sixties, it is my own opinion that it has been rather a curse. I do not merely mean that the impression that has been given to non-economists (through the mediation of statisticians) that there is something natural about a constant growth rate has been a curse. That is obvious; maybe it will be one of the (few) advantages of the present economic crisis that it will teach us to get over it. I also mean that it has encouraged economists to waste their time upon constructions that are often of great intellectual complexity but which are so much out of time, and out of history, as to be practically futile and indeed misleading. It has many bad marks to be set against it.

I must however admit that I have myself spent much time on steady state economics—the Harrod type, the Joan Robinson type, the Kaldor type, the von Neumann type, the Solow type—one after another. I felt that I had to learn them, and the best way to learn them is to write out one's own version. But in the successive versions which I have produced, I have always been making some effort to get away.

Thus in my *Trade Cycle* book (1950) I began with my version of Harrod. I am not particularly proud of that book, but it does have the virtue that it makes some attempts to get back *into* time. One is by introducing lags, though that is a device which is more appropriate in econometrics than in economic theory. By making *present* behaviour depend upon *past* experience, one does something to re-introduce the flow of time; but, I fully admit, not very much. Another route of escape was my concept of Autonomous Investment—a concept which equilibrists, very naturally, have found hard to swallow. As first introduced, it looks like a piece of steady state economics; and there, admittedly, it is out of place. But I did go on, in the later parts of the book (which have received much less attention) to allow Autonomous Investment to change autonomously. I believe that at that point my model did become less deterministic, and so less equilibrist.

The next stage in the story, so far as I personally am concerned, was my *Capital and Growth* (1965), written fifteen years later. It is a long gap, and of course it is true that during these years much that is relevant had been done by others. A large part of *Capital and Growth* is just a survey of what they had been doing. They had taken the capital stock of the Harrodian steady state—much too "macro" in its original form—and had broken it down into its components: capital goods of different specifications, different durabilities, and different "vintages." They had been able to do this by a massive injection of matrix algebra. I had to learn the matrix algebra, which had come into fashion since the days of my mathematical education—and it took me quite a time! They had also developed a new kind of "dynamic equilibrium" in which not even ratios are kept constant; a plan, a consistent plan, is nevertheless developed between time 1 and time 2. (This goes back to von Neumann and to Ramsey and includes much work descended from them: turnpike theorems, optimum saving theorems and the like.) Though these are not steady state theories, they are nevertheless equilibrium theories. One point of time is not like another, even in the ratio sense; yet the whole of the plan is looked at together. The plan is mutually determined; there is no movement from past to future, except in the sense that there is also a movement from future to past. There is no room for the unexpected.

I had to learn these things; and the greater part of *Capital and Growth* is occupied with setting out my version of them. But there are some signs, even in *Capital and Growth*, that I was trying to get away. There are many of them in the opening chapters (which are chiefly of a critical character); and there are some, even in the latter part of the book, though that is mainly concerned with the steady state, or with the other kind of "dynamic equilibrium." There is the monetary chapter (XXIII); but that really belongs to the theory of markets, to which I shall be coming later. There is a funny chapter on *Interest and Growth* (XXII), which tries to break away; but it is an unsuccessful break-out since it is still using the tools of steady state economics, which are obviously unsuitable. Most important is the chapter called *Traverse* (XVI). This was a first attempt at a formal theory of an economy which is not in a steady state, not in "Growth Equilibrium"—an economy which has a history, so that things actually happen. Since it is a system in which the actors do not know what is going to happen next, it at once appears that flexibility (which disappears from sight in the steady state) is a matter of major importance. The method that is used in that chapter is not, as I have since become convinced, very suitable; but I do not regret having made the attempt. Some quite interesting things did come out. I was able, in particular, to throw some new light (or what to me was new light) upon the *role* of prices—to show how different it is in an uncertain world from what it appears to be in equilibrium economics.[9]

So we come to *Capital and Time* (1973), as I promised. People, I can see from reviews, have not known quite what to make of it; it probably needed a preface (such as I have been giving, in fact, in this essay) so that it could be explained. The whole of the second part of *Capital and Time* is called *Traverse*; it corresponds to that single chapter in *Capital and Growth*. It is in fact the case that the chief (almost the whole) purpose of the latter book is to seek a better way of doing what I was trying to do in the former *Traverse* chapter. In that former chapter I was trying to build a theory which should at least be rather more *in time,* while using a fairly conventional steady state model as a basis. It did not do. So I tried, in the later book, to build my *Traverse* on a different steady state model, which I hoped, and I think I showed, could get one just a little further. But this new steady state model (descended from Böhm-Bawerk through one of the less read chapters of *Value and Capital*)[10] would, I knew, be unfamiliar to most of my readers. So the whole (or nearly the whole) of the first part of *Capital and Time* is taken up with explaining it.

But this first part is *not* the important part. Taken by itself, its conclusions are quite negative. It just shows that you get the same steady state results in my model as in other models, a thing which was to be expected *a priori* but needed to be demonstrated in detail. The results come out rather neatly, so it may be that it will be found (even by equilibrists) to be quite useful, if only for teaching purposes. But that is all.

Even in Part II, I had to start very slowly. If I had started with a fine set of plausible assumptions, drawn from the real world, I am sure I should have got nowhere. I had to build up my model bit by bit. I began from a steady state (but that was simply because I had to have something firm, which I thought I understood, from which to start), but the point of the steady state (in Part II) is that it is to be *disturbed*. I made a lot of use—perhaps too much use—of what I called a Simple Profile, a production plan which admitted the construction of a plant and then its utilisation, but not much else. It is not surprising that some of the results which I got with the Simple Profile were much the same as those which others have got by more conventional methods. I am again not ashamed of my "fixwage" hypothesis, with which I still think it was proper to begin; I did indeed push on quite a long way beyond it. Nor am I ashamed of the "static expectation" assumption, which made firms choose their plans on the basis of today's prices, or rather price ratios; that again I think was the right way to begin. Though I did not do much to modify this assumption, I don't think it would be hard to modify it. But this is no place to discuss these matters in detail. What I want to emphasise is that in Part II I was trying to build something up. It ends with a chapter called "Ways Ahead"; that was meant as a signal that I was sure I had not finished the job.

Most of my critics have been (and no doubt will be) equilibrists; but there is one, for whom I have great respect, who has opened fire from the other flank. Professor Ludwig Lachmann, of the University of Johannesberg, South Africa, is (like Professor Hayek) a chief survivor of what I distinguished as the Mengerian sect of the Austrian school. It is clear that his view of me is like Menger's view of Böhm-Bawerk. He cannot, of course, abide the steady state.[11] Even the modest uses of it which I have made (and perhaps, until now, I have not sufficiently emphasised that they are meant to be very modest uses), even these fill him with dismay. Even the explanations which I have now been giving (and which are meant, incidentally, to assure him that I am more on his side than on the other) will, I fear, fail to placate him. His ideal economics is not so far away from my own ideal economics; but I regard it as a target set up in heaven. We cannot hope to reach it; we must just get as near to it as we can.

There is one further thing I want to say about *Capital and Time*. I was trying in Part II to analyse a growth process *sequentially*; there were things which emerged almost as soon as one tried to do that, even if one was not succeeding in doing it very well or very completely. I began, for instance, to understand why there had been so much trouble with that old distinction between autonomous and induced inventions, a distinction for which I must admit I had myself some responsibility in days gone by.[12] It is a static distinction, quite out of time, though it concerns a matter where some time-reference is essential. When one puts it back *into time,* it looks quite different.

As I said in the book:

the technology, and the technological frontier, now become suspect. . . . The notion of a technology, as a collection of techniques, laid up in a library to be taken down from their shelves as required, is a caricature of the inventive process. . . . Why should we not say that every change in technique is an invention, which may be large or small? It certainly partakes, to some degree, of the character of an invention; for it requires, for its application, some new knowledge, or some new expertise. There is no firm line, on the score of novelty, between shifts that change the technology and shifts that do not.[13]

One can say that, and still admit a distinction between autonomous and induced invention, but the distinction must now be of a more dynamic character. An induced invention is a change in technique that is made as a consequence of a change in prices (or, in general, scarcities); if the change in prices had not occurred, the change in technique could not have been made. I now like to think of a major technical change (one that we may agree to regard as autonomous, since, for anything that we are concerned with, it comes in from outside) as setting up what I now call an Impulse. If the autonomous change is an invention which widens the range of technical possibilities, it must begin by raising profitability and inducing expansion; but the expansion encounters scarcities, which act as a brake. Some of the scarcities may be just temporary bottle-necks which in time can be removed; some, however, may be irremovable. Yet it is possible to adjust to either kind of scarcity by further changes in technical methods; it is these that are the true *induced inventions.* The whole story, when it is looked at in this way, is *in time,* and can be in history; it can be worked out much further, and can, I believe, be applied.[14]

That is rather a mouthful; it deserves a lecture to itself; but there I must leave it. For I have still to say something (it cannot, at this stage, be very much) about the other "deficiency" which, as I explained, was left unfilled in the thirties. I must turn, that is, to the theory of *markets.*

How—just how—are prices determined? In *Value and Capital* (even in the "dynamic" part of *Value and Capital*) I had been content to be what is now called neo-Walrasian; prices were just determined by an equilibrium of demand and supply. And I am afraid that for many years I got no further, or very little further. When I was asked to review Patinkin's book, which really raised the issue, I quite failed to see the point.[15] It was only by slow degrees that it began to sink in.

Walras himself, it is true, had been much less obtuse. He had seen that for a market to work in his way (the way in which so many others have followed him) some market *structure* was necessary. But the market structure which he posited was very special. One would be tempted to think that it was invented by Walras just to give the right result if there were not some evidence that there did exist examples of markets which did work in much this way, and could well have been familiar to him.[16] One, in fact, may have been the Paris Bourse itself!

These however would be very sophisticated markets, requiring a lot of organisation; for who is to pay the official who is to "cry" the prices, or (as Clower would call him) the "auctioneer"?[17] There must be a prior agreement among the parties to play the game according to these rules; but how is such an agreement to come about? A proper theory of markets must clearly include the Walras-type market as a particular case; but I think it needs to start much further back.

The simplest form of exchange is barter; and (since Edgeworth) we know how that works. One might begin with a market (or pre-market)—a sort of village fair—in which all transactions were barter transactions between a pair of individuals, each giving up something which he wants relatively less in exchange for something which he wants relatively more. But such simple barter, as the textbooks have long been telling us, is bound to leave some opportunities for advantageous trading unexploited; so one must go on from that to introduce some form of triangular trade. At that point, two things happen. One is the evolution of some form of money; in a more complete account than I can offer here, that would have to be fitted in.[18] The other is that there arises an opportunity for the development of specialised merchanting—a merchant being defined as one who buys not for his own use but in order to sell again. It is easy to see that once the market has passed a certain size, so that problems of communication become important, there will have to be specialised merchants (or, perhaps, some substitute for them).

I am very convinced that for the purpose in hand, the specialised merchant is the key figure. When Gerschenkron reviewed my *Theory of Economic History,* he entitled his review "Mercator Gloriosus" [19]—indicating that from his point of view, the point of view of the historian, I had made too much of the merchant. I dare say that he is right. But I am sure that from the point of view of economic understanding I was right. The role of the merchant in the development of market organisation is crucial.

Once merchants exist there are three kinds of dealings to be distinguished: (1) dealings between merchants, (2) dealings between merchants and non-merchants, and (3) direct dealings between non-merchants, which in some particular cases may still survive. The most obvious example of direct dealings between non-merchants, surviving into otherwise sophisticated economies, is the market in private dwelling-houses. We rarely find house-merchants holding stocks of dwelling-houses (for rather obvious reasons); but there remains a problem of communication, which is dealt with in another way. This is by the appearance of house agents, a particular kind of commission agent, who has the function of bringing buyer and seller together, and consequently of advising them of the price at which they should trade. He charges a commission to cover the cost of his services (which may formally be paid by the buyer or by the seller, but the price is in fact so adjusted that it falls to some extent on both). In a complete theory of markets, the commission agent would have to find a place.

The market for dwelling-houses is a notoriously "imperfect" market; the most perfectly organised markets are at the other end—the markets on which specialised traders trade with one another. It is here that we should look for the Walras-type market and for other sophisticated types. For when merchants habitually trade together, they develop needs for assurance about the carrying-through of their dealings—needs for legal assurances about property and contract, and other related matters—and it is worth their while to pay something in order to get these rules policed and enforced. All this is very important, but it is just one end of the spectrum of market structures.

At the centre, however, is what remains: dealings between merchants and non-merchants. It is here that we meet the shopkeeper and the wholesaler. They buy to sell again, so must buy before they sell, so they must hold stocks. The holding of unsold stocks is expensive, so their appearance is again an indication that information is imperfect. They are giving those who buy from them the service that they can buy the things they want when they want them. The provision of that service is expensive; for the costs that they incur in providing it they properly charge.

In this sort of market, with sharply specialised merchants, there is no question who fixes prices; it is the merchant himself. When he finds his stock running down, so that he is in danger of failing to meet the demands that may be made upon him, he will first try to get more from other merchants; if they have ample stocks, all is well; but if their stocks also are running down, he will have to offer higher prices, to the other merchants or to outside producers, in order to get more stock. Then he will charge a higher price to consumers in order to cover the rise in his costs. Such a market may well be quite similar, in many ways, to the textbook competitive market; but until we take uncertainty and costs of information into account we cannot show how it works.[20]

I believe that there was a stage in the development of capitalism when a market such as I have been describing was the typical market—for consumers' goods, and for many sorts of producers' goods also. But I greatly doubt if it can still be regarded as the typical market. What has upset it is the taking over of the mercantile function by the producers themselves. The manufacturers do it directly, the primary producers indirectly, through the formation of their own associations or by selling organisations equipped with political power. This is of course the point at which the question of monopoly becomes so important. But that, again cannot in general be understood unless we look at it *in time,* as an aspect of the evolutionary process we have been considering. Why is it that the theory of monopolistic competition, or imperfect competition, to which so much attention was paid in the thirties, now looks so faded? Because it is quite shockingly *out of time.*[21]

There is a practical conclusion from what I have just been saying to which I should like to draw attention. You have a long tradition in the United States of anti-monopoly action; and in my own country, in recent years, it has been ineffectively imitated. I do not think it has been much of a success, even with you. On the line of thought I have been sketching out, one can see why. It is an attempt to go back from the late stage of capitalism—the producer-dominated stage—to the earlier stage, before the producers took over. But this ealier stage depended for its functioning upon a merchant class, an independent merchant class; and that cannot be raised from the dead by a stroke of the pen, or by an Act of Congress. It would have to grow up; to bring it back would be quite a job.

One final salute—to Georgescu. He has chosen a cosmic way of demonstrating the irreversibility of time.[22] Since he was addressing himself to a science-based culture, that (I am sure) was a good way of going about it. For my part, I am very ignorant of science; though I have dabbled in mathematics my spiritual home is in the Humanities. It is because I want to make economics more human that I want to make it more time-conscious; and since I am approaching the task from that end I am content with a more earthy way of going about it. We are nevertheless, I believe, on the same side. We are both of us evolutionists, but not straight-line, or "exponential," evolutionists. It is the *new* things that humanity has discovered which makes its history exciting; and the new things that may be found in the future, before humanity blows itself up, or settles down to some ghastly "equilibrium," make a future worth praying for, and worth working for.

150

Notes

1. *Value and Capital,* 2nd ed. (Oxford: Clarendon Press, 1946), p. 130. The poem from which I took the quotation purports to be a translation from Horace, but the correspondence with its "original" is far from close.

2. I discussed this matter in a note first printed in *Economica* 9 (New Series), no. 34 (May 1942), and reprinted in *Capital and Time* (Oxford: Clarendon Press, 1973), pp. 164–66.

3. *History of Economic Analysis* (New York: Oxford University Press, 1954), p. 847.

4. *Grundsätze der Volkswirtschaftslehre* (Translated by Dingwall and Hoselitz as *Principles of Economics*), chapters 7 and 8. There can be no doubt that Menger would have been on the side of Marshall, rather than on that of Pareto, with respect to the point about consumer theory discussed above, and essentially for the reason given. I owe the beginnings of my understanding of this to conversations with Professor Rosenstein-Rodan.

5. *The General Theory of Employment, Interest and Money* (New York: Harcourt, Brace and Co., 1936), p. 155.

6. I make no claim that I am the first to say this; it seems to me to be in substance the main point which emerges from the influential book by Axel Leijonhufvud, *On Keynesian Economics and the Economics of Keynes* (New York: Oxford University Press, 1968).

7. "Mr. Keynes and the Classics," *Econometrica* 5 (1937), reprinted in my *Critical Essays in Monetary Theory* (Oxford: Clarendon Press, 1967) and elsewhere.

8. *The Collected Writings of John Maynard Keynes,* vol. 14 (London: Macmillan, 1971), p. 79; also in my "Recollections and Documents," *Economica* 40, no. 157 (February 1973).

9. *Capital and Growth* (New York: Oxford University Press, 1965).

10. Chapter XVII.

11. See his review of *Capital and Time* in the *South African Journal of Economics* 41, no. 3 (September 1973), "Sir John Hicks as a Neo-Austrian."

12. See my *The Theory of Wages* (London: Macmillan and Co., Ltd., 1932), Chapter VI.

13. *Capital and Time* (Oxford: Clarendon Press, 1973), p. 120.

14. I have tried to draw some more practical consequences in a paper entitled "The Future of Industrialism," *International Affairs* 50, no. 2 (April 1974).

15. "A Rehabilitation of 'Classical' Economics," *Economic Journal* 67, no. 266 (June 1957).

16. So I was told by Keynes himself. I had sent him the article on Walras which I had published, entitled "Leon Walras," *Econometrica* 2 (1934). I have a letter from him about it dated 9 December of that year. The substantial part of the letter is as follows:

There is one small point which perhaps I may be able to clear up. . . . You enquire whether or not Walras was supposing that exchanges actually take place at the prices originally proposed when these prices are not equilibrium prices. The footnote which you quote [p. 345 of my paper, p. 44 of the 4th French edition of the *Elements* which I was using] convinces me that he assuredly supposed that they did not take place except at the equilibrium prices. For that is the actual method by which the opening price is fixed on the Paris Bourse even today. His footnote suggests that he was aware that the Agents de Change used this method and he regarded that as the ideal system or exchange to which others were approximations. As a matter of fact, this is also the method by which opening prices are fixed on Wall Street. It is unfamiliar to us because the only London example which I can think of is the daily "fixing" of silver by the bullion brokers. In all these cases there is an application of Edgeworth's principle of re-contract, all those present disclosing their dispositions to trade and the price which will equate offers and demands is arrived at by an independent person, known in New York as the specialist.

It is much to be desired that the methods of trading on organised markets, in different countries and at different times, should be studied systematically.

17. Robert Clower and Axel Leijonhufvud, "The Coordination of Economic Activities: A Keynesian Perspective," *The American Economic Review* 65, no. 2 (May 1975): 184.

18. I started the job in the first lecture of *The Two Triads* [*Criticial Essays in Monetary Theory* (Oxford: Clarendon Press, 1967)]. See also my *A Theory of Economic History* (Oxford: Clarendon Press, 1969).

19. *The Economic History Review,* 2nd Series, 24, no. 4 (November 1971).

20. See my chapter on "The Methods of Marshall," *Capital and Growth,* Chapter 5.

21. I made an attempt to start the business of bringing it back into time in "The Process of Imperfect Competition," *Oxford Economic Papers,* New Series, 6, no. 1 (February 1954); but I do not pretend that I got very far.

22. Georgescu-Roegen, *The Entropy Law and the Economic Process* (Cambridge: Harvard University Press, 1971).

7

Speeding Up of Time with Age in Recognition of Life as Fleeting

Paul A. Samuelson

A child claims that summer drags forever. His grandfather regrets how fast the summer flew by. To a Watsonian behaviorist in psychology or a Paretian behaviorist in economics, this may be deemed a matter of talking at cross purposes, of comparing cheese with incommensurable chalk.

However, it is a testable matter of fact whether people do, autobiographically, report that "time seems to pass more quickly as I grow older." Many have so reported. And, independently, various writers have hit upon a Weber-Fechner type of purportive logarithmic "explanation." Commonly, the argument goes much as follows.[1]

Posit that one begins life with a clean slate. (Ethologists will hardly agree.) Let each passing day, or month, or year of objective calendar time, t, bring with it a more or less constant average rate of new "sensations," "experiences," or bits of stimulus somehow measured. By any age, t, one has accumulated the lifelong integral of such "experience."

Then, by hypothesis, the sense of the speed at which, subjectively, actual time passes may be posited to be determined by the *percentage of incremental experience received, in comparison with total recorded inventory of past experience.*

This sounds vague, but it can be reduced to operationally meaningful, refutable form. Write $\dot{X}(t)$ for the instantaneous rate at age t of new current sense perceptions, somehow measured (as for example by how many photons are falling on the retina of the eye or the camera of the brain). Then the integral of sense perceptions ever received by age t is

$$X(t) = \int_0^t \dot{X}(u)du \tag{7.1}$$

$$= kt, \quad if \ \dot{X}(u) \approx k, \text{ a constant} \tag{7.2}$$

By appropriate choice of time units, we could make k equal to unity.

Now consider a special "subjective or internal time," θ, with the posited property that two calendar intervals will seem subjectively of the

---

I owe thanks to the National Science Foundation for financial aid, and I have an intellectual debt to Nicholas Georgescu-Roegen of Vanderbilt University for his subtle appreciation of the deep issues underlying my final section and his helpful criticisms throughout.

153

same duration if and only if in each such interval there has been the same percentage (or logarithmic) increment of accumulated experience:

$$\theta_3 - \theta_2 = \theta_2 - \theta_1 \quad \text{if and only if}$$
$$\ln X(t_3) - \ln X(t_2) = \ln X(t_2) - \ln X(t_1) \tag{7.3}$$

Taking Newtonian limits, we thus hypothesize the following rate relations between θ, X, and t:

$$\frac{d\theta}{dt} = c^{-1} \frac{d[\ln X(t)]}{dt}$$

$$= c^{-1} \frac{d[\ln(kt)]}{dt}$$

$$= c^{-1}t^{-1}$$

$$\frac{dt}{d\theta} = ct \tag{7.4}$$

$$t = t_0 e^{c\theta} \tag{7.5}$$

$$\theta = c^{-1}\ln(t/t_0) \tag{7.6}$$

By convention, we may set $\theta = 0$ at age of first recalled memory, say at age 4 with $t_0 = 4$; the scaling constant c depends on the arbitrary dimensional units we choose to measure subjective time in—so that we can set $c = 1$ if we agree on the proper (inessential) rate correspondence at age t_0 between the two time magnitudes. However, any positive scaling will do as well as any other.

All the ambiguous talk about "photons, sensations, experiences, and bits of stimulus" can be dispensed with once we realize that the objective testable assertion of (7.5) about reporting of subjective judgments can be summed up as follows:

People do (or don't) report that between ages four and eight the passage of subjective time is about equal to that between eight and sixteen, and that between sixteen and thirty-two, . . . , and that between arbitrary age t^* and age $2t^*$: similarly, time elapsed from t^* to bt^* must seem the same as from t^{**} to bt^{**}, for all (b, t^*, t^{**}).

Since it is a common observation that the very old, particularly when health is failing, begin to complain about the slowness of time, the logarithmic hypothesis at best might apply only up to late middle age.

Square Root and Power Rules

All the above is by way of review. Suppose, however, persons alternatively report:

Between four and nine there seems to be the same duration of subjective time as between nine and sixteen—*not* as between nine and twenty and one quarter as the Weber-Fechner rule required. Moreover, between four and twenty-five, time flew by just as it did between nine and thirty-six, or between sixteen and forty-nine, . . . , or between ages $(t^*)^2$ and $(t^* + 1)^2$.

Evidently my θ is then following a square-root rather than logarithmic rule. In place of (7.3), (7.4), and (7.5), I seem to have the square-root-rule relations:

$$\theta_3 - \theta_2 = \theta_2 - \theta_1 \leftrightarrow t_3^{\frac{1}{2}} - t_2^{\frac{1}{2}} = t_2^{\frac{1}{2}} - t_1^{\frac{1}{2}} \tag{7.7}$$

$$d\theta/dt = \frac{1}{2} c^{-1} t^{-\frac{1}{2}} \tag{7.8}$$

Inessential dimensional constants aside, we can summarize such regularities in the square-root rule that is the alternative counterpart to (7.6)'s logarithmic rule:

$$\theta = t^{\frac{1}{2}} \tag{7.9}$$

More generally, people could be tested to see whether they follow $t^{\frac{1}{2}}$ or t^α for α any positive position, or t^α/α for any nonzero α less than or equal to one:

$$\theta = t^\alpha/\alpha \quad 0 \neq \alpha \leqslant 1 \tag{7.10}$$

For $\theta \to 0$, this can be made to approach $\ln t$.

For time to seem to slow down rather than speed up with age, we would have to posit $\alpha > 1$. If calendar and subjective time seem always to agree, $\alpha = 1$.

We can test, and not prejudge, whether time speeds up, by examining the curvature of reported

$$\theta = f(t) \tag{7.11}$$

where $f(t)$ is a concave (from below) function if time does seem to pass faster with age, or is a convex function if it seems to slow down with age. If the decade of the thirties drags in comparison with early and subsequent decades, $f(t)$ would have to go through an inflection point of changing curvature then.

The Forward Look

My main purpose here is not to rederive the logarithmic rule, nor even to generalize it to a square-root or unspecified-power rule. Rather it is to analyze a quite different mechanism that might help explain the subjective speeding up of time that people report after forty.

A historical incident will illustrate what is involved. Eric Bell[2] writes the following account about the great algebraist, Evariste Galois (1811–1832), who was killed in a duel at the age of 21. All night before his hopeless duel, Galois

. . . had spent the fleeting hours feverishly dashing off his scientific last will and testament, writing against time to glean a few of the great things in his teeming mind before the death which he foresaw would overtake him. Time after time he broke off to scribble in the margin, ''I have not the time; I have not the time,'' and passed on to the next frantically scrawled outline. What he wrote in those desperate last hours before dawn will keep generations of mathematicians busy for hundreds of years.

Weill's *Knickerbocker Holiday* reports the same message in the love song

It's a long, long time from May to December
But the days grow short when you reach September.

What is emphasized here is not the backward-looking duration from birth to each age but rather the perceived elapsing time interval from that age to life's end.

If humans, like the one-hoss shays of Oliver Wendell Holmes's poem, were destined to live to one certain age—say, the Biblical three score and ten—each passing year would reduce life expectancy by just that much. The subjective sense that this next year you will have lost 1/20 of remaining life, then 1/19, . . . , and then 1/2 might be expected to be perceived as a speeding up of the passing of calendar time with age.

It is usually not given to us to know exactly when we shall die. However, one does not have to be a trained actuary to know that the force of mortality greatly increases with age (at least after one passes through the shoals of infancy). Life expectancy decreases with age:

$$de^0(t)/dt < 0 \qquad (7.12)$$

for most values of t, where $e^0(t)$ represents the average number of years a person of age t may expect to live before dying.

One simple approximation for the subjective speeding up of time would be to postulate

$$d\theta/dt = be^0(t), b > 0 \qquad (7.13)$$

$$\theta = f(t) = b \int_0^t e^0(u)da, f'(t) < 0$$

$$t = f^{-1}[\theta] = g(\theta), g''(\theta) > 0 \qquad (7.14)$$

In the unrealistic one-hoss shay case of sudden death:

$$\theta(t) = b \int_0^t (70 - u)du = b(70t - 1/2t^2), 0 < t < 70 \qquad (7.15)$$

Early in life, calendar time and subjective time would agree in this case rather closely (as if, in (7.10), α were near to unity). Later in life, time would seem to flit by ever faster; until, at 69-plus, it could reach a Galois-like intensity.

The early writers on probability recognized that chance elements in mortality caused one to lose less than a year of expectancy with each passing year. Realistic actuarial tables today keep $e^0(t)$ positive at all ages, albeit shrinking rapidly for centenarians. A crude example, simpler than the formulas of Gompertz and other actuaries, would be the case where

$$\theta(t) = \int_0^t e^{-u}du = 1 - e^{-t} \qquad (7.16)$$

$$t = -1n(1 - \theta) \qquad (7.17)$$

This would entail at all ages a positive acceleration term, $d^2\theta/dt^2$, as is required if time is to seem to speed up as one grows older.

To show that it would not be possible to distinguish from report data between the backward- and the forward-looking hypotheses, note the similarity of implications of (7.13) and (7.11):

$$d\theta/dt = be^0(t), be^{0'}(t) < 0 \qquad (7.18a)$$

$$d\theta/dt = f'(t), f''(t) < 0 \qquad (7.18b)$$

Also, one can replace $be^0(t)$ by some monotone-increasing function of $e^0(t)$, such as $\theta[e^0(t)]$, or use some other parameter of shrinking life left.

Qualifications

Young people, it is said, believe they will live forever. So, perhaps, the hypothesis of subjective speeding up of time from the perception of years-of-remaining-life flitting by should be reserved for the older ages only. How old?

D'Alembert, in his rather absurd attempt to resolve the famous St. Petersburg Paradox, proposed that people (do? or ought to?) treat sufficiently small positive probabilities as literally zero. When challenged to specify how small they would have to be for this, Buffon suggested that a man of fifty-six in good health does not wake up and think he will die that day. So any probability below the force of mortality at fifty-six for one day, reported by Stigler (1950, n. 126) to have been $p = 0.0001$ in the eighteenth century and $p = 0.00005$ in 1950, can be taken to be zero.[3] (Since men do not cancel their term insurance each morning, this is indeed absurd.) However, the fact that Buffon has not met with more scornful readers may suggest that only after age sixty is the presence of the grim reaper most consciously felt.

Similarly, at extreme old ages, the release of death may be increasingly welcomed. And time may again seem to drag as observable alertness diminishes and vital signs decelerate. No simple hypothesis should be expected to be able to fit the full diversity of life-cycle experience.

Problem of Existence of Subjective Time

Thus far I have been taking for granted that there may really exist for some of us a coherent notion of subjective time, $\theta = f(t)$. My present effort would not be worthy of him whom it seeks to honor, Nicholas Georgescu-Roegen, if I left this deep issue at the implicit and unresolved stage.

Therefore, I now propose to explore the testable conditions that are necessary and sufficient for the very existence of such a (θ, t) structure.

Begin with the testable hypothesis that a given individual reports that, when given any two arbitrary ages of life, t_1 and t_3, the individual is always able to report to you an intermediate age, t_2, which he feels does "subjectively split" the interval into two subintervals of equal seeming duration:

Axiom A: $t_2 = M(t_1,t_3)$ is an observable function with the following properties:

A_1: $M(t_1,t_3)$ is to be continuous (and perhaps "smooth")

A_2: $M(t_1,t_3) \equiv M(t_3,t_1)$, a harmless symmetry condition

A_3: $M(t_1,t_3'') > M(t_1,t'_3)$ if $t_3'' > t_3'$

A_4: $M(t,t) \equiv t$, a "mean," with $Min(t_1,t_3) \leqslant M(t_1,t_3)$
$\leqslant Max(t_1,t_3)$

Axiom A does not suffice to ensure that a subjective time function, $\theta = f(t)$, does exist. We must stipulate more about the $M(\ ,\ )$ function if $t_2 = M(t_1, t_3)$ is always to agree with

$$\theta_3 - \theta_2 = \theta_2 - \theta_1 \leftrightarrow f(t_3) - f(t_2) = f(t_2) - f(t_1) \qquad (7.19)$$

Equation (7.19) says, in effect, that the $M(t_1, t_2)$ mean must be a so-called associative mean. Thus, the percentage-increment-of-experience paradigm could be summed up in the language of the geometric mean: namely, time between 4 and 8 seems to pass on quickly as between 8 and 16 because 8 is the geometric mean of 2 and 16: $8 = \sqrt{(2 \times 16)}$, $\log 8 = \frac{1}{2}(\log 2 + \log 16)$; and likewise for times between a and $\sqrt{(ab)}$ in comparison with those between $\sqrt{(ab)}$ and b.

For $\theta = f(t) = -t^{-1}$ in (7.10) or (7.11) or (7.19), the autobiographer replaces the geometric mean by the "harmonic mean" in splitting any time interval into two seemingly long subintervals. Then the time between 4 and 6.4 seems of the same duration as between 6.4 and 16, because 6.4 $= (\frac{1}{2}2^{-1} + \frac{1}{2}16^{-1})^{-1}$, the harmonic mean—or more generally, $(a, c > a)$ are split by b, the harmonic mean, $(\frac{1}{2}a^{-1} + \frac{1}{2}b^{-1})^{-1} = b$.

If there is neither speeding up nor slowing down of subjective time, we have the ordinary arithmetic mean

$$b = M(a, c) = \frac{1}{2}a + \frac{1}{2}c \qquad (7.20)$$

Time would seem to slow down with age if $f(t)$ were a convex rather than concave function, like the "quadratic mean" of Pythagoras, $b = (\frac{1}{2}a^2 + \frac{1}{2}c^2)^{\frac{1}{2}}$.

The most general case of a so-called associative mean has been discussed by mathematicians, as in Hardy-Littlewood-Polya (1934, Theorem 215). In the present context, equations (7.11) and (7.19) say that b "subjectively splits" a and c, $a \leqslant c$, into two equal subintervals (a,b) and (b,a), if and only if

$f(b) = \frac{1}{2}f(a) + f(c), f(x)$
        strictly increasing and continuous, implying $a \leqslant b \leqslant c$ (7.21)

Abel's Identity

But really, Axiom A does not require that a relation like (7.21) correspond to one's reported $M(t_1, t_2)$ function. There may not be a coherent subjective time sense, $\theta = f(t)$. Why should my autobiographical reportings, even if made after calm and careful reflection, satisfy all the straitjackets of the paradigm that posits the true existence of a definite sense of subjective time?

The task of deductive analysis is to point out what are the testable restrictions on empirically observable data of the subjective-time paradigm. The task of empirical observers is to test, and possibly refute or fail to refute, these testable relations. Therefore, to Axiom A must be added the following form of the Abel (1826) Identity.

> Axiom B: If t_1 and t_5 are "subjectively split" by $t_3 = M(t_1, t_5)$, t_1 and t_3 are "split" by $t_2 = M(t_1, t_3)$, and t_3 and t_5 are "split" by $t_4 = M(t_3, t_5)$ then it must be the case (a testable, refutable condition) that t_2 and t_4 are just split by $t_3 = M(t_2, t_4)$. Mathematically, this implies that the functional identity of Abel (1802–1829) holds on $M(t_1, t_2)$ in the form
> $$M(M(t_1, M(t_1, t_5)), M(M(t_1, t_5), t_5)) \equiv M(t_1, t_5)$$

If this holds, given any finite interval of calendar time, we can divide the continuum into as many fine equal-subjective-time intervals as we desire: thus, select any two nearby ages on the interval; call them t_0 and t_{0+h}. By solving the following relations for
$[t_{0+2h}, t_{0+3h}, \ldots, t_{0+nh}, \ldots]$, and for
$[t_{0-h}, t_{0-2h}, \ldots, t_{0-nh}, \ldots]$, we have our desired equal θ intervals:
$[\theta_0 - nH, \theta_0 - (n-1)H, \ldots, \theta_0 - H, \theta_0, \theta_0 + H, \theta_0 + 2H, \ldots, \theta_0 + nH]$:

$$t_{0+h} = M(t_0, t_{0+2h}), \ t_{0+2h} = M(t_{0+h}, t_{0+3h}), \ \ldots$$
$$t_{0+(n-1)h} = M(t_{0+(n-2)h}, t_{0+nh}) \ t_0 = M(_{0-h}, t_{0+h}),$$
$$t_{0-h} = M(t_{0-2h}, t_0), \ \ldots, t_{0-(n-1)h} = M(t_{0-(n-2)h}, t_{0-nh}) \quad (7.22)$$

Graphical Construction

Figure 7–1 depicts contour lines of the $M(t_1, t_2)$ function, free of any unobservable solipsistic magnitudes. If only Axiom A applied to a person who reported a "speeding up of time," the smooth contours could be any curves that are convex near the 45-degree line. These contours are shown in Figure 7–1a, for which there exists no coherent sense of subjective time, $\theta = f(t)$. This is because the mean, $M(t_1, t_2)$, is not capable of there being written as an "associative mean."

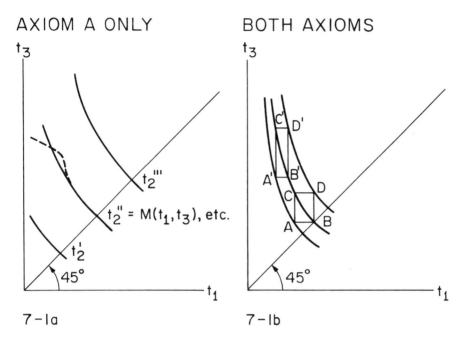

AXIOM A ONLY

t_3

t_2'''

$t_2'' = M(t_1, t_3)$, etc.

t_2'

45°

t_1

7–1a

BOTH AXIOMS

t_3

C' D'

A' B'

C

A D

B

45°

t_1

7–1b

Figure 7–1. Contours of the $M(t_1, t_3)$ Function. The contours shown connect all pairs of points (t_1 and t_3) that are split by equal t_2 = $M(t_1, t_3)$. In 7–1a arbitrary contours that satisfy Axiom A are shown as convex near the 45° line of symmetry. (Note the broken non-convex segment shown as a possibility for the middle contour away from the 45° line.) In 7–1b, along with Axiom A there is added the important Abelian Axiom B, so that there exists a coherent notion of subjective time, $\theta(t)$, and so that the $M(t_1, t_3)$ function is an "associative mean." From the two lower contours, by completing the Georgescu box ABC-and-D, we can derive the equally-spaced contours of "subjective time." (By selecting two initial contours close enough together, we can make our grid of measurement as fine as we like.)

162

Figure 7–1b imposes Axiom B as well as Axiom A. The resulting contours are compatible with the existence of a surface that generates those contours, and is capable of being written in the Gossen-Jevons additive form

$$M(t_1, t_2) = f^{-1}[\tfrac{1}{2}f(t_1) + \tfrac{1}{2}f(t_2)] \tag{7.23}$$

We may then avail ourselves of the Georgescu device, discussed in Georgescu-Roegen (1952) and Samuelson (1974), of constructing from any two close-together contours the implied equal-spacing contours by repeated "completing of the Georgescu box."[4] Without Abel's testable identity being satisfied, the whole construction would fail to apply.

Cardinal-Utility Increments

There is another way of looking at the problem of the operational implications for observable behavior of the existence of a subjective time scale. It has the merit of tying up the discussion with now-classical economic discussions of the possible cardinality of utility.

Pareto, three-quarters of a century ago, realized that consumer demand could be understood in terms of a person's merely having to decide whether one batch of goods is (ordinally) worse or better than another batch of goods, without having to be able to decide whether the increment in something called "utility" was greater or less in going from batch A to B than the increment in "utility" in going from C to D. Pareto (1909), Bowley (1923), Frisch (1926), Lange (1934–35), Phelps Brown (1934), Bernardelli (1934–35), R. G. D. Allen (1935), Samuelson (1938), Alt (1936), and many others realized the following:

If (U_1, U_2, U_3, U_4) are indicators of four levels of "utility," $U_1 < U_2 < U_3 < U_4$, then any monotone stretching of this U scale, call it $u = f(U)$, $f'(\ ) > 0$, would give new consistent indicators of "utility," $u_1 = f(U_1) < u_2 = f(U_2) < u_3 = f(U_3) < u_4 = f(U_4)$. However, the algebraic signs of increments of indicators of utility would agree if and only if $f(\ )$ is restricted to being a *linear* stretching: $f(U) \equiv a + bU$, $b > 0$; $|b| > 0$; i.e.,

sign of $\{[f(U_2) - f(U_1)] - [f(U_3) - f(U_4)]\}$ always agrees with
sign of $\{[U_2 - U_1] - [U_3 - U_4]\}$

if and only if $f''\{U\} \equiv 0$. $\tag{7.24}$

Samuelson (1938) pointed out, however, that it already begs the case to talk of ΔU and Δu increments. Going from batch of goods

$(q_1^a, \ldots, q_n^a) = Q^a$ to $(q_1^b, \ldots, q_n^b) = Q^b$, or alternatively from $(q_1^c, \ldots, q_n^c) = Q^c$ to $(q_1^d, \ldots, q_n^d) = Q^d$, a person might be able to make comparisons without those comparisons referring to the *difference* of some scalar magnitude, $U(Q^b) - U(Q^a)$ or $U(Q^d) - U(Q^c)$. Under certain regularity conditions, the person has a function of the $2n$ variables, $(q_1^b, \ldots, q_n^b; q_1^a, \ldots, q_n^a)$ that relates these "steps' in his mind or preference: call this

$$V(X; Y) = V(x_1, \ldots, x_n; y_1, \ldots, y_n), \text{ or}$$
$$v = \phi\{V(x; y)\} = v(X; Y), \phi'\{ \ \} > 0, \phi''\{ \ \} \gtreqless 0 \quad (7.25)$$

This is postulated to have the property:[5]

$$\phi\{V(Q^a, Q^b)\} > \phi\{V(Q^c, Q^d)\} \text{ when } (Q^a \text{ to } Q^b) \text{ is deemed "more}$$
significant'' than $(Q^c \text{ to } Q^d)$.

Likewise for $\phi\{V(Q^d; Q^d)\} > \phi\{V(Q^a; Q^b)\}$ or $\phi\{V(Q^a; Q^b)\} = \phi\{V(Q^c; Q^d)\}$.

What I showed almost forty years ago is the following: There will exist some $\phi\{ \ \}$ and $f\{ \ \}$ that make $\phi\{V(X; Y)\} \equiv f\{U(Y)\} - f\{U(X)\}$ if and only if the following variant of Abel's identity is verifiably true:

Abel-Samuelson: Whenever Q^a-to-Q^b is deemed equally significant to Q^c-to-Q^d, it must be the case that Q^a-to-Q^c is deemed equally significant to Q^b-to-Q^d.

Alternative Axioms for Subjective Time

Figure 7–2 applies this same logic to the question of the existence of a coherent subjective time scale, and *all* that this implies for observable behavior. It plots in the space of (t_1, t_2) contours of all the points of "seemingly equal subjective time" intervals. Thus, the 45° line represents the passage from any initial time to itself, the shortest possible subjective time interval. With the convention $t_1 \le t_2$, we need only fill in the upper half of the positive quadrant.

The contours are positively sloped, in contrast to the usually negatively sloped indifference contours of the economist: this is because an increase in initial t_1 can only be compensated for by an increase in terminal t_2 if we are to be on the contour of equal-seeming time duration. The seeming speeding up of subjective time with age imposes no simple curvature condition on these contours.

Figure 7–2a obeys only the first axiom of the new formulation.

Axiom I: Reportable contours of equal time duration are indicated by the function

$$\tau = \tau(t_1, t_2), \; t_1 \leqslant t_2$$

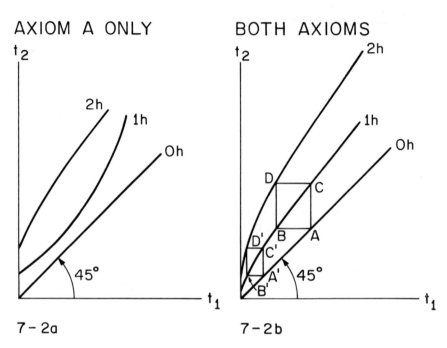

AXIOM A ONLY — 7–2a

BOTH AXIOMS — 7–2b

Figure 7–2. Contours of $\tau(t_1, t_2)$. The contours connect pairs of points (t_1 and t_2) that have the same subjective-seeming duration of time between them. Thus, the points on the 45° line each correspond to zero subjective-seeming duration of time, since on that line t_1 and t_2 correspond to the same instant of time. In 7–2a, the contours only satisfy Axiom I and actually correspond to no coherent sense of subjective time. In 7–2b, however, the contours also satisfy the Abelian Axiom II: now with a coherent sense of subjective time, the Georgescu boxes, like ABC-and-D, can be used to construct, from the 45° line of $0h$ and the contour for $1h$, the new contour for $2h$. Likewise, from nh and $(n-1)h$, one can complete the box to construct the $(n+1)h$ contour. By selecting the $1h$ contour near enough to the 45° line, we can make the grid as fine as we like.

where

I.1 $\tau(t_1, t_2)$ is continuous in its arguments

I.2 $\tau(t_1, y)$ is monotone strictly increasing in y and $\tau(x, t_2)$ is monotone strictly decreasing in x

I.3 $\tau(x, x) \equiv \tau(y, y)$

Nevertheless, from Axiom I alone we cannot find a stretching of $\tau(t_1, t_2)$ that puts it in the form needed for a coherent subjective time structure. We must add a second refutable axiom to rule out Figure 7–2a and rule in Figure 7–2b.

Axiom II: If $\tau(a, b) = \tau(c, d)$, then necessarily $\tau(\text{Min}[a, c], \text{Max}[a, c]) = \tau(\text{Min}[b, d], \text{Max}[b, d])$

By "completing the Georgescu box," formed as at A on the 45° line and B and C on a nearby arbitrary contour, labeled $\theta = h$ we can calculate the D point on the $\theta = 2h$ contour. The whole of that new contour is constructed by letting A slide on the 45° line from the origin out to infinity. Then, apply the Georgescu box technique to points generated from $\theta = h$ to $\theta = 2h$, to get points on $\theta = 3h$. Clearly, by prescribing our initial $\theta = h$ contour arbitrarily near to the 45° line, we can in effect make h arbitrarily small, and thus trace out the existent subjective time scale,

$$\theta = f(t) = \psi\{\tau(t_1, t_2)\}, \ \psi'(\tau) > 0, \tag{7.26}$$

to as great accuracy as can be desired. (Experimentally, as Georgescu-Roegen reminds me, it is realistic to expect "threshold" effects so that few of us would be able to gauge minute equivalent subjective-time intervals. But this is to say that, at the fine scale level, we do do not verify the existence of a coherent set of autobiographical reports about seeming durations: our axioms, by their violation, reveal the absence of subjective-time structures when they do not exist!)

Mathematically, Axioms I and II are equivalent to putting the following (testable!) restrictions on continuous, monotone $\tau(t_1, t_2)$:

$$\tau(y,y) = \tau(x,x) \le \tau(x,y), \ y \ge x > 0$$
$$\begin{cases} \tau(a,b) = \tau(c,d), \ d \ge b \ge a \le c \\ \text{if and only if} \\ \tau(a,c) = \tau(b,d) \end{cases} \tag{7.27}$$

This strong Abelian condition can be satisfied for a $\tau(t_1, t_2)$ function if and only if

$$\tau(t_1, t_2) = f^{-1}[\tfrac{1}{2}f(t_1) + \tfrac{1}{2}f(t_2)] \tag{7.28}$$

where $f(t)$ is a uniquely determined function, up to the linear transformation $a + bf(t)$ $b > 0$, and where $f^{-1}[x]$ is the inverse function defined by $x = f(t)$.[6] Axioms A and B on $M(t_1, t_2)$ are essentially equivalent to Axioms I and II on $\tau(t_1, t_2)$.

Conclusion

The discussion here has been artfully arranged so that no phenomena of introspection, which are in principle unobservable, are ever involved. Even a radical behaviorist will, on reflection, find no cause for legitimate complaint.

Whether actual human beings do or do not satisfy the various axiomatic hypotheses to a tolerable degree of approximation is not a task for the logician to decide. The matter must be put to the test of experience, once the analyst has clarified how that can be done.

Notes

1. For the Weber-Fechner law, see any psychology text; or, in economics, G. J. Stigler (1950), which discusses the views of d'Alembert that I later comment on and also discusses the St. Petersburg Paradox. On the plane from Boston to Nashville for the Georgescu Festschrift, I discovered in Georgescu (1971) the words: "There is some evidence that the hours seem shorter as we grow older because—as has been suggested [by K. Pearson (1899)]—the content of our consciousness increases at a decreasing [percentage?] rate."

2. The quotation comes from Eric Bell (1937, Chapter 20 on Galois, p. 375).

3. G. J. Stigler (1950).

4. See N. Georgescu-Roegen (1952). Debreu (1960) later also gave some conditions for strong separability of variables, but in contrast to those of Georgescu-Roegen (1952) they are only applicable to a function of more than two variables. See also P. A. Samuelson (1974).

5. Georgescu-Roegen (1954) points out in his n. 66 that "lexicographic" orderings can exist, which cannot be described by a single-scale

cardinal indicator function or by any of its monotonic stretchings. I agree that the present formulation, therefore, still needs to be qualified to avoid what Georgescu calls the "ordinalist error." Debreu (1954) has also given valuable analysis of Eilenberg conditions necessary or sufficient if a transitive preference ordering is to be representable by one numerical function (and hence, after stretchings, by an infinity of such numerical functions).

6. See Samuelson (1947), Chapter 5, Equation [15]) for an alternative test for independence. If $M(t_1, t_3)$ has continuous partial derivatives of requisite order, the Abel identity can be shown to have for its full empirical implications the condition $\partial^2 \log M(t_1, t_3)/\partial t_1 \partial t_3 \equiv 0$. The similar condition on $\tau(t_1, t_2)$ is that $\partial^2 \log \tau(t_1, t_2)/\partial t_1 \partial t_2 \equiv 0$.

Bibliography

Abel, Niels Henrik. 1826. "Recherche des fonctions de deux quantités variables indépendantes x et y, telles que $f(x,y)$, qui ont la propriété que $f(z, f(x,y))$ est une fonction symetrique de z, x et y." *Journel fur die reine und angewandte Mathematik,* herausgegeben von Crelle, Bd. I, Berlin. Reproduced as Chapter VI in *Oeuvres Complètes de Niels Henrik Abel* (ed. L. Sylow & S. Lie) (Christiania: Grondahl & Son, 1881).

Allen, R. G. D. "A Note on the Determinateness of the Utility Function." *Review of Economic Studies* 2 (1936): 155–58.

Alt, F. "Über die Messbarkeit des Nutzens." *Zeitschrift für Nationalökonomie* 7 (1936): 161–69.

Bell, E. *Men of Mathematics.* New York: Simon & Schuster, 1937.

Bernardelli, H. "Notes on the Determinateness of the Utility Function." *Review of Economic Studies* 2 (1934–35).

Bowley, A. L. *Mathematical Groundwork of Economics.* Oxford: Clarendon Press, 1924.

Brown, E. H. Phelps. "Demand Functions and Utility Functions: A Critical Examination of Their Meaning." *Econometrica* 2, no. 1 (1934): 51–58.

Debreu, G. "Representation of a Preference Ordering by a Numerical Function." In R. M. Thrall et al. (eds.), *Decision Processes.* New York: Wiley, 1954.

——— "Topological Methods in Cardinal Utility Theory." In Arrow, K. J., Karlin, S., and Suppes, P. (eds.). *Mathematical Methods in the Social Sciences, 1959 (Proceedings of the First Stanford Symposium).* Stanford, California: Stanford University Press, 1960.

Frisch, R. "Sur un problème d'économie pure." *Norsk Matematish Foreignings Skrifter* 1, no. 16 (1926): 1–40.

Georgescu-Roegen, N. "A Diagrammatic Analysis of Complementarity." *Southern Economic Journal* (1952): 1–20.

―――― "Choice, Expectations and Measurability." *Quarterly Journal of Economics* 68 (1954): 503–34.

―――― "Threshold in Choice and the Theory of Demand." *Econometrica* 26 (1958): 157–68; reproduced as Chapter 5 in *Analytical Economics: Issues and Problems*.

―――― *Analytical Economics: Issues and Problems*. Cambridge, Mass.: Harvard University Press, 1966.

―――― *The Entropy Law and the Economic Process*. Cambridge, Mass.: Harvard University Press, 1971.

Hardy, G. H., Littlewood, J. E., and Polya, G. *Inequalities*. Cambridge: The University Press, 1934.

Lange, O. "The Determinateness of the Utility Function." *Review of Economic Studies* 1 (1934): 218–28; 2–3 (1934–35): 76–77.

Pareto, V. *Manuel d'economie politique*. Paris: V. Giard & E. Briere, 1909.

Pearson, K. *The Grammar of Science*. London: Scott, 1892.

Samuelson, P. A. "Complementarity: An Essay on the Fortieth Anniversary of the Hicks-Allen Revolution in Demand Theory." *Journal of Economic Literature* (1974): 1255–89.

―――― *Foundations of Economic Analysis*. Cambridge, Mass.: Harvard University Press, 1947.

―――― "The Numerical Representations of Ordered Classifications and the Concept of Utility." *Review of Economic Studies* 6 (1938): 65–70, 344–56; reproduced in *The Collected Scientific Papers of P. A. Samuelson* I, Chapter 2, 15–20.

Stigler, G. J. "The Development of Utility Theory." *Journal of Political Economy* 58 (1950): 307–27, 373–96; reproduced as Chapter 5 in Stigler, G. J. *Essays in History of Economics*. Chicago: University of Chicago Press, 1965.

Bibliography of Nicholas Georgescu-Roegen

Bibliography of Nicholas Georgescu-Roegen

Books and Monographs

Metoda Statistică. Bucharest: Biblioteca Institutului Central De Statistica, 1933, pp. 506.

Un Quantum-index pentru Comertul Exterior al României. Bucharest: Institutul Central De Statistică, 1938.

Activity Analysis of Production and Allocation. Coeditor with T. C. Koopmans et al. New York: John Wiley & Sons, 1951, pp. 404.

Analytical Economics: Issues and Problems. Cambridge, Mass.: Harvard University Press, 1966, pp. xvi, 434.

La science économique: Ses problèmes et ses difficultés. Paris: Dunod, 1970, pp. xvi, 300.

The Entropy Law and the Economic Problem. Pamphlet. University of Alabama, 1971, p. 16.

The Entropy Law and the Economic Process. Cambridge, Mass.: Harvard University Press, 1971, pp. xviii, 450.

Analisi economica e processo economico. Firenze: Sansoni, 1973, pp. xvi, 282.

Energy and Economic Myths: Institutional and Analytical Economic Essays. Oxford: Pergamon Press, in press.

Production and Institutions in Agriculture. Montclair, N.J.: Allanheld, Osmun and Co., forthcoming.

Bioeconomics. Princeton University Press, forthcoming.

Articles

"Sur un problème de calcul des probabilités avec application à la recherche des périodes inconnues d'un phénomène cyclique." *Comptes Rendus de l'Académie des Science* 191 (July 7, 1930): 15–17.

"Le problème de la recherche des composantes cycliques d'un phénomène." Dissertation. *Journal de la Société de Statistique de Paris* (October 1930): 5–52.

"Further Contributions to the Sampling Problem." *Biometrika* (May 1932): 65–107.

171

"Sur la meilleure valeur a posteriori d'une variable aléatoire." *Bulletin de la Société Roumaine des Sciences* 33–34 (1932): 32–38.

"Tehnica numerelor indice pentru nivelul general al preţurilor." *Buletinul Statistic al României* 4 (1932).

"Note on a Proposition of Pareto." *Quarterly Journal of Economics* (August 1935): 706–14.

"Fixed Coefficients of Production and the Marginal Productivity." *Review of Economic Studies* (October 1935): 40–49.

"Marginal Utility of Money and Elasticities of Demand." *Quarterly Journal of Economics* (May 1936): 533–39.

"The Pure Theory of Consumer's Behavior." *Quarterly Journal of Economics* (August 1936): 545–93.

(With R. Turpin and A. Caratzali.) "L'influence de l'age maternel, du rang de naissance, et de l'ordre des naissances sur la mortinalité." *Premier Congrès Latin d'Eugénique* (1937): 271–77.

"La corrélation entre l'age maternel et le sexe de l'enfant dans les naissances simples et gémelaires." *Congrès International d'Eugénique.* Bucharest, 1938.

"Inventarul Agricol al României." *Enciclopedia României* 3 (1939): 334–43.

"Comerţul Exterior al României." *Enciclopedia României* 4 (1943): 458–60, 472–95.

"Preţurile in România." Ibid., pp. 928–33.

"Costul vieţii in România." Ibid., pp. 934–38.

"Venturile individuale in România." Ibid., pp. 891–903.

"Avuţia Naţională a României." Ibid., pp. 967–72.

"Probabilitatea văzută de un statistican." *Analele Institutului Statistic al României* 2 (1945): 11–21.

"Modificări structurale in venitul naţional al României in urma celui de al doilea război mondial." *Analele Institutului Statistic al României* 3 (1946): 3–27.

"Further Contributions to the Scatter Analysis." *Proceedings of the International Statistical Conferences* 5 (1947): 39–43.

"A supra Problemei 5527." *Gazeta Matematică* 52, Commemorative issue (October 1947): 126–33.

"Further Contributions to the Scatter Analysis." Reprinted in *Econometrica* 16 (1948): 40–43.

"The Theory of Choice and the Constancy of Economic Laws." *Quarterly Journal of Economics* 64 (February 1950): 125–38.

"Leontief's System in the Light of Recent Results." *Review of Economics and Statistics* (August 1950): 214–22.

"The Aggregate Linear Production Function and Its Applications to von Neumann's Economic Model." Chap. 4 in *Activity Analysis of Production and Allocation*. New York: John Wiley & Son Co., 1951, pp. 98–115.

"Relaxation Phenomena in Linear Dynamic Models." Ibid., Chap. 5, pp. 116–31.

"Some Properties of a Generalized Leontief Model." Ibid., Chap. 10, pp. 165–73.

Review of W. W. Leontief, *The Structure of American Economy*. In *Econometrica*, 19 (1951): 351–53.

"A Diagrammatic Analysis of Complementarity." *Southern Economic Journal* (July 1952): 1–20.

"Toward Partial Redirection of Econometrics." *Review of Economics and Statistics* (August 1952): 206–11.

"Note on Holley's Dynamic Model." *Econometrica* (July 1953): 457–59.

"Multi-Part Economic Models: Discussion." *Econometrica* (July 1953): 469–70.

"Note on the Economic Equilibrium for Nonlinear Models." *Econometrica* (January 1954): 54–57.

"The End of the Probability Syllogism?" *Philosophical Studies* (February 1954): 31–32.

"Choice and Revealed Preference." *Southern Economic Journal* (October 1954): 119–30.

"Choice, Expectations and Measurability." *Quarterly Journal of Economics* (November 1954): 503–34.

"Limitationality, Limitativeness, and Economic Equilibrium." In *Proceedings of the Second Symposium in Linear Programming*, Vol. I. Washington, D.C.: 1955, pp. 295–330.

Review of Maurice Allais, *Traité d'économie pure*. In *American Economic Review* 46 (1956): 163–66.

"Economic Activity Analysis" (review article). *Southern Economic Journal* 22 (1956): 468–75.

"The Nature of Expectation and Uncertainty." Chap. 1 in *Expectations, Uncertainty, and Business Behavior*, ed. Mary Jean Bowman, New York: A Social Science Research Council publication, 1958, pp. 11–29.

"Threshold in Choice and the Theory of Demand." *Econometrica* 26 (January 1958): 157–68.

"On the Extrema of Some Statistical Coefficients." *Metron* 19 (July 1959): 1–10.

"Economic Theory and Agrarian Economics." *Oxford Economic Papers*, N.S., 12 (February 1960): 1–40.

"Mathematical Proofs of the Breakdown of Capitalism." *Econometrica* 28 (April 1960): 225–43. (A special issue of essays in honor of Ragnar Frisch.)

Review of E. Levy, *Analyse structurale et méthodologie économique*. In *American Economic Review* 52 (1962): 1123–24.

"Some Thoughts on Growth Models: A Reply." *Econometrica* 31 (January-April 1963): 230–36, 239.

"Measure, Quality, and Optimum Scale." *Essays on Econometrics and Planning Presented to Professor P. C. Mahalanobis*. Oxford: Pergamon Press, 1964, pp. 231–56.

"Economic Theory and Agrarian Economics." Reprinted in C. Eicher and L. Witt, *Agriculture in Economic Development*. New York: McGraw-Hill, 1964, pp. 144–69.

"Measure, Quality, and Optimum Scale." Reprinted in *Sankya*, Series A, Vol. 27, Part I (1965): 39–64.

Review of Michio Morishima, *Equilibrium, Stability and Growth: A Multi-Sectoral Analysis*. In *American Economic Review* 55 (1965): 194–98.

"Further Thoughts on Corrado Gini's *Delusioni dell'econometria*," (an invited paper for the *International Statistical Symposium in Honor of Corrado Gini*, Rome, 1966). *Metron* 25 (1966): 265–79.

"Chamberlin's New Economics and the Unit of Production," an invited contribution for *Monopolistic Competition: Studies in Impact*, Essays in honor of Edward H. Chamberlin, R. E. Kuenne, ed. New York: John Wiley & Sons, 1967, Chap. 2, pp. 31–62.

"Teoría Económica y Economía Agraria." English translation: "Economic Theory and Agrarian Economics" (1960), followed by a 1966 postscript. *El Trimestre Económico* 34 (1967): 589–638.

"Théorie économique et économie politique agraire." English translation: "Economic Theory and Agrarian Economics" (1960), followed by a 1966 postscript. *Economie Rurale* 71 (1967): 51–76.

"An Epistemological Analysis of Statistics as the Science of Rational Guessing." *Acta Logica* 10 (1967): 61–91.

"O Estrangulamento: Inflação Estrutural e o Crescimento Econômico." *Revista Brasileira de Economia* 22 (March 1968): 5–14.

"Utility," an invited contribution for the *International Encyclopedia of*

Social Sciences, vol. 16. New York: Macmillan and Free Press, 1968, pp. 236–67.

"Revisiting Marshall's Constancy of Marginal Utility of Money." *Southern Economic Journal* 35 (1968): 176–81.

"Process in Farming versus Process in Manufacturing: A Problem of Balanced Development." In Ugo Papi and Charles Nunn, eds. *Economic Problems of Agriculture in Industrial Societies.* (Proceedings of a conference held by the International Economic Association in Rome, 1965.) London: Macmillan, 1969, pp. 497–528. "Discussion." Ibid., pp. 528–33.

"Economic Theory and Agrarian Economics." Reprinted with a "Postscript 1966" in *Economics of Underdeveloped Agriculture,* ed. Tara Shukla. Bombay: Vora & Co., 1969, pp. 318–73.

"Economie, Matematică și Cunoaștere." *Viața Economică* 7, no. 27 (July 1969): 21–22.

"A Critique of Statistical Principles in Relation to Social Phenomena." *Sociological Abstracts* 17, no. 5, suppl. 6 (August 1969): 9.

"Relations Between Binary and Multiple Choices: Some Comments and Further Results." *Econometrica* 37, no. 4 (October 1969): 726–28.

"The Institutional Aspects of Peasant Communities: An Analytical View." Chap. 4 in *Subsistence Agriculture and Economic Development,* Clifton R. Wharton, Jr. ed. Chicago: Aldine Publishing Company, 1969, pp. 61–99.

"A Critique of Statistical Principles in Relation to Social Phenomena." *Revue Internationale de Sociologie,* Actes du XXII Congrès de l'Institut International de Sociologie, Series II, 5, no. 3 (December 1969): 347–70.

"Uma Anályse Crítica da Função de Produção Neoclássica." *Revista de Teoria e Pesquisa Econômica,* Istituto de Pesquisas Econômicas da Faculdade de Economia e Administração da Universidade de São Paulo, 1, no. 1 (April 1970): 11–35.

"Economia Producției." *Progresele Științei* 6, no. 1 (January 1970): 12–16. (Invited lecture delivered before the Romanian Academy.)

"The Economics of Production." Richard T. Ely lecture. *American Economic Review, Papers and Proceedings of the Eighty-second Annual Meeting* 60, no. 2 (May 1970): 1–9.

"On the Case of Catalytic Labor." *International Economic Review* 11, no. 2 (June 1970): 315–17.

"Economic Theory and Agrarian Economics." In *Leading Issues in Economic Development: Studies in International Poverty,* edited by

Gerald M. Meier. New York: Oxford University Press, 1970, pp. 68–72.

"Structural Inflation-Lock and Balanced Growth." *Economies et sociétés, Cahiers de l'Institut de science économique appliquée* 4, no. 3 (March 1970): 557–605.

"Amintiri despre Gazeta Matematică." *Gazeta Matematică* 75, no. 10 (October 1970): 389–90.

"Demonstrazioni matematiche del crollo del capitalismo." Appendix V in Paul M. Sweezy et al., *La Teoria dello sviluppo capitalistico.* Torino: Boringheri, 1970, pp. 497–521. [English translation: "Proofs of the Breakdown of Capitalism." *Econometrica* 28 (April 1960): 513–21.]

"The Measure of Information: A Critique." *Abstracts.* IVth International Congress of Logic, Methodology and Philosophy of Science, Bucharest: 1971, pp. 139–40.

"Analysis versus Dialectics in Economics." In *Ensaios Econômicos, Homagem a Octávio Gouvêa de Bulhões,* Micea Buescu, ed. Rio de Janeiro: APEC, 1972, pp. 251–78.

"Process Analysis and the Neoclassical Theory of Production." *American Journal of Agricultural Economics* 54, no. 2 (May 1972): 279–94.

"Economics and Entropy." *The Ecologist* 2, no. 7 (July 1972): 13–18. (Reprint of *The Entropy Law and the Economic Problem,* Distinguished Lectures Series, no. 1, Alabama University, 1971.)

"O impasse da inflação estrutural e desenvolvimento equilibrado." *Revista Brazileira de Economia* 26, no. 3 (July-September 1972): 109–46. [English translation: "Structural Inflation-Lock and Balanced Growth." *Economies et societes,* Cahiers de l' I.S.E.A. (Geneva: Librairie Droz), IV (March 1970), pp. 557–605.)

"Utility and Value in Economic Thought." *Dictionary of the History of Ideas,* 4 vols. New York: Scribner's, 1973, vol. 4, pp. 450–58.

"The Entropy Law and the Economic Problem." Chap. 1 in Herman E. Daly, ed., *Toward a Steady-State Economy.* San Francisco: W. H. Freeman, 1973, pp. 37–49. (Reprint of *The Entropy Law and the Economic Problem,* Distinguished Lectures Series, no. 1, University of Alabama, 1971.)

Review of John S. Chipman, Leonid Hurwicz, Marcel K. Richter, and Hugo F. Sonnenschein, *Preferences, Utility, and Demand.* In *Journal of Economic Literature* 11, no. 2 (June 1973): 528–32.

"The Economics of Production." In Richard E. Neel, *Readings in Price Theory.* Cincinnati: South-Western Publishing Co., 1973, pp. 192–207. [Reprint of "The Economics of Production," Richard T. Ely lecture, *American Economic Review* 60 (May 1970): 1–9.]

" 'Land of Plenty' and Rationing.'' *The Tennessean* (December 5, 1973).

"Teoria econômica e economia agrária.'' In Carlos Peláez, ed., *Ensaios sobre café e desenvolvimento econômico.* Rio de Janeiro: Instituto Brasileiro do Café, 1973, pp. 379–420. [English translation: "Economic Theory and Agrarian Economics.'' *Oxford Economic Papers,* N. S., 12 (February 1960): 1–40 and of "1966 Postscript.'']

"Economy of Power Lesson from Crisis.'' *The Tennessean,* Business and Industry Section, Special Issue, January 13, 1974.

"Was geschieht mit der Materie im Wirtschaftsprozess.'' In *Recycling: Lösung der Umweltkreise?*, *Brennpunkte* (publication of the Gottlieb Duttweiler Institut) 5, no. 2 (1972): 17–28.

"Economic Theory and Agrarian Economics.'' In *Essays on Coffee and Economic Development.* Rio de Janeiro: Instituto Brasileiro do Café, 1973, pp. 359–99.

"Fisiologia do desenvolvimento economico.'' In *Painéis internacionais sobre desenvolvimento socioeconômico* (International Colloquium for the 21st Anniversary of BNDE), APEC Editora, Rio de Janeiro: 1974, pp. 335–47.

"Mechanistic Dogma and Economics.'' *Methodology and Science* 7, no. 3 (1974): 174–84.

"L'economia politica come estensione della biologia.'' (Lecture delivered in Aula Magna of the Faculty of Economy and Commerce, University of Florence, May 14, 1974.) *Note Economiche,* ed. Monte dei Paschi di Siena, 1974, No. 2, pp. 5–20.

"Dynamic Models and Economic Growth.'' (Paper read at the International Colloquium on "Equilibrium and Disequilibrium in Economic Theory,'' Institute of Advanced Studies, Vienna, July 3–6, 1974.) *Economie appliquée* 27, no. 4 (1974): 529–63.

"Energy and Economic Myths.'' (Lecture delivered on November 8, 1972, at the School of Forestry and Environmental Studies, Yale University, in the Series Limits to Growth: The Equilibrium State and Human Society.) *Southern Economic Journal* 41, no. 3 (January 1975): 347–81.

"The Entropy Law and Economics.'' In Jiří Zeman, ed., *Entropy and Information in Science and Philosophy.* Amsterdam: Elsevier, 1975, pp. 125–42.

"Energy and Economic Myths.'' *The Ecologist* 5, nos. 5 and 7 (June and August-September 1975): 164–74, 242–525.

"A Critique of the Measure of Information.'' (Keynote address to Section 5, Third International Congress of Cybernetics and Systems, Bucharest, August 1975.) *Summaries of Papers* (1975): 75–76.

"Dynamic Models and Economic Growth." *World Development* 3 (November-December 1975): 765–83.

"Energía y los mitos económicos." *El Trimestre Económico* 42, no. 4 (October 1975): 779–836.

"Vilfredo Pareto and His Theory of Ophelimity." In *Convegno Internazionale Vilfredo Pareto* (Roma, October 25–27, 1975). Rome: Accademia Nazionale dei Lincei, 1975, pp. 223–65.

"Discussion." (International Colloquium for the Commemoration of Sadi Carnot, Paris, June 11–13, 1974. Proceedings forthcoming.)

"Economic Growth and Its Representation by Models." *Atlantic Economic Journal* 4, no. 1 (Winter 1976): 1–8.

"The Measure of Information: A Critique." (to be published in *Modern Trends in Cybernetics and Systems*. England: Abacus, and Romania: Editura Tehnica.)

"Economics or Bioeconomics?" (Paper read at the AEA meeting, Dallas, December 29, 1975.)

"A Different Economic Perspective." (Paper prepared for the AAAS meeting, Boston, February 21, 1976.)

"Technology and Economic Policy." In Howard L. Hartman, ed., *Proceedings of Centennial Symposium on Technology and Public Policy*, Vanderbilt University, Nov. 6–7, 1975, pp. 43–50.

About the Contributors

Kenneth E. Boulding is Professor of Economics, University of Colorado, and former president of the American Economic Association (1968).

John S. Chipman is Professor of Economics, University of Minnesota, and a Fellow of the Center of Advanced Study in Behavioral Sciences, 1972–73.

Sir John R. Hicks is Professor Emeritus, All Souls College, Oxford University, and Nobel Laureate (1972).

Simon Kuznets is Professor of Economics Emeritus, Harvard University, Nobel Laureate (1971), and former president of the American Economic Association (1954).

James C. Moore is Associate Professor of Economics, Krannert Graduate School of Industrial Administration, Purdue University.

Paul A. Samuelson is Institute Professor, Massachusetts Institute of Technology, Nobel Laureate (1970), and former president of the American Economic Association (1961).

Joseph J. Spengler is James B. Duke Professor of Economics Emeritus, Duke University, and former president of the American Economic Association (1965).

Jan Tinbergen is Professor Emeritus, Erasmus University, Rotterdam, and Nobel Laureate (1969).

About the Editors

Anthony M. Tang is Professor of Economics and former chairman of the Department of Economics and Business Administration at Vanderbilt University. He started his undergraduate study (1941–42) at L'Université L'Aurore, Shanghai, China, and completed his bachelor's degree (1949) at Loyola University, New Orleans, Louisiana, His Ph.D. (1955) is from Vanderbilt University. While on leaves of absence from Vanderbilt, whose faculty he joined in 1954, he served as visiting professor or lecturer at Osaka University (1959–60), University of California at Berkeley (1963–64), Chinese University of Hong Kong (1966–68), National Taiwan University (1974–75), and University of Michigan (1976–77). He is the author of articles and books and has served as editor or a member of editorial boards of journals. His research and teaching interests are in the economic development and problems of the southern region of the United States; international economic development with emphasis on the role of agriculture; and Soviet-type economies, especially regarding comparative policies and performance of the agricultures of the People's Republic of China and the Soviet Union in priority industrialization context.

Fred M. Westfield is Professor of Economics at Vanderbilt, where he also received his B.A. degree in 1950. His Ph.D. is from M.I.T. Before returning to Vanderbilt in 1965, he was on the faculty of Northwestern University. His research interest has been in micro-economics; his work has been published in the *American Economic Review, Quarterly Journal of Economics,* and *Review of Economics and Statistics,* among others, and as contributions to various volumes. A winner of a Ford Faculty Research Fellowship, he has also served as consultant to the Harvard University Development Advisory Service, The World Bank, and to various government agencies in the United States and abroad. He has been a frequent faculty member of the American Economic Association's Economics Institute at the University of Colorado.

James S. Worley is Professor of Economics and Business Administration and the director of the Graduate Program in Economic Development at Vanderbilt University. He was associate provost of the university from 1968 until 1971 and served as chairman of the Department of Economics and Business Administration from 1971 until 1974. He received his B.A. and M.A. from Vanderbilt University, and his Ph.D. from Princeton. In 1958 he joined the Vanderbilt faculty, having taught earlier at Wofford College and Princeton University. He has taught on several occasions at the Economics Institute, University of Colorado. In connection with his

181

duties as the director of the Graduate Program in Economic Development at Vanderbilt, he has visited many developing countries as well as most of the countries in Western Europe. His research and teaching interests are in money and financial institutions (including monetary and fiscal policies for economic development) and industrial organization (especially the relationship between the structure of industry and technological change). He also maintains an active interest in the development of the southern region of the United States.

Related Lexington Books

Peter Albin, *The Analysis of Complex Socio-Economic Systems*, 176 pp., 1975

Richard Edwards, David Gordon, and Michael Reich, *Labor Market Segmentation*, 336 pp., 1975

Ronald E. Grieson, *Public and Urban Economics*, 432 pp., 1976

George N. Halm, *A Guide to International Monetary Reform*, 144 pp., 1975

Edgar Owens, and Robert Shaw, *Development Reconsidered*, 208 pp., 1972

Martin F. J. Prachowny, *Small Open Economies,* 160 pp., 1975

Alan A. Powell, *Empirical Analytics of Demand Systems*, 152 pp., 1975

Peter L. Watson, *The Value of Time*, 128 pp., 1974